GOLD AND GRAND DREAMS

Quesnel Forks, showing the junction of the North Fork and South Fork rivers, ca. *1898.*
(A-3697, BCA)

GOLD AND GRAND DREAMS

CARIBOO EAST IN THE EARLY YEARS

MARIE ELLIOTT

HORSDAL & SCHUBART

Horsdal & Schubart Publishers Ltd.
Victoria, BC, Canada

Front Cover: *Forks of Quesnelle, 1864*, watercolour by Frederick Whymper, (PDP 112, BCA).
Back Cover: Old building at Quesnel Forks, photo by the author.

This book is set in American Garamond Book Text.

Horsdal & Schubart wishes to acknowledge the Canada Council for the Arts, Heritage Canada through the Book Industry Development Program and the British Columbia Arts Council for their financial support of our publishing program.

Printed and bound in Canada by Printcrafters, Winnipeg, Manitoba.

Canadian Cataloguing in Publication Data

Elliott, Marie, 1938-
    Gold and grand dreams

Includes bibliographical references and index.
ISBN 0-920663-71-0

    1. Cariboo (B.C.: Regional district)—History. I. Title.

FC3845.C3E35 2000   971.1'75   C00-910829-7
F1089.C3E35 2000

Printed and bound in Canada

Acknowledgments

W HEN I FIRST visited Quesnel Forks in 1989 I was fascinated by the historical significance of the little ghost town, and by its beautiful location on a gravel delta, at the junction of the Quesnel and Cariboo rivers. Further explorations to Horsefly Creek, Keithley Creek, and the Snowshoe Plateau increased my understanding of East Cariboo's mining history and the difficulties faced by the first gold seekers and government officials. As I discovered more information about the people who lived in East Cariboo I wanted to share their fascinating stories. Wherever possible, I have used their own words, while always keeping in mind that the majority of the population — the indigenous people and the Chinese — had their histories, too.

Many friends and institutions have helped me with research over the last ten years. I thank them all, but especially Archivist Frances Gundry who guided me to useful sources at the British Columbia Archives, and was great company while exploring the Cariboo. Dr. L.C. Struik, Geological Survey of Canada, answered many questions about geology. Dave Falconer, R.C. Harris, and Gary and Lana Fox searched out and mapped the original gold rush trails and generously shared their time and knowledge. Alan and Donna Purdy, Margaret Murray Henderson and Lucy Robinson at Likely, and John and Anna Roberts and Kris Andrews at Williams Lake offered encouragement and friendly welcomes. June Wall at Quesnel provided photographs and helpful information on her Quesnel Forks ancestors. Dale Hunchak introduced me to her great-grandmother Martha Hutch and her family, who lived at Keithley Creek. Don Tarasoff at B.C. Heritage Trust, Martin Segger and Brad Morrison shared their research on Quesnel Forks. Al Lompart, Crown Land Registry, was most helpful in locating maps. Bill Quackenbush, Curator at Barkerville, and Dr. David Lai and Mavis Leung, at the University of Victoria, greatly assisted with the interpretation of Chinese documents. The staff at U.B.C. Special Collections, Williams Lake Archives, Barkerville Archives, California Historical Society, Oregon Historical Society, the New England Historic Genealogical Society, the Geological Survey of Canada, National Archives of Canada, and the Hudson's Bay Archives kindly helped with special requests. The staff at the British Columbia Archives have been outstanding in making their records available through the Internet, especially the Vital Statistics section, and they have dealt efficiently and cheerfully with all research requests. Reverend Robert Nind and Philip Nind, Mrs. Judith Curthoys and Mrs. P. Hatfield in England, and Mrs. M. McCulloch in Queensland, Australia, pieced together Philip Henry Nind's family and school history and later career. Marlyn Horsdal greatly improved the manuscript with her sensitive editing. Last but not least, my children, Carol and Robert, have alway been patient and supportive.

For ease in reading I have used Quesnel Forks, rather than the various spellings over the years: Forks of Quesnelle, Quesnelle City, and Quesnelle Forks. Similarly, Quesnelmouth has been used for simplicity. Cariboo East was the official title of the region in the 1860s, but East Cariboo was the common description and thus it is used in the text.

CONTENTS

Quesnel River mining area, Gustavus Epner map.
(CW-A 1913, BCA)

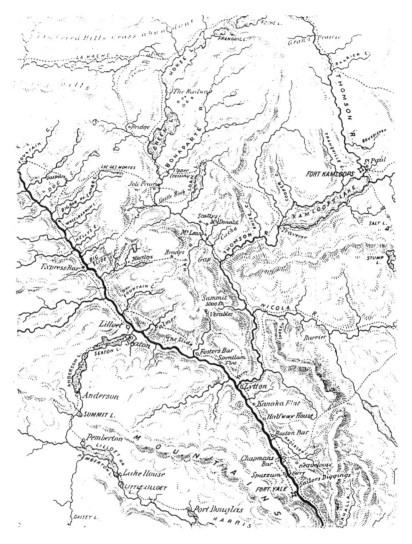

Lillooet/Fraser River trails, Gustavus Epner map.
(CW-A 1913, BCA)

For Margaret Murray Henderson and David G. Falconer

USA PURCHASED ALASKA 1867

INTRODUCTION

THE GLIMMERING LIGHTS of Quesnel Forks welcomed four weary travellers as they made their way down the hill to the village, on a winter evening in early February 1863. Indian Jim, French Joe, John "Cariboo" Cameron and Robert Stevenson had tramped 20 miles on snowshoes that day, from the mouth of Keithley Creek, pulling a sleigh laden with precious cargo. Cameron's winter earnings from his claim, a 50-pound sack of gold, was lashed to a coffin containing the body of his young wife, Sophia. Sophia could have been buried in the hillside portion of Cameron's claim at Williams Creek, which later became an official cemetery, or in the established Quesnel Forks cemetery. But as she lay dying of typhoid fever she begged a promise from her husband. She would not be the first white woman buried in the Cariboo; she would be taken home to Ontario.

Two Irish women, Catherine Lawless and Johanna McGuire, greeted the cold and tired men, the former providing overnight accommodation at her boarding house. Because there had been a number of deaths from smallpox at Quesnel Forks, Johanna urged them not to proceed any farther, but the next day they went on. Trekking south through the Cariboo in temperatures of 30 degrees below zero (F), they found the disease had claimed most of the natives at Beaver Lake and James Loway at Lac La Hache. The 400-

mile journey via Lillooet and Harrison Lake was arduous, but they arrived safely in Victoria on March 7.

For almost a hundred years Quesnel Forks provided a welcome haven for unique individuals like Cariboo Cameron, Robert Stevenson and Johanna McGuire. The first white gold seekers, Chinese placer miners, Jewish merchants, native packers, and hardy women stayed for a few days, a few years, or a lifetime. Now, all that marks the rich sequence of events are the graves in the cemetery, and the tumble-down cabins of Chinese miners, built on the gravel delta where the Cariboo gold rush began in 1859.

There are many ghost towns in British Columbia. Some, like Slocan and Phoenix, came into existence quickly, to take advantage of rich mineral deposits in the Kootenays. Indigenous sites, such as Ulkatcho and Kluskus in the Chilcotin, were occupied seasonally, for centuries. As once-thriving communities they offered shelter and sustenance; as part of a commercial network, they were linked intrinsically to other villages and sites nearby, and to major supply centres hundreds of miles away.[1]

For the most part, the men and women who lived in these villages had no idea they were contributing to history as they coped with earning a living, with illness, loneliness and death. From our vantage point more than a hundred years later, we see them as courageous, resilient, and willing to gamble. The development of our province depended on their enterprise and cooperation; with sufficient documentation, it is worth investigating the role they played in the rural history of British Columbia. What special reasons created a mining camp, a fishing village, or a summer gathering place and what made these places come to an end? Moving from a place, we can study a region, then the province with a clearer understanding of British Columbia's diversity. As western historian Patricia Limerick affirms, "without the local and regional levels of meaning, the more general levels are unrooted, ungrounded, abstract, and unconvincing."[2]

Quesnel Forks is located in the centre of East Cariboo which is bounded by the Cariboo Mountains on the east and the Fraser River on the west. For millions of years, glaciers from two or more ice ages wore down the Cariboo Mountains and the Quesnel Highlands, scouring out depressions for lakes and rivers, and depositing a thick layer of till over the landscape. These gold-bearing deposits shaped the future of the province.

The Fraser River gold rush brought about the formation of the colony of British Columbia; the Cariboo gold rush ensured its survival. Surface deposits of flour gold between Hope and Lytton were quickly depleted in 1858, when thousands of white and Chinese prospectors from California joined resident native men and women to work the gravel bars. Within a year, miners wanting larger stakes carried their searches elsewhere. Rushes to the Similkameen and Rock Creek in 1860 caused some excitement, but the rich discoveries to the north, along the Quesnel and Horsefly rivers, and Keithley Creek in 1859 and 1860, claimed most of the transient population.

Governor James Douglas wrote dolefully from Lillooet in September 1860, "The fate of the Colony hangs at this moment upon a thread, abundance of the precious metal is the only thing that can save it from ruin."[3] Within a month, his concerns evaporated. Eager crowds gathered at the docks in New Westminster and Victoria, to stare in amazement as bedraggled miners staggered down the gangplanks, laden with $2,000,000 in Cariboo gold. For the next few years, until gold seekers tapped the wealth of Williams and Lightning creeks, the East Cariboo placers, indirectly through road tolls and import taxes, financed law and order, government administration and road building. Thereafter, a consistent payout of gold kept prospectors in the region. Even today, the placer deposits of the Quesnel and Cariboo River areas remain one of the most important sources of gold in the Cariboo mining district.

Natural history and social history are firmly enmeshed in the story of East Cariboo. To understand the importance of the region, one must first look at the land and its natural resources. The area around Quesnel Lake is classified as the Interior Cedar-Hemlock biogeoclimatic zone. This is the most productive zone in the province, with the greatest variety of coniferous tree species. Dense stands of western hemlock, western red cedar, spruce and subalpine fir give way to Douglas fir and lodgepole pine on drier sites. The abundance of trees was a positive factor supporting the gold rush. Lumber for stores and cabins, mining flumes, wing dams, water wheels, bridges and ferries could be obtained easily.

When the gold seekers moved higher up the mountains, they fought their way through forests of spruce and fir and thickets of willow and wild rhododendron to reach the beautiful open parkland of the subalpine, at about 5,000 feet. Large expanses of grassy meadows, and rivulets and ponds on the Snowshoe Plateau nourished hundreds of pack animals and livestock in the summer. The breathtaking variety of wildflowers and distant view of snow-clad mountains soothed many weary, homesick young men.

Besides adequate timber reserves and pasture for animals, miners needed a dependable water supply for washing gold out of the gravel. At such high elevations, annual snowmelt from the mountains guaranteed enough water for sluicing on the major creeks and rivers in East Cariboo for part of the summer. The intensive hydraulic mining that commenced in the 1890s brought much heavier demands.

Provisions were scarce for the first few years of the Cariboo gold rush, but if a prospector knew how to hunt, trap, or fish, there was an abundance of food. Grizzly and black bears, lynx, caribou, mule deer, rabbits, beaver and muskrat frequented most areas. Feathers littered every campsite along the trail because grouse, ducks and other game birds were available in season. Moreover, the Quesnel Lake-Horsefly River system was a major sockeye-producing area, and many other lakes contained fish year round.

For thousands of years prior to the arrival of the miners, Secwepemc (Interior Salish) men and women hunted and fished in East Cariboo. Various sites in the Quesnel Lake and Horsefly areas contain evidence of seasonal cache pits and circular house sites. Unfortunately no detailed archaeological studies have been made of the fishing culture and we can only assume that occupation dates back 5,000 years or more. On his initial exploration of the South Fork River and Quesnel Lake, Philip Henry Nind, the first assistant gold commissioner, noted a native fishing camp on an island near the junction of the north arm of Quesnel Lake. Besides fishing from canoes, the Secwepemc may have operated a fish trap at the foot of Quesnel Lake that was taken over during the gold rush by Isaiah Mitchell.

In addition to abundant fish species, the Quesnel Lake/Horsefly area was rich in beaver colonies. Both native men and women traded a variety of furs at Fort Alexandria. Fishing, hunting and trapping were probably seasonal, with the natives wintering in pit houses near the Fraser River at Au Rapid, La Barge and Canoe.

The early French Canadian fur traders called the Cariboo Mountains "Siffleur Monts" because of the whistling marmots that inhabited the area. Unaware of Hudson's Bay Company cartography, the gold seekers named the mountains for the herds of caribou that grazed through the upper timberline.[4] Initially, "Caribou country" referred to the region from Cariboo Lake northward to Williams Creek, but the name eventually was applied to all of the area from 100 Mile House north to Quesnelmouth, and from the Cariboo Mountains west to the Fraser River.

If you could grasp one edge of the Quesnel Highlands and pull the Highlands and Cariboo Mountains out flat, you would have a surface that extended 550 miles to the Pacific Ocean. Plate tectonics, the process whereby land masses accrete onto one another, gradually compressed East Cariboo into 6,000-foot-high mountains, 200 miles in width. The last upheaval occurred at the time that the Rocky Mountains were formed, approximately 50,000,000 years ago. During the mountain-building process, geothermal activity dissolved gold, like salt in solution. When the hot liquid rose upward into cooler, limestone rock, the gold precipitated out. Geologist L.C. Struik has mapped the Downey succession of the Barkerville terrane as the main gold belt. It extends 50 miles, from Cariboo Lake to Wells, near Barkerville.[5]

Recent analysis of gold samples from placers south of the Cariboo and Quesnel rivers, by geologists K.C. McTaggart and John Knight, suggest that another important source of lode gold may have been located on Spanish Mountain, which is in a different terrane. The Quesnel terrane is volcanic in origin, and contains several deposits of copper-gold and copper-molybdenite ores that are currently being mined.

Except for the higher altitudes, thick stratified till covers most of the land surface in the Cariboo. Eroded from the Quesnel Highlands and Cariboo Mountains by two or more ice ages, 15,000,000 to 10,000,000 years ago, it filled ancient river beds, such as the Bullion Pit mine site, 300 feet deep. The high banks of silt, sand and gravel along the Fraser and Quesnel rivers are remnants from the infilling of a giant lake that encompassed Quesnel Forks, Williams Lake, and the Fraser River valley north to Prince George.[6]

During the ice ages glaciers broke down the quartz ledges on the Snowshoe Plateau and elsewhere, creating small deposits (lenses) of gold in the nearby creeks. Flakes and larger pieces, often in a quartz matrix, washed downstream, mixed with sand and gravel. When ice dams blocked lakes and rivers, gravel deposits built up along the river banks in a series of benches, and at the mouths of creeks in fan-shaped deltas. Each ice age produced deposits that were eroded and infilled by streams during interglacial periods.

The complicated erosional process created a jumble of fragmented gravel layers, some gold bearing, some not, turning East Cariboo into a giant casino. If a claim paid off, the "players" remained; if it didn't, they moved on, looking for better stakes. Just as gamblers become hooked on the thrill of winning, the men and women who earned their living from placer mining became addicted, too. Many of them spent their entire lives on the creeks, hoping to "get even."

The one location where gold could be found with any certainty was on bedrock, either mixed with clay, caught in potholes in the rough surface, or trapped under boulders. For miners, trying to reach bedrock was similar to playing the slot machines. After days and months of excavation — a costly investment in time and money — they might gain a handsome reward or lose everything. In addition to the bedrock of the present rivers and creeks, prospectors searched for buried channels that may have been an earlier water course, usually located at some height above the present river bed.

The gold from each creek, whether Keithley or Harvey Creek on the south side of the Snowshoe Plateau, or Williams or Lightning Creek on the north side, bore its own special identification. Modern geologists analyze the chemical content of gold specimens and compare it to gold in source rock, but old-time prospectors claimed they could tell by the colour, size and appearance of the gold where it had originated. Depending on how far the gold had travelled, samples could still contain pieces of quartz or be flattened and smooth. Placer gold varies in fineness from about 775 to about 950 (per one thousand parts of alloy); vein gold, from 850 to 910.[7] Gold was worth $17 to $20 an ounce between 1859 and 1930.

Cutting through the thick overburden, the Quesnel River system drains the golden heart of British Columbia, an immense area covering more than 4,000 square miles. The present drainage system has been in place for at least 10,000 years — long enough for gold to be washed downstream to the junction with the Fraser River, where rich gravel bars attracted the attention of the first non-native prospectors in 1859.

There seems little doubt that the men and women who rushed to the Cariboo between 1859 and 1865 knew they were making history. Many of the white and Chinese immigrants had already taken part in the California or Australia gold rushes and the local Fraser River gold rush. All around the world, newspapers reported their adventures and published the letters they sent home to loved ones. Even to have walked a few hundred miles on the gold rush trail, then turned back, was enough to boast about for the rest of their lives. For after all, they had "seen the elephant" or "Jinshan — the mountain of gold."[8]

On reading first-hand accounts in diaries and letters written home, one discovers that there was an immediate sense of community and intimacy about the Cariboo gold rush. It was much smaller than the California or Australia rushes, and it attracted groups of men who had already worked together or were acquainted with one another. (At the height of the Cariboo gold rush in 1863, there were probably no more than 2,500 white men and women and 1,000 Chinese in the region, whereas gold rushes in California and Australia had each drawn more than 100,000 people.)

Because a large mining claim increased the odds of striking it rich, three or more men formed a mining company, often of their own nationality, whether Canadian, American, French, German, Chinese, or British. Working together, building sluices and washing gravel, required a high degree of cooperation and trust, especially in primitive hydraulicking operations. When bank cave-ins were deliberately created as part of the hydraulicking process, miners risked their lives on a daily basis.

Furthermore, three gold rushes within a decade involved men who were still young and strong. The Cariboo gold rush attracted veterans of several "wars," once again setting forth to to do battle with natural forces. They brought with them all the placer mining expertise needed to work the gravels of the Cariboo: innovative methods of hydraulic mining and the most practical ways to build sluices, long toms and Cornish wheels. They knew how to "read" gravel deposits, and search out buried channels and nugget patches. And they knew the value of lode gold, usually in the form of quartz reefs. When the placer deposits were mined out, the reefs of East Cariboo held promises of further wealth. (Mining in California, between 1850 and 1860, developed in this fashion.) Jewish merchants and Latin American packers had also honed their skills during the earlier gold rushes. When they reached the Cariboo, the great distances and transportation difficulties between supplier and retailer did not discourage them.

Once a gold rush begins, it is impossible to stop the human tide. As the immigration to California in 1848 and to Australia in 1851 illustrated all too well, men and women will overcome incredible obstacles in the exciting rush for spoils. When the influx of prospectors led to the formation of the colony of British Columbia in 1858, Governor Douglas and Judge Matthew Baillie Begbie wisely borrowed from gold mining laws already established in Australia and New Zealand to formulate British Columbia's Gold Fields Act and Regulations.[9] Nevertheless, the Fraser River gold rush was a proving ground in many ways. It tested the ability of the colonial government to administer the new mining laws, the ingenuity of private enterprise to provide food, supplies and transportation, and the gold seekers themselves — winnowing out those men and women who could not survive the rigours of placer mining in the wilderness, who would not coexist peacefully with fellow miners and thousands of native inhabitants.

Centuries earlier, the native people of the Cariboo had forged their own sense of community and a close affinity with the land and its resources. They faced major upheavals to their way of life from the gold seekers. We are only now beginning to appreciate gold rush history from their perspective and to note their adaptations and contributions to it. A mystique of gold rushes is that the immigrating hordes "conquer" a new frontier. In reality, the gold seekers found on reaching British Columbia that the indigenous people and the land demanded respect and adaptation. Moreover, these two demands were enforced by British law.

By the tally of Jesuit priest Father John Nobili, who visited Fort Langley and accompanied the Hudson's Bay fur brigades as far north as Babine Lake between 1845 and 1848, there were approximately 3,000 Interior Salish in the country from the Okanagan to Fort Alexandria. The most numerous group were the Couteau, so called because they wore knives on cords around their necks. They lived along the Fraser River, numbering 1,530; and at the Fountain, numbering 1,127. He recorded 1,255 natives at Fort Alexandria; some were Shuswhap (or Atnahs) but most were Carriers (or Porteurs).

Under British law, all men and women were considered equal. Douglas and Begbie went to great efforts to stress this fact. At the beginning of the Fraser River gold rush, Douglas visited mining camps at Hope and Yale in late May 1858, and again in September to impress the law upon the miners. Over 190 white miners and approximately 400 natives were engaged in placer mining at Yale in June. There had been some altercations between the two groups and Douglas stressed that "the laws would protect the rights of the Indian, no less than those of the white man." Begbie was proud of the fact that, unlike California, native men and women could and did lay charges against white men and have their day in court. The miners soon learned that if there were no white witnesses, convictions would be made solely on native testimony.[10]

Not enough can be said about the prior influence of the Hudson's Bay Company on the social attitudes and status of the various indigenous peoples. A close relationship with the land made the natives sensitive to the dangers to their food supply and to their trading practices with the HBC, especially if the annual salmon migration in late summer was interrupted. The rich fishing sites at Lytton, the Fountain and Pavilion had furnished dried fish for trading with the HBC for 30 years. Although the HBC guns the natives acquired in trade were not of the best quality, many men were armed and could have carried out guerrilla attacks on the newcomers, as happened in northwestern California and Queensland, Australia, during the same time period. But after nearly four decades of contact with the HBC, trading at the various land forts or with its ships, natives were prepared to barter, not fight with the miners. The exception was the band located at Okanagan Forks which had routinely harassed Hudson's Bay personnel as they passed through their territory, and now attacked the gold seekers. To ensure good relations along the fur brigade route south from Fort Alexandria to Fort Vancouver, leaders of the HBC brigades made small payments in the form of tobacco and clothing to the various groups of natives, as they passed through their territories. When miners began using the brigade trails, they were expected to continue this courtesy.[11]

There were numerous altercations with white miners during the Fraser River gold rush of 1858,[12] and for the first years of the Cariboo gold rush. Fortunately, conflicts in the Cariboo never reached the point where armed miners threatened to destroy villages and kill natives as happened in the Fraser Canyon in 1858. When refusal to barter with the Nlaka'pamux or Thompson natives precipitated the death of a French miner south of Lytton, Captain H.M. Snyder, at Yale, undertook a "march of peace" in August 1858 that improved relations.[13]

A year later, rumours reached Victoria of a possible uprising near Lytton. Douglas advised Henry Maynard Ball, the assistant gold commissioner stationed there, to use prudence when dealing with the local natives who were "well acquainted with our laws and customs" and had always been treated with kindness by the government. Douglas warned Ball not to place much value on the miners' reports of native unrest. If necessary, he should obtain the services of an interpreter from HBC Factor Donald McLean at Kamloops to gain an explanation from the local natives. Chief Spintlum at Lytton should also be involved.[14]

Many of the early prospectors in the Cariboo came from California, but only one incident in 1860 suggests the harsh discrimination that reduced the aboriginal population of California from 90,000 in 1850 to 29,000 in 1870. At a mining site near the mouth of the Quesnel River, a notorious troublemaker, Moses Anderson, formerly one of General Walker's filibusters, callously shot a native boy when he refused to take him to a native woman. Dr. J.B. Wilkinson (who was also a miner) saved the boy's life. Anderson quickly left the country.[15]

Mutual dependence helped maintain some sort of equilibrium between white and indigenous residents in the Cariboo. Both native men and women soon found employment packing supplies for merchants, and the women earned extra income making moccasins and snowshoes. Unlike the Fraser River gold rush, in East Cariboo the natives do not appear to have taken part in placer mining, and further stability was gained when the earliest settlers, Peter Dunlevy, James Sellers, Thomas Moffitt and William Pinchbeck, formed partnerships with local aboriginal women and fathered children. Native generosity kept many starving miners alive, as they returned empty-handed from the goldfields — a fact not widely publicized.[16]

Through the colonial correspondence, mining claims registers and, later, the federal census reports of 1881 and 1891, we come to appreciate the contribution made by Chinese miners to the Cariboo gold rush and to the settlement period. They first arrived from California with the vanguard of white miners in 1858, and within a year they were emigrating directly from Canton. Some Chinese remained on the lower Fraser River to work the claims abandoned by the white miners, but gradually, more and more found their way up the Fraser River, beyond Lillooet.

During the California and Australia gold rushes, the Chinese, like the indigenous people, had been treated harshly. They were often driven from their claims and their possessions destroyed. As they worked their way up the Fraser River in 1859, Assistant Gold Commissioner Thomas Elwyn, at Lillooet, expressed concern for their safety to Governor Douglas. Elwyn heard a rumour that miners working on the Quesnel River would not allow Chinese beyond Fort Alexandria and he was unsure how far his jurisdiction carried. Douglas placed the onus for safety on the miners, responding that if the Chinese wanted protection they must stay closer to Elwyn's location.[17]

Natives also took part in harrassing Chinese miners. When Douglas visited Lillooet in September 1860, the Grand Jury presented a list of requests. Among them was protection for the Chinese from natives or others. Two Chinese miners had been murdered by natives because they had assaulted a native woman. The jury felt that the Chinese were an economic advantage and welcome citizens.[18] Two months earlier, at Lytton, Ball reported to the Colonial Secretary that the natives were inclined to treat the Chinese miners "as inferior beings to themselves, and all badly disposed white men will have every opportunity of committing outrages on them."[19]

The Chinese used good sense in shadowing the white miners, rather than being in the vanguard. They generally took over abandoned claims, thus avoiding harassment by white miners who were always looking for a new strike. The British law of equality gave them further protection, but certainly not immunity from prosecution. Begbie's first court case in the Cariboo, at Quesnel Forks in 1861, involved three Chinese miners charged with the murder of one of their countrymen.

It would be easy to dismiss the miners as ne'er-do-wells and troublemakers, looking for a quick gain. The problems caused by Moses Anderson proved that there was indeed a criminal element amongst the hundreds who worked their way north in 1860. However, the majority of the miners wanted law and order so they could carry out as much mining as possible during the short season. Claims were easily jumped, and could not be bought and sold with any degree of security unless they were legally registered.

Furthermore, many of the gold seekers had been raised in good homes in Great Britain, Europe, eastern Canada and the United States, where they had acquired family values and a Victorian-era respect for religion, law and order. At Ferguson's Bar in September 1860, and at Antler Creek in 1861, miners were quick to send petitions to Nind and Judge Begbie when they felt that matters were getting out of control. Begbie attributed the general tranquillity of the population to the classes of men involved in mining, and to their good sense. He thought well of the visible minorities — the industrious Chinese and Negro miners.[20] Dr. John S. Helmcken, son-in-law of James Douglas, concurred. "The Germans and Frenchmen who came to the mining regions were not gutter spawn," he told William Trimble, "but often younger sons of good families, or peasants; and they were well trained to obedience to law."[21]

The cooperation of the native population, the desire for law and order on the part of the miners, and the foresight of Begbie and Douglas in replicating the tested mining laws of Australia and New Zealand, were the major factors that ensured stability in British Columbia's gold mining areas for decades to come. It was also important that the right men were chosen to administer the mining laws.

Douglas advised the Colonial Office in London that he wanted to hire men acquainted with the geography of British Columbia, who had a knowledge of Indian character, and "a sufficient degree of intelligence to administer the law with propriety and discretion."[22] The colonial government was well served by the first administrators sent to the Cariboo (initially named the Alexandria District) and to Lytton and Lillooet: Philip Henry Nind, Thomas Elwyn, Peter O'Reilly, Oliver Hare, and Henry Maynard Ball. Of Anglo-Irish stock, all but Nind had received training in the army, or with the constabulary. They were energetic, hardy outdoorsmen, and excellent horsemen. Most importantly, they were fair and level-headed in dealing with mining disputes.[23]

The gold mining regulations were well suited to the isolated mining camps where only one or two government officials and an equal number of police constables supervised upwards of 2,000 miners. Assistant gold commissioners held the powers of stipendiary magistrates to arbitrate claims, and to hear all mining disputes. With the help of police constables, they issued mining licences, registered claims, collected taxes, and supervised the sale of Crown Land and the construction and maintenance of roads and public works. They also acted as Indian agents, with the power to lay out reserves. Miners who were unhappy with the magistrate's decisions could appeal judgments on disputes worth more than £20 to the Supreme Court, held by Begbie once or twice a year, when he made his circuits.

In rural areas, where the population was spread over many square miles, assistant gold commissioners took on extra duties as coroners and unofficial social workers, ensuring that law and order was maintained, the dead properly interred, and the insane, aged and destitute cared for. After confederation, the duties of assistant gold commissioners were divided between government agents and gold commissioners, the latter responsible for administering mining legislation.

We tend to think of gold rush society as a temporary phenomenon — in a few short years the men and women rush on, leaving the countryside abandoned. East Cariboo history does not support this theory. Packers, miners and merchants, many with native wives, remained on the creeks or nearby in the Williams Lake, Soda Creek and Chilcotin areas to the end of their days. At Lac La Hache, 150 Mile House and Quesnelmouth they were joined by ex-Hudson's Bay employees and their part-native families. Over the years they gained improvements for the region by petitioning the provincial government for better roads and ferry service, mail delivery, health care, and police protection.

Because natives had lived in the Cariboo for thousands of years, they had a natural sense of community that may have been threatened by the influx of miners, but never extinguished. Beset by smallpox and white man's alcohol, they maintained their traditions in the face of difficult odds. They are always there, even though the story of Quesnel Forks and East Cariboo is structured mainly around the men and women who formed the backbone of the mining community: government officials, merchants, mining engineers, and prospectors. Native men and women provided the needed interpreters, guides, companions, and labour for the gold rush and settlement periods.

For written records, we rely on assistant gold commissioners Nind, Elwyn, Hare, and William Stephenson whose official, detailed correspondence described mining conditions from 1860 to 1914. And without personal letters from William Barry, John Hobson, Jim May and George Hargreaves, and the wonderful diaries of Robert Scott and Joel Palmer, we would miss the three-dimensional aspect that makes regional history so appealing.

This history of East Cariboo ends at William Stephenson's death in January 1916. A new era was beginning as stage coaches and ox trains gave way to passenger cars. The long-awaited railroad, with a terminus at Williams Lake, would be completed three years later in 1919. Ranchers sought new ways to manage their farms since it was no longer necessary to provide grain for hundreds of pack animals and horse teams.

Today, East Cariboo continues to flourish, and ever hopeful prospectors still search for "glory holes." But on the gravel delta at the junction of the Quesnel and Cariboo rivers, the old log buildings have all but lost their fight against the elements. As a lone prospector checks out a patch of black sand on the river bank, only the ghosts of Quesnel Forks cheer him on.

CHAPTER ONE

1859

"I think there is hiyou gold up here."[1]

James Jasper May

THE IRISH IMMIGRANTS who came to North America, to escape
the potato famine, brought with them a strong will to succeed.
Members of Hannah Barry's family in San Francisco were no exception.
When news of the Fraser River gold rush reached California in early
1858, two of her sons, Thomas and James, travelled north to open a
saloon at Fort Yale, in what would soon become the colony of British
Columbia. Financial backing for their venture most likely came from a
relative, Theodore A. Barry, who owned a wholesale and retail liquor
business in San Francisco. Theodore and his partner, Benjamin A.
Patten, managed the most elegant "gentlemen's saloon" in the city.[2]

A future brother-in-law, Sam Adler, and other merchants joined
Tom and James on Front Street at Yale, which was the head of steamer
navigation on the Fraser River. The colonial government soon installed
magistrates and a revenue officer. Early government attempts at law
and order, coupled with the warmth and cheer at the saloons and

1

stores, made Yale an important base for eager prospectors working on nearby claims at Hills Bar and Emory Bar, or heading up river to the many sites above Boston Bar.

In their eagerness to explore farther north, the prospectors who had wintered over at Yale ventured up the Fraser Canyon in January and February 1859, pulling sleds loaded with supplies. By spring, the Barry brothers were catering to a fresh invasion of gold seekers who pressed beyond The Forks (Lytton), Cayoosh (Lillooet) and the Fountain to Fort Alexandria and the Canal (Quesnel) River. Freebooting survivors of General Walker's Nicaragua invasion shared the trail to the upper country with well-bred immigrants from England, who didn't know "paydirt from top dirt,"[3] and experienced miners from Hill's Bar such as Captain Bowen, Ned Campbell and James Moore.

About this time an Irish woman arrived at Yale. She went by the name of Johanna McGuire, and may have been the woman Bishop

Sam Adler.
(F-07320, BCA)

2

George Hills heard about on his visit to Fraser River mining sites in 1860. Several stories claim that Johanna had a dual personality: pious and caring when sober; foul mouthed and slatternly when inebriated. Johanna was just as strong willed as the Barry brothers and she, too, joined in the rush to the Cariboo.[4]

Throughout the summer and fall there were weekly, sometimes daily newspaper reports about the Quesnel River gold discoveries. By year end, Forks of Quesnelle was a familiar name not only to the Barry brothers at Yale but to residents of New Westminster, Victoria, Portland and San Francisco.

Information began appearing in Victoria newspapers in July 1859 confirming the rich diggings on the Quesnel River, where miners were making ten to fifty dollars a day. In early August the Victoria *Colonist* published a letter from Jim May to his friend "B.", dated June 15, 1859, Fort Alexandria:

> I embrace this opportunity of writing you a few lines to let you know that we are well and hope you are enjoying the same blessing. The water is very high now, and we cannot work; but I think it will not be hard to find ten or fifteen dollar diggings when the water falls. We are located on Canal River, about twenty five miles above Fort Alexander [*sic*]. I think there is hiyou gold up here, and if you and the boys come you had better buy your grub at the Forks and pack it on animals to this place. If you come you had better buy enough to last you until cold weather sets in.[5]

The prevailing mood was cautious while water was high during spring runoff. It was foolish for men to travel 400 miles north only to be "humbugged." But once the rivers began to subside, further reports filtered down from reliable travellers such as James Batterton, the expressman. "Quesnel River fever" caught the Barry brothers and other merchants at Fort Yale, Lytton and Lillooet unprepared for both the initial rush, and then the depression that set in when most of the miners headed north. A Lillooet resident complained, "If I had been a trader, and brought up with me 20,000 pounds of bacon and ditto of flour, I could have got rid of all the bacon before breakfast, and had an empty house by dinner time."[6]

Working north from Lillooet, prospectors took advantage of an intricate network of aboriginal trails to reach Fort Alexandria and the Quesnel River. One ancient route parallelled the banks of the Fraser River to Alkali Lake and thence to Williams Lake, where it connected with the Hudson's Bay brigade trail to the fort. Other routes led over Pavilion Mountain to Cutoff Valley (Clinton) or followed Hat Creek to the Bonaparte Valley, where they tied into the brigade trail at Green Lake. A third group of gold seekers arrived at the Bonaparte Valley after working their way up the Fraser and Thompson rivers from Yale.

Until spring runoff raised the height of the Fraser River, the miners who reached the vicinity of Fort Alexandria in 1859 were able to prospect the exposed gravel bars up river to the junction with the Quesnel River. There, the richness of Ferguson's Bar and Long Bar left no doubt that a major source of gold lay eastward. Placer gold production for the colonies of Vancouver Island and British Columbia more than doubled, from $705,000 in 1858, to $1,616,072 in 1859. The output increased to $2,228,543 in 1860, and with the Antler Creek and Williams Creek strikes, to $2,668,118 in 1861. The richest year for British Columbia was 1863, with $3,913,563. Thereafter, the total amount declined annually.[7]

By the end of the summer Benjamin MacDonald, Jim May,[8] Thomas "Dancing Bill" Latham, John Rose and William Ross Keithley were among the eager miners who reached the gravel delta at the junction of the North and South Forks of the Quesnel River (now called the Cariboo and Quesnel rivers). Here was the moment of truth. Most of the gravel banks and stream beds up river from the delta contained gold in paying quantities, i.e., at least ten dollars a day per man. Some of the gold was coarse, like buckshot. They were moving in the right direction toward one of the ancient mother lodes — the quartz reefs of the Snowshoe Plateau. Dancing Bill, said to be a nephew of Governor Milton S. Latham of California, discovered a small creek draining into the South Fork, three miles above Quesnel Forks.[9] Latham's Dancing Bill Company commenced working low-grade gravel that paid off consistently for the next 40 years.

At the same time as the Quesnel River area was being explored, other miners followed the Beaver River Valley to the Horsefly River. They located a rich placer ten miles upstream from Quesnel Lake.

James Moore, one of the first miners on Hill's Bar at Yale in 1858, established the Blue Lead mine at Horsefly with partners Henry Ingram and Archie Rutherford. They were joined by John McLean, John McClellan, Mike Keenan, Joseph Paterson, Dennis Cain, Col. Dixon, Jim Waldon, Otto Lloyd and T.S. Hill. Presently other miners arrived. Ira Crow, Dave Gardiner, George Hide and William Carlyle worked in the vicinity for a brief time then built a raft and drifted down Quesnel Lake to explore the Quesnel River.

Although Moore mentions Ira "Hiram" Crow in his account, he omits Peter Curran Dunlevy, James Sellers, Tom Moffitt and Tom Menefee who, according to Alexander McInnes, were the discoverers of the Horsefly gold deposits. Stories of these first arrivals at Horsefly River were published in the *Ashcroft Journal* in January 1896, when Moore was living near Quesnel Forks and Dunlevy at Soda Creek. The fact that the stories do not correlate make them suspect. Was one old pioneer trying to top the other? Unfortunately, mining records for the Alexandria District do not contain any of the early Horsefly claims.

The gold seekers bound for Quesnel Forks had to overcome numerous difficulties before reaching their destination. The two most important challenges — repeated annually throughout the gold rush years — were establishing and maintaining trails and locating enough pasture for horses, mules and livestock. The centuries-old aboriginal trail network, and the Hudson's Bay Company fur brigade trail from Kamloops via Green Lake to Fort Alexandria, greatly assisted miners venturing into the Cariboo region. But conditions changed dramatically once prospectors left the brigade trail, destined for Quesnel Forks. The aboriginal trails leading northeast from the brigade trail to Beaver River Valley and Quesnel Lake terminated at beaver ponds and fishing sites, not gold placers.

A new, more direct route from Beaver Valley to the river bank opposite Quesnel Forks had to be made through 20 miles of burned and fallen timber and mosquito-infested swamps. Thirty-two-year-old Kentucky adventurer Timoleon Love acted quickly to brush out a rough trail through the morass to his ferry landing opposite Quesnel Forks. But he left maintenance to the packers who spent little if any time removing downed timber in their haste to get through. Forced over this tortuous route, mules, horses and livestock created huge mudholes that claimed hundreds of animals during the first three years of the gold rush. Judge Begbie reported seeing five loaded packhorses drowning at one time, and young men often mentioned this grim part of the journey in their diaries and letters home to loved ones.

Once the gold seekers reached the Quesnel River they had to pay ferry tolls. Rates were 50¢ for a passenger, 50¢ per one hundred pounds for freight, and $1.50 for loaded animals. Timoleon Love secured his enterprise by journeying to Lillooet for a ferry licence in June 1860. He then sold out to James Locke and Benjamin Hart for $600. During the same year John Tow established a second ferry crossing ten miles below Quesnel Forks on the Quesnel River. Tow's ferry connected with a trail that followed the high ridge beyond the North Fork River to Davis' Crossing at Keithley Creek, approximately eight miles above Cariboo Lake. Packers and miners endured the awkwardness and danger of the ferries for two years, until Thomas Barry and Sam Adler bridged the South Fork River to Quesnel Forks in March of 1861.

Locke and Hart next applied, unsuccessfully, for a charter to build a road from Lillooet to the Thompson River or the Cariboo. Locke, a native of Waterville, New York, died in the squalid New Westminster prison in November 21, 1862, awaiting trial for a $6,000 debt and possible embezzlement. His death led to changes in the law of British Columbia, ensuring that men and women could not be sent to debtor's prison.

More than anything else, the importance of good pasture and solid footing for animals determined the direction of the trails. Between Williams Lake and Quesnel Forks the only decent pastures for animals were at Beaver River Valley and Little Lake. Packers Richard Dorsey and Joseph and A. Deschilles established the first stopping place in Beaver Valley in 1860, followed by Peter Dunlevy and Jim Sellers in 1861. Dunlevy and Sellers planted a large vegetable garden and sowed fields of grain. Their generous meals of fresh beef, mutton, lake trout, churned butter, and locally grown vegetables earned them the reputation as the best stopping house in the Cariboo.

At Williams Lake, Thomas Davidson also commenced farming. After three long weeks on the trail to the Cariboo, weary travellers and packers found his stopping house and grassy fields, at the foot of the lake, a pleasant respite. Assistant Gold Commissioner Philip Nind chose the area for his headquarters when he arrived to dispense law and order in August 1860. The first jail in the Cariboo, built there in 1861, also became the first post office for the region. Police Constable George Gompertz took on duties as postmaster, supervising the distribution of mail east to Quesnel Forks and Antler Creek. It cost three shillings (75¢) to send a letter from New Westminster to Quesnel Forks.

When packers reached the vicinity of Quesnel Forks, they camped in the lush meadows at Little Lake because there was no pasture for animals at the Forks. The steep hill down to the South Fork River, opposite the village, was best attempted in the morning. With luck, animals could be unloaded at the ferry terminal and returned to the meadows by evening of the same day. A popular stopping house operated by O'Brien and one of Walker's filibusters, Robert Hamilton "Hamy" Smith, sprang up at the Little Lake site. It featured a store and stables for 14 horses that in good times generated $1,800 a month.[10]

Legalizing claims presented another problem. During the Fraser River gold rush, miners at Yale made their own mining laws for a year before Governor James Douglas proclaimed the Gold Fields Regulation Act in August 1859. Drafted by Judge Begbie, the Act gave Douglas authority to install assistant gold commissioners who could register claims, collect mining licences, and act as magistrates to arbitrate claims.

Three hundred miles north of Yale, Cariboo miners waited almost two mining seasons for the arrival of a government official. The nearest assistant gold commissioner, Thomas Elwyn, was located 150 miles away at Lillooet with orders to remain at his post.[11] Assistant gold commissioner Philip Henry Nind did not reach Quesnel Forks until late September 1860, forcing the miners to police themselves and to establish a method of marking their claims. They solved the latter problem easily by naming creeks after themselves — the most practical way to set a mining claim on a map. This method also ensured that their names or company titles were preserved for posterity: Dancing Bill's Gulch, Rose Gulch, and Morehead, Hazeltine, Sellers, Keithley, Weaver and Harvey creeks.

Nind and Elwyn were sympathetic toward the Cariboo miners who had difficulties following the Gold Fields Regulation Act. The Act set down 25 feet by 30 feet as the size of a claim, with a limit of one claim per miner plus one discovery claim. The miners in the Cariboo staked 100-foot-square claims, and allowed one discovery claim and one claim by purchase. Nind did not enforce the 25-foot claim, agreeing with the miners that it was too narrow for bench claims. When Elwyn took over from Nind in the spring of 1862, Douglas requested him to stop the miners from abusing the mining laws. Elwyn replied from Quesnel Forks:

> I am aware that the claims are larger than allowed by law, & also that each Free Miner can legally hold only one claim. I beg however most strongly to recommend that no existing titles should be interfered with, 1st because it would be an injustice towards those who have either taken up or bought claims under the existing custom; and 2nd because I believe there is no force in the two Colonies sufficient to effect such a change. I am directed by His Excellency if on investigation the above abuses are found to exist "to institute measures to put an end to them." I neither can, nor dare, carry out these orders.[12]

The mining regulations that worked so well on the Fraser River did not cover dry diggings in the Cariboo where the right to dump tailings, to tunnel or to carry water over a neighbouring claim needed defining. The Gold Fields Act allowed for the creation of local mining boards when there was a sufficient permanent population, and Nind hoped that practical amendments to the Act could be made by such boards.

Few men paused any length of time to work a claim if it was not paying well. The minute news broke of a rich strike on another creek, they dashed off in that direction. When the ground proved worthwhile, groups of three or more were the most successful because they could stake a number of claims together to ensure a large placer-mining operation. Once staked, the claims could not be left vacant for more than 72 hours or mining rights were forfeited. In order to preserve their investments during the winter when most miners returned south, the assistant gold commissioner laid over claims, usually from October 1 to the following May or June. The laying-over process allowed miners to seek a warmer climate during the winter yet still retain their mining rights. But they had to be "on the ground" by the proclaimed date in the spring and re-register their claims for the coming season or someone else could "jump" them.

The miners came from every level of society, and from many nations. Pursuit of gold put them all on a common level. Americans such as William Ross Keithley, James May, Isaiah Mitchell, Nemiah T. "Black Jack" Smith and Thomas "Dancing Bill" Latham met up with John Rose, a Scot, and Benjamin "Black or Siwash" MacDonald, born near Fort Edmonton to Hudson's Bay Company Chief Factor Archibald McDonald and his part-native wife Jane.[13] In the fall of 1860, Benjamin staked one of the first claims on the north side of the Snowshoe Plateau at Antler Creek. He sold out to his partners for $3,000 in 1861, and joined up with his half-brothers Ranald and Allan to operate a pack train, with headquarters on the Bonaparte River near Cache Creek. (In 1861, Ranald applied for a charter for a toll road from Bella Coola across the Chilcotin to Quesnelmouth, but did not follow through with his plans.)

Despite strenuous efforts by packers and merchants, by the end of the summer there were still only enough provisions for the daily needs of the miners. A six-month grubstake, sufficient to tide them over the winter, was almost impossible to obtain or afford. Many miners had made their "pile" and left for homes in eastern Canada or the warmer climate of San Francisco. Others chose to winter over at Lillooet, New Westminster, and Victoria, vowing to return north as soon as possible in the spring. Without any law enforcement or assistant gold commissioner to register their claims, they had managed to cooperate peacefully. A few determined miners such as Thomas Latham, William Keithley and John Rose remained in the Cariboo to work dry bench diggings which paid $20 to $100 a day, although, healthwise, staying on was not good for them. They needed a break from the miserable diet of bacon, beans and bannock in order to build themselves up for a new round of backbreaking labour the following year. Keithley would last until June 1862 before poor health forced him to take a leave of absence.

By November, Judge Begbie estimated there were no more than 2,000 white people left in the colony of British Columbia. At Yale, James Barry was content to accept the downturn in customers and continue the saloon business,[14] but his brother Tom and Sam Adler craved the excitement of a mining frontier. As Tom and Sam followed gold rushes to the Cariboo, Omineca and Cassiar regions in the years to come, they would be joined by more relatives: brothers William, John and Michael Barry, and Moses Adler.

The supreme test of the colonial government lay ahead next mining season. Would the system of assistant gold commissioners and police constables that managed the Fraser River gold rush in 1859 work as well 400 miles away? Would eager prospectors starve when tenuous supply lines failed to provide enough food? And would there be enough fodder for horses, mules and livestock? These problems troubled few of the miners as they headed south at the onset of winter. Tales of their adventures only served to excite the urban populations, resulting in a flood of humanity the following year.

CHAPTER TWO

1860

"Years hence, on railroads and steamers, men will
remember the struggles they had in the virgin
forests and beaver swamps of British Columbia."[1]
Judge Matthew Baillie Begbie

THE ENTREPRENEURS WHO arrived at Quesnel Forks with
the gold seekers in the spring of 1860 brought with them enough
financial capital to ensure that the Cariboo gold rush had a sound
mercantile base. Although they held interests in claims from time to
time, they were not miners, they were capitalists. The first toll-bridge
owners, the saloon keepers, and the Jewish and Chinese merchants
set up shop at Quesnel Forks and made it the most important
commercial centre in the Cariboo for the next three years.
Expressmen and packers, and a gold escort, made it the terminus of a
400-mile supply route that began at New Westminster. One estimate
gave $900 per ton as the total packing cost to lay goods down at
Quesnel Forks in 1859. Two years later the cost had been reduced to
$700 per ton.

A letter from Forks Canal (Quesnel Forks), May 21, 1860, to Sutton and Helmering, wholesale liquor and cigar dealers at Fort Hope, set the scene:

> Gents: We received your favor of May 13th; was glad to hear from you. All well here; have been here about four weeks. Robinson has been at Horse Fly since we came to the upper country. We rather slipped up on that operation; Horse Fly proved a failure. We only took part of our stock to that place; the remainder arrived last week by pack train, French Ned, safe and in good order. We shall locate about three miles from the Forks of Canal. On the south branch of Rose's Bar, I think the chances are good for a good trade. I started mining — got a very good claim, but sold out yesterday for five hundred dollars, clear of all expenses. Johnson the butcher, George Weaver and Dave Potts have claims on the same gulch, and are all doing well.
>
> The miners here are striking good diggings daily and I do think that we will have plenty of diggings for any number of miners who may come up. The great drawback to this country is the great difficulty in getting to it.
>
> Provisions are very high, staple articles rating about 70 cents per pound, and are considered low at that rate, in comparison to what they have been. When I first arrived here all kinds of supplies were scarce, and rating at about $1.50 per pound. That was the principal cause of so many persons leaving here for the lower country. They could not stay and prospect without considerable money. Prospecting is expensive, being confined principally to ravines and gulches, but in nearly all cases successful where persons have had the means to give it a fair trial.
>
> There are any quantity of one horse whisky sellers from Oregon and Similkameen. We have no doubt but what we will do well.
>
> [Hiram] Robinson and [James] Sellers
>
> P.S. I forgot to give you a description of the character of the gold we get; it is all coarse. Dave Potts & Co. have taken out the largest pieces as yet, some of them over fifty dollars solid gold — I believe three pieces — and quite a large number of nuggets weighing from 20 to 40 dollars. Besides this, a number of other companies have taken out nearly as large pieces.[2]

After modest beginnings at Yale, Thomas Barry, in partnership with Samuel Adler, cut a broad swath through the Cariboo, acquiring and selling saloons and the 150 Mile stopping house. Their most enduring legacy in the Quesnel Forks area was the South Fork River bridge. Although replaced a number of times, it served the public until the 1940s.

As soon as travelling was feasible, Barry and Adler looked over prospects in the Cariboo, including a visit to Horsefly. By the end of June they had secured a charter from the colonial government to build the South Fork bridge. For payment of an annual rental fee of £80 ($400), they gained the right to collect tolls for five years. They were to relinquish the bridge to the colonial government should it wish to take over management. To fill in the months until bridge construction could begin at low water in November, the two men built a saloon at the north end of the bridge site. There must have been some rousing times at the Bridge House for it featured two first class billiard tables, and two young owners who enjoyed entertaining. Adler played the violin and was a fine raconteur; Barry had a good singing voice and could readily defend himself in a fight.

Another ambitious immigrant from California, William Ballou, was indirectly involved with Quesnel Forks. He began his career as a one-man express company during the California gold rush. With San Francisco partners he started Ballou's Express during the Fraser River gold rush in 1858, extending service to Lillooet in 1859. At Lillooet, Ballou connected with Dan Braly (Braley) and Company's Pony Express which served Quesnel River and the Cariboo twice monthly, including "every mining camp and public place en route." James Batterton was Ballou's expressman, operating from Yale north.[3]

Many of the first merchants at Quesnel Forks were Jewish. J. Boas, D.J. Hamburger, S.D. Levi, David Sokolosky, Herman Lewin, Isadore Braverman and Herman Schultz had established headquarters in Victoria or New Westminster, possibly with San Francisco partners. Non-Jewish businessmen included Schultz's partner Jasper Trickey, merchant William Morehead; tinsmith Edward Griffin; butchers and traders Frederick Black and William Carlyle; restaurant and hotel owners Andrew Jackson Abbott and T.S. Handley; and packers Josiah Crosby Beedy and Frank Fulford (who, like Barry and Adler, owned a saloon with a billiard table). Abbott and Handley also owned a 320-acre ranch at Lac La Hache.

Chinese miners came to the Cariboo increasingly from 1860 onwards. When Nind visited the Fraser River mining sites, following his arrival in the Alexandria District in August 1860, he found them working a gravel bar near the mouth of the Quesnel River. The Chinese refused to take out mining licences, possibly because they had very little money. Nind did not sell his first licence to them until April 1861.

Estimates of the number of Chinese miners in the Cariboo during the gold rush range up to 6,000. This number is exaggerated because

Jasper N. Trickey, merchant at Quesnel Forks in 1862.
(G-05781, BCA)

scarcity of provisions during the first years curtailed a large population. However, once the Cariboo gold rush died down and the
transient white miners moved on, the Chinese took over. By 1877 the
Cariboo was virtually a Chinese province, with over 50% more
Chinese than white miners (1510 versus 949). The first federal census
for the Cariboo, in 1881, confirmed that they outnumbered white
settlers almost two to one. The Quesnel Forks/Keithley Creek area
had the largest population of Chinese in the province after Victoria
and Nanaimo.[4]

The increase in Oriental miners attracted the services of merchants
Kwong Lee and Ei Tie. The Kwong Lee Company had its beginnings
in San Francisco, but was now based in Victoria, importing tea, rice
and other foodstuffs from China. In time they would build their own
opium factory. During the Fraser River gold rush they established a
warehouse and store at Yale, and upon moving north to Quesnel
Forks, invested in stores, real estate and mining operations in the
Quesnel Forks, Keithley Creek and Quesnelmouth areas. To maintain
a dependable supply line, Kwong Lee transported goods to the
Cariboo with their own teams of oxen. Ei Tie may have been related to
another Victoria merchant and opium manufacturer, King Tie. Like
Kwong Lee, Ei Tie followed the gold rushes, with a store at Yale, then
at Quesnel Forks. He owned a pack train, and built a warehouse at
the north end of the South Fork bridge. In 1873, Oliver Hare, the
first government agent at Quesnel Forks, converted this building into
a residence with a jail.

One thousand miles away in Oregon, cattle ranches had multiplied
since white settlement began in the 1840s. When news of the Fraser
River gold rush reached Oregon, a hardy, energetic band of packers
quickly organized herds of cattle and sheep to drive north on the two
Hudson's Bay Company brigade routes. One of the earliest traders
and packers was General Joel Palmer, famous for guiding wagon
trains across the western plains on the Oregon Trail in the 1840s, and
later for his role as Indian Superintendent in Oregon. He was a
handsome man, with a square jaw and deep-set eyes. At age 50, he
still possessed an amazing energy and willingness to gamble on new
projects. His leadership skills while conducting wagon caravans, and
his commisary experience during the Indian Wars in Oregon, enabled

15

him to locate suppliers and put expeditions together efficiently and safely. In 1858 he took one wagon train to the Fraser River via the HBC brigade route through the Okanagan to Fort Thompson (Kamloops). The following year he made two trips, one to the Fraser River, and the second to Fort Alexandria. He returned to the Cariboo in 1860 and 1861.

Although Palmer got as far as Fort Alexandria in 1859, he did not venture into Quesnel Forks. He spent August and September at La Fontaine (the Fountain), near Lillooet. When Palmer returned to Oregon, his lengthy report, emphasizing the importance of the

General Joel Palmer.
(OHS 843)

Quesnel River, was published in the *Oregon Statesman* in February 1860: "On this river and its two forks are, perhaps, the richest gold mines yet discovered in British Columbia," he boasted, urging farmers and merchants to supply the Fraser River and Similkameen gold rushes via the Columbia River route. (Meanwhile, Governor Douglas reported to the Colonial Office in London that something must be done to halt the thrust of Oregon provisions into British Columbia.[5]) In early spring, 1860, Palmer set about equipping more pack trains for a return to Fort Alexandria, contracting for 37,660 pounds of freight and hiring 14 men to help with the packing at $40 a month. When Palmer sold his mules to Cook and Kimball at Lytton in July, he valued one train of 34 mules and one bell mare at $5,150, and a second train of 32 mules and one bell horse at $4,750.[6]

In June 1860, Palmer took cattle and several small pack trains from his corral at Mud Lake to Quesnel Forks, over "the worst trail possible to conceive." He stopped at Beaver Valley and spent one afternoon cutting out logs and detours. In order to spare his horse, he walked the last ten miles to the South Fork River. At Quesnel Forks he found, "ten log and shingle or clapboard houses, consisting of stores and restaurants, and probably thirty or forty tents." Although nearly all the front lots along the South Fork River had been claimed, he managed to secure one for $25. While building a cabin on it, he rented a house from Timoleon Love in order to sell the goods he had packed in.[7]

Palmer was a religious man of the Quaker faith. He attended church regularly while at home in Oregon, but readily adjusted to Sunday in the Cariboo which was considered "a day of trade and amusement." At first business was not as brisk as he expected, the men being "idlers, gamblers and miners, some just arriving and others coming in from the diggings." Prospecting parties returning from the North Fork reported good claims 40 miles distant, but all provisions and mining equipment had to be packed in because there was no decent trail and no grass for animals. When Palmer set the rate for flour at 55¢ a pound, other merchants undercut his price to 35¢. Once he moved into his own quarters, trade improved to $200 to $300 a day. A week later he returned to his Mud Lake and Fort Alexandria trading posts to distribute the remainder of his goods. Over the course of his stay at Fort Alexandria he provided the Hudson's Bay Chief Trader, John Saunders, with $288 worth of supplies.[8]

During July and August, Palmer took 62 pack mules to Lillooet for more merchandise. He returned to Fort Alexandria and did not visit Quesnel Forks again until mid-September, when he sold out to business partners David C. Kelley and W.H. Wright. They purchased "dry goods, groceries, provisions, horses, mules and cattle, and houses and tools. Those that are at Cariboo, Little Lake, Horsefly, Mud Lake, Alexandria and Bonaparte, and those at the Forks of Quesnelle River." The Quesnel Forks invoice amounted to $4,249.65, including one beef carcass that weighed 420 pounds and sold for 15¢ a pound. Palmer returned to his home in Oregon via Lillooet and Victoria, to prepare for another trip to the Cariboo the following year. At New Westminster, he stayed at the Mansion boarding house, operated by Catherine Lawless. Perhaps it was Palmer's obvious success that encouraged Lawless and her son to try their luck in the Cariboo the following year.[9]

While businessmen and packers established themselves during the first years of the Cariboo gold rush, the newspaper reports naturally focused on the gold discoveries. For example, George Harvey arrived at Quesnel Forks on March 10. With three men he worked on the North Fork at the mouth of Sellers Creek, taking out $2,300 in three weeks. When the river began to rise, he sold out and prospected with William Keithley along Cariboo Lake. They found paydirt on the creeks that now bear their names. Keithley had worked on "his" creek the previous year and Harvey had already explored the Fraser River as far as the mouth of the Cottonwood River north of Quesnelmouth. With only a prospector's rough knowledge of geology and his California mining experiences, he accurately predicted the location of the Cariboo gold belt north of Cariboo Lake, two decades before professional geologists mapped the region.

At high water, the Quesnel River runs from ten to 12 miles an hour, and in many places it is rough and turbulent. Tragedy struck the Dancing Bill Company on the South Fork River during spring freshet. On June 10, the *Colonist* published a second letter from James May, this one addressed to Antonia Spizer:

James Jasper May.
(G-04489, BCA)

I write to inform you that Bartholomew and his partner, also Scotty, were drowned whilst crossing the river. They had a claim in the company known as the Dancing Bill Company. You had better come up and attend to it. Bartholomew told me this morning that the claim was paying $13 per day to the hand.[10]

Scotty, Bartholomew and his nameless partner were probably the first miners to be buried in the Quesnel Forks cemetery. James May, their informant, lived much longer. A tall, lanky American from Missouri, May spent the rest of his life placer-mining in the Cariboo, Big Bend and Omineca regions of British Columbia. May and another well-known gold rush pioneer, packer Jean Caux, known as Cataline, ended their days at Hazelton.

Expressman James H. Batterton wrote from Forks of Quesnelle River August 20, 1860:

> Business is dull here at present, from the fact that many of the miners have left for the Cariboo country. Of the few left, none seem to be dissatisfied with their prospects. On the South Fork, at Rose's Gulch, some five miles above the Forks, there have been pieces weighing from two to three ounces taken out. On the North Fork the gold is finer, but pays equally as well.[11]

Batterton went on to report that Harvey with four men had cleaned up $2,100 in six days on Harvey Creek and that at Keithley Creek Black and Company "(four men — two shoveling, one bailing, and one sluice-forking), took out eighteen ounces and two dollars." The Horsefly country was too flat to allow good water drainage, preventing James Moore's Blue Lead Company from making much of a profit. Alert to any good mining prospects, Batterton applied to the colonial government for permission to dam Quesnel Lake, in order to mine ten miles of the South Fork river bed.

In September the *Colonist* noted: "Fort Alexander is now a one horse town. A town has been started at the Forks of Quesnelle and called the Forks City. It is filled with miners every Sunday buying provisions." William Davidson at Williams Lake, and Peter Dunlevy and Jim Sellers at Beaver Lake were supplying vegetables and grain. William Walkem, "Special Correspondent" for the *Colonist*, reported that there were about 600 white miners above Alexandria, "of which four hundred were on the Quesnel River or in the Cariboo and two hundred on the Fraser." A small party of Chinese were also working on the Quesnel River.[12]

Law and order for the Cariboo eventually received government attention. In April, Henry Maynard Ball, assistant gold commissioner at Lytton, had urged the colonial government to provide police protection for miners working on the upper Fraser, and at Lillooet, Elwyn echoed his concerns. Ball was an experienced veteran of the Australia gold rush, well aware that troublemakers could oust men from a good claim if there was no law enforcement. The government immediately offered him the position of assistant gold commissioner for the new Alexandria Mining District. Ball declined. (He would later spend 15 years in government service in the Cariboo: two years at Quesnel and 13 at Barkerville.) In place of Ball, the government chose Philip Henry Nind, a clerk with the Colonial Secretary's office in Victoria. He was hired in July, and reached Williams Lake in August, accompanied by Police Constable William Pinchbeck.

Nind received instructions from the Colonial Secretary to use his good judgment. The country was too distant from Victoria for detailed advice. Douglas seemed more concerned by the number of Oregon packers heading for the Cariboo, and wanted Nind to ensure that they had paid customs duties. Without waiting for all their belongings to arrive by packhorses, Nind and Pinchbeck went to the mining area on the Fraser River, between Fort Alexandria and Quesnelmouth, to register claims, issue mining licences, and deal with criminal cases. By this time a French miner had been killed and, in a

Philip Henry Nind, first assistant gold commissioner, Alexandria (Cariboo) District.
(G-04005, BCA)

separate incident, Moses Anderson had wounded a young native boy. The miners caught the murderer of the Frenchman, but released him because there was no jail, and no guarantee that their expenses would be reimbursed. Anderson evaded capture and left the country.

Nind was a young, ambitious recruit, only a few years older than Elwyn. The eldest of 14 children born to Reverend Philip H. Nind, Oxfordshire, he had been educated at Eton and obtained his MA from New Inn Hall, Oxford, in 1858. A keenly intelligent man, with a strong sense of duty and allegiance to the Crown, Nind was an excellent choice as the first assistant gold commissioner in the Cariboo. (Expert horsemanship and an iron constitution were basic requirements for all colonial employees in the field.) His detailed reports to Governor Douglas were written clearly and without exaggeration. William Pinchbeck was also a good choice for the first police constable. A native of Yorkshire, England, he had mined and operated a hotel in California. From these experiences he had gained empathy for the democratic nature of the American mining camps. While at Hope, prior to being hired by Nind, he signed a petition demanding responsible government for the mainland colony. Other British subjects who signed the petition were future Cariboo miners William "Billy" Barker from England and Robert M. Scott from Ontario.

When Nind finally reached Quesnel Forks in September he was accompanied by Judge Begbie and a court registrar. The group travelled on horseback from Mud Lake to Beaver Valley, thence to Little Lake where they established a base camp. Begbie was on a reconnoitering trip to determine where court could be held in 1861, and to size up the country. Although he did not hear any cases, the miners must have been impressed with his energy and desire to learn as much as possible about the mining frontier. When Begbie returned to New Westminster he reported to the Colonial Secretary that Quesnel Forks would be the centre of the mining region next year. But in his assessment of all the routes to the Cariboo, there was only one word to describe the trail to the Forks: "Horrible! Years hence, on railroads and steamers, men will remember the struggles they had in the virgin forests and beaver swamps of British Columbia."[13]

Quesnel Forks had grown only slightly since Joel Palmer's visit in June. There were now 17 inhabited houses, one being built, and three or four tents. Nind reported that eight or ten acres had been cleared, "and an industrious Frenchman [Pierre Voute] has planted vegetables, which however with the exception of turnips and radishes have not ripened. The population during the latter part of the summer has probably averaged between forty and fifty, though there may have been more in the month of October as miners were then beginning to collect here previous to emigration."[14]

Because all the first arrivals of 1859 — Keithley, Rose, MacDonald, and Weaver — had moved on to other creeks, Nind travelled to Keithley Creek on September 26, following the original trail to Davis' Crossing. William Keithley had discovered gold there the previous July and William Hazeltine and George Weaver were using piped water, possibly the first hydraulic operation in the Cariboo, to work a well-paying river-bank claim. At Keithley, Nind heard the first reports of gold found on Antler Creek by Rose, MacDonald and Bowen, forecasting the rush over the Snowshoe Plateau during the coming winter.

There were only 30 or 40 miners at Keithley Creek; many had left early for the south, fearing cold weather. Paul Somers was one who departed for eastern Canada before Nind's arrival. After spending a month in preparation on Harvey Creek, Somers' group of five men washed out a total of 720 ounces of gold.

When Nind returned to Quesnel Forks he issued trading licences to Barry and Adler, Ricard, Frederick Black, David C. Kelley, Bennett and Abbott, and Locke and Hart. He issued liquor licences to Barry and Adler, Ricard, Black, Spinks, and the first white woman recorded at the Forks, Johanna McGuire.

Entrepreneurs besieged Nind with requests for ferry licences and bridge charters. Locke and Hart wanted a licence to operate ferries on both the North and South Forks; John Tow, a licence for a ferry across the Quesnel River ten miles below Quesnel Forks; Lucius DeCastle Loucks and Isaiah Mitchell made separate applications for licences to operate ferries on the North Fork. In addition, Mitchell wanted to run a ferry on the Cariboo Lakes, to connect with mining camps at Goose Creek, Keithley Creek and Harvey Creek. A native of New England, Mitchell had spent most of his adult life building and sailing ships, but John Lachapelle, also a boat builder by trade, gained the ferry concession. Lachapelle called his stopping place

Cariboo House. Within two years he increased his holdings to include two ferryboats, one canoe, a scow, and a hay ranch at Swamp River. He sold out to Lucius Loucks in 1863 and moved to Victoria. (Loucks knew the value of investment in transportation, having worked as a clerk for the first railway in Canada West.) Even the smallest enterprise was considered: Joseph Raleigh (Rawley) gained a licence to operate a rowboat ferry at Keithley Creek. He had already built a house at Little Cariboo Lake.

After issuing the trading and liquor licences, Nind met Isaiah Mitchell who had been mining on the Horsefly River during the summer. Mitchell took him up the South Fork to his boat cache. At Rose's Bar they found one company making "between sixteen and twenty dollars a day to the hand." At French Bar Nind registered the claims of Louis Lefevre, Bernard Passama, Bartoleme Jourdan, Antoine Capdeville and Victorieau Silvien. A month later Jourdan died at Williams Lake from eating wild parsnip root. His belongings included a bag of gold worth $215.00.[15]

Exploring along the shore of Quesnel Lake with Mitchell, Nind climbed a bald hill and drew a map of the lake. He was looking for an easier route to the mountains that might avoid the difficult trail to Quesnel Forks. As far as he was concerned, a more central location for a village was needed "than a flat lying between two swift rivers which can only be approached by terrific hills, is many miles distant from pasture, and forces the trail to the mines, on which it is principally dependent, over a country where no money or labour can ever make even a moderately good road." A few years later Mitchell would make a "cutoff trail" from the Cariboo Road via Horsefly but it never gained the popularity of the older, established route through Quesnel Forks to the Snowshoe Plateau.[16]

Meanwhile, at Victoria, Governor Douglas waited anxiously for word from Nind. In a despatch to London dated October 25, 1860, Douglas mentioned that he still hadn't received a report. Nind wrote two weeks later, November 9, immediately on his return to Williams Lake. Along with his report he requested advice on how to handle the many ferry applications. He wanted them sorted out by next February, before the expected invasion of miners made resolution difficult. Nind summed up 1860 optimistically: "This year has been an experimental one, chiefly consumed in prospecting, but it leads to the belief that we are on the eve of a great discovery which may hereafter people the Northeast portion of British Columbia with tens of thousands. I conceive it however probable that the north branch may be found next year to penetrate the very heart of extensive goldfields, explorations seeming to indicate that the confines only of auriferous rock have been reached."[17]

Before turning his energy to building a small, 16- by 14-foot cabin for the winter (with the help of his two constables, Seymour and Pinchbeck), Nind recommended to Douglas that a gold escort be instituted the coming year to strengthen the government presence. For a few hours or a few days, Quesnel Forks offered a safe haven for returning miners. But when it came time to "hit the trail" again, they feared the long hill leading up the bluffs on the south side of the South Fork River, where they were easy prey for robbers.

Despite the great distances and disparities in nationalities, there was ready camaraderie amongst the miners. Few, if any, worked alone. They had partners or were members of larger groups and when they became sick or injured, help was generously given. When John McLellan of the Blue Lead claim at Horsefly left for San Francisco because of illness, a collection was taken up amongst miners and businessmen in the Quesnel Forks area. McLellan wrote from San Francisco: "It is from the miners and residents of British Columbia, alone, that I could expect such unbounded generosity as was manifested to me on this most desirable occasion."[18]

Final reports for the year came from Nind and Batterton. On December 23, Batterton wrote to the *Colonist*:

> The weather this Fall has been very mild compared with that of the two preceding. Very little rain had fallen up to the time of my leaving (17th Nov.) No snow in the valley of the Quesnelle and but little on the mountains this side.
>
> The mining prospects are good. The few parties that were out prospecting late this Fall seem to have found better prospects than heretofore struck in this country. The best prospects have been obtained some 30 miles beyond the Cariboo country, on the head waters of a stream that is supposed to empty into Swamp river.[19]

Nind wrote to the Colonial Secretary that William Keithley had made a fresh discovery on a bench about 12 miles above Quesnel Forks on the North Fork, taking $1,300 from 1,000 buckets of gravel. Keithley, Isaiah P. Diller and company remained over the winter working the claim. When the paystreak gave out the following June they sold it to Gray and Company and moved on to Williams Creek.

The future did indeed look prosperous, not only for miners like William Keithley, but for entrepreneurs like Thomas Barry and Isaiah Mitchell. In September Barry legally dissolved his partnership with brother James at Fort Yale, casting his lot with Sam Adler. Twelve miles up the North Fork, Mitchell abandoned the idea of a ferry across the river and commenced building his bridge, using handmade winches.

Barry and Adler ended the year with a Christmas celebration at Abbott's restaurant. In the centre of the small, one-room shack stood a six-legged table of whip-sawn pine. "The furniture was all home-made, and so constructed as to give one the idea that it was hurriedly finished on a Saturday night, or that the carpenter knew nothing of his business." The ten men in attendance included blacksmith John Peebles, and mining partners Mike Brown, Jim Costello, Kansas John Metz, and Murt Collins who had registered claims on Keithley Creek earlier in the year. Pork and beans, pancakes, and "plum duff without the duff" made up the plain bill of fare. Sam and Tom supplied whiskey hot, whiskey cold, and brandy neat to ensure that their lively group of friends always remembered their first Christmas at Quesnel Forks.[20]

CHAPTER THREE

1861

"It was patent to all who were old residents that
English Law if transgressed was not to be evaded
with the same impunity as Californian Law."[1]
Philip Henry Nind

THE DISCOVERY OF gold on Antler Creek, in October 1860, by
S.M. Bowen, James May and Benjamin MacDonald, was impossible to
keep quiet. By December of 1860, local merchants Peter Dunlevy,
James Sellers and Tom Moffitt had claims staked on speculation; and
by March of 1861 most of the important sections of the creek had
been taken up. Quesnel Forks held its place this year as the major
supply centre in the Cariboo as thousands of miners once again
trekked through to the new sites.

When Philip Nind returned to Quesnel Forks on March 3, 1861,
following a new trail from Little Lake, he found considerable activity.
Barry and Adler's bridge across the South Fork was still under
construction, as was Isaiah Mitchell's bridge on the North Fork. Nind
did not remain long at the village because the majority of the miners

were awaiting his arrival on Keithley and Antler creeks. As he travelled along the bank of the North Fork to Mitchell's bridge, he noticed wing dams and water wheels erected by the miners who had wintered over at the Forks. Mitchell later applied for a charter to collect tolls on his bridge, claiming he had spent $2,100 on its construction and on building the connecting trails.

With Constable William Pinchbeck, Nind visited Keithley and Diller's claim and others at Keithley Creek before crossing the 6,000-foot summit of the Snowshoe Plateau to Antler Creek. He spent six days at Antler registering mining claims, back-dating the discovery claims of John Rose, Benjamin MacDonald and Jim May to October 8, 1860. There was as yet only one log cabin, built by Rose and MacDonald; "the rest of the miners were living in holes dug out of the snow which was between six and seven feet deep."[2]

When Nind commenced resolving disputes, the miners at Antler Creek accepted his judgments without protest. He reported, "It was patent to all who were old residents that English Law if transgressed was not to be evaded with the same impunity as Californian Law. No one cared to risk the loss of what might be a fortune to him, besides this, there was an absence of every kind of intoxicating liquor." Nind may have found fewer troublemakers because they were now soldiers; the American Civil War commenced this year and lasted until 1865.[3]

Nind returned to Quesnel Forks, en route to his Williams Lake headquarters, to find that Barry and Adler had completed their bridge at a cost of $5,000. He wrote to the Colonial Secretary, "Mr. Adler has shown much enterprise in endeavouring to secure the traffic of the ensuing year to the Forks of Quesnelle, as it is by no means certain that travel will adopt this route to the Northern mines." The tolls for crossing over the 300-foot bridge were 25¢ for foot passengers and one dollar for packed horses or mules. Native men and women passed over free if they were not packing for white men. Nind believed he had issued mining licences to nine-tenths of the population during his circuit.[4]

By the end of March, pack trains could travel as far as Beaver Lake where native men and women were earning seven to nine dollars a day carrying loads to Quesnel Forks. Nind felt "mercantile interests [were] now centered at Quesnel Forks and efforts will be made to secure to it the trade of the upper country." From Quesnel Forks to Antler a team of 20 natives earned $50 to $70 each packing 100 pounds.⁵ Until animals reached the Forks in late April, provisions were expensive. Flour sold at $40 per 100 pounds and bacon at 75¢ per pound, almost twice the price of goods at Beaver Lake, 20 miles away. By May, yeast powders, boots, smoking pipes and gold pans were sold out. Even the simple luxury of a frying pan was impossible. An enterprising laundryman charged six dollars per dozen pieces to wash clothes.

Snow still lay on the hillside going down to the Quesnel River when Argus, a travelling correspondent for the *Colonist*, arrived at Quesnel Forks in May. His description of the village conforms to a painting done by Frederick Whymper in 1864. A narrow levee, "barely sufficient for pack trains to unload" ran in front of the buildings which faced the South Fork River. Argus predicted that the buildings would have to be moved once a survey was made. There were 150 miners in town, and about 800 to 900 men in the rest of the Cariboo. "I have noticed several parties of men starting out with over 100 lbs. on their backs, which they will have to carry over a most difficult country. Owing to the quantity of fallen timber on the apology for a trail, a man, to make a successful trip, must be a sort of Blondin on a small scale, and well skilled in tight rope dancing."⁶ Animals could only get in to the Forks if packers brought barley with them, which was expensive at 12 1/2 cents a pound. Tom Menefee, packing from Lytton, was about to take a string of 30 horses to Antler, expecting some difficulty on the Snowshoe Plateau.

In early May, Joel Palmer also arrived back at Quesnel Forks. He and business partner, David Kelley, hiked through ice and snow to Antler Creek in two days. When they visited the various mining claims, Palmer estimated that only half of the 250 men on the creek were working because of the deep snow. Four or five claims were paying heavily. One claim, with four men, recovered $580 in a day. Other claims, using sluices, produced from $40 to $50 per day.

With "serious regret," Palmer sold his half interest in the packing and cattle business to Kelley and departed for Oregon. Although the profits from his share fell short of the capital invested, $12,964, Palmer's saddlebags held $8,200 in gold, and $270 in coin. From the sale of a horse and various collections along the way, the amount increased to $11,412 in gold, and $588 in coin by the time he reached Yale.[7] Nind was absent at mining sites on the Fraser River and regretted missing Palmer when he stopped at Williams Lake, en route south. At Lytton, Palmer met up with Governor Douglas who was touring the Fraser Canyon and Thompson River valley. Douglas was duly impressed with the large amount of gold, as were the miners at Hope. Palmer noted in his diary, "They appear to have a golden dream of the importance of their country."[8] Once again, Palmer stayed at the boarding house of Catherine Lawless in New Westminster before catching the steamer to Victoria.

Argus visited the mining site at the mouth of Keithley Creek in early June. He found, "a small town of five log houses and about twenty tents situated on a flat.The settlement is known by the name of Black's Store, a party of that name having established a trading post there." In July he reported, "High Living is now the order of the day on Keithley's Creek, beef and milk being within reach of the public — the former at 41 cents per pound, and the latter at $1.50 a quart. Nearly 2000 head of cattle have been brought here this year from Oregon." The small nucleus of a townsite did not develop, but the favourable location was later acquired by merchants Vieth and Borland who turned the flat into a large, well-run ranch.[9]

Expressman Dan Braley also travelled as far as Antler Creek. He reported to the *Colonist* that Hi Robinson and Company had taken out $950 in two days; Dennis Cain and Company $300 day per man, and Dud Moreland $230 in one day. He estimated that there were 1,200 men at Quesnel Forks and in the Cariboo.

With the snow melted, it now became a matter of urgency to get a decent pack trail established to Antler to prevent starvation. A combined effort of public subscription and government grant succeeded in opening up the route. (The same strategy had been used at Yale the previous year when a bridge over the Coquihalla and a trail between Yale and Hope were completed. Not only the merchants and citizens of Yale, but William Ballou, the expressman, Judge Begbie and Nind subscribed. Begbie's contribution was the most generous, at $250.)[10] Merchants at Keithley and Antler creeks subscribed $800 for the Antler Creek trail. At the suggestion of Begbie, Nind solicited a petition from the Antler Creek miners for improvement of the trail, then submitted it to the colonial government with his recommendations. While on a visit to Lillooet in early June, Colonial Secretary W.A.G. Young intercepted Nind's letter and sent his approval immediately. At a meeting at Quesnel Forks on June 23 the residents learned that the government had granted $2,000 (£400). At the same time it made a grant of $2,000 to improve the trail from Lillooet to Williams Lake. (Packer Frank Fulford gained this latter contract, to complete a 12-mile section from Lillooet to "The Slide".)

The residents of Quesnel Forks nominated Frederick Black, Sam Adler, David Kelley, Thomas Davidson and Thomas Spence to make a survey, and to superintend construction of the Antler Creek trail. They chose the same route Nind had used in March, from Quesnel Forks to Keithley Creek via Mitchell's Bridge, then from Keithley Creek over the Snowshoe Plateau. The work began immediately, clearing away fallen trees and corduroying swampy sections, and was finished by the end of July. Black and his business partner William Carlyle took responsibility for provisioning and paying the labourers, because Nind did not have enough money on hand. The merchants at Quesnel Forks were so eager to attract miners that they improved parts of the older trail from the Forks to the Cariboo Road at their own expense. Black and Carlyle cleared away the burned and downed trees between Beaver Lake and Little Lake at a personal cost of $900, and Barry and Adler upgraded the portion from Beaver Lake to their South Fork bridge.

The idea of damming the Quesnel River in order to mine ten miles of the river bed, from Quesnel Lake to Quesnel Forks, gained government support this year as well. James Batterton appears to have been the first one to express an interest, but Thomas Spence won formal government approval.[11] The great plan was all speculation, however. Construction of a dam strong enough to hold back the waters of the deepest lake in British Columbia required large amounts of international capital that would not be possible until 1896. Furthermore, Spence had other important interests. Together with Joseph Trutch and Gustavus Blinn Wright, he was one of the main contractors building the Cariboo Road in 1862. In 1865, Trutch, by then Chief Commissioner of Lands and Works, appointed Spence to supervise road maintenance in the Cariboo.

Although the mining population was now at Keithley and Antler creeks, Nind wanted a police constable stationed at Quesnel Forks because of the unsavoury characters passing through. He posted Charles Seymour at the Forks in May and June. Seymour spent his days selling mining licences which were paid for in the only available currency, gold dust. Lacking a jail or other government accommodation, he spent his nights sleeping on the floor of Barry and Adler's saloon. One evening he did not secure his bag of gold dust properly before retiring, and by morning £60 had vanished. The gold was never recovered and eventually the Treasury in London wrote it off. [12]

Seymour also recorded claims to the first lots in Quesnel Forks. On May 29, 1861, Locke and Hart paid $2.50 to record one lot down river from Black and Carlyle. This is possibly the same lot claimed earlier by J.H. Walker, which had 32-foot frontage, and was recorded March 18, 1861. [13]

The Cariboo gold rush posed two main concerns for the colonial government: starvation and lawlessness. But snug in their Victoria offices, government officials had little sympathy for the police constables and assistant gold commissioners who maintained law and order and kept the lines of communication open. Constable George Gompertz claimed extra allowance for living at Quesnel Forks — meals had cost him two dollars each and board at the restaurant $20 per week. Constables were paid only £20 ($100) per month. Nind also complained about the high cost of living when he was away from his headquarters at Williams Lake. He was given distant duty allowance of $15 a day, but protested that it was not enough. Since his arrival at Williams Lake in August 1860 he had been away 137 days visiting mining sites. Nind and William Pinchbeck avoided using local restaurants by packing their own provisions and hunting game. After much procrastination, the government increased distant duty allowance to $25 a day for Nind and $15 a day for constables. [14]

The miners' religious needs received attention from both Roman Catholic priests and Anglican ministers, although few men cared to take time off work during the frantic mining season to attend their services. Roman Catholic priest Father Grandidier borrowed a horse from retired Hudson's Bay Factor Donald McLean at Bonaparte to travel to the mining sites. He met with little success except at

Williams Creek where there were some Irish miners. While passing through Beaver Valley, Grandidier dared to spend the night at Peter Dunlevy's stopping house. The miners ridiculed him when he knelt to say his prayers before sleeping in the common room, but Dunlevy, a Roman Catholic, quickly intervened.[15] Anglican ministers Reverend Christopher Knipe and Reverend Lundin Brown also visited East Cariboo during the summer. Brown preached at Quesnel Forks for a number of Sundays before returning to Lillooet.[16]

In spite of the difficult trails, sporadic food supplies, mosquitoes and muskeg, the spring and summer of 1861 was an exuberant time. Rich creeks on the north side of the Snowshoe Plateau were discovered every few weeks. First Antler, then Cunningham, Grouse, Stevens, Williams, Lowhee and Lightning produced gold from surface gravel that rivalled the palmiest days of the California gold rush. To the consternation of many new miners a number of claims were held by speculators who knew how to make a quick profit. For example, William Rankin bought a claim on Antler May 7, from Quesnel Forks merchant F.L. Fellows for $1,000. Rankin sold it to Duncan McMartin on May 30 for $1,500.[17] James Sellers of Beaver Lake was strongly criticized for buying into claims on speculation, preventing legitimate miners from working them.

Special Correspondent for the *Colonist* wrote on June 26, 1861:

> I must again remark on the evils attending the absence of a Gold Commissioner or legal authority in these parts. Every day complaints are heard on that head. Not everyone can spare time sufficient to enable them to go such a long distance as Williams Lake to transact any little business they may have with the Commissioner. In a large and new mining district like Cariboo, it is imperative that there should be some recognized authority to take immediate notice of any appeals that may be made, and to act as arbitrator in the hundred and one mining disputes which are bound to arise in a mining district.[18]

The excitement at Antler Creek affected the very existence of Fort Alexandria. Throughout the mining season packers had tried to lure away Hudson's Bay Company labourers with offers of a better salary and better food. When one man, Howse, deserted to Davidson's ranch at Williams Lake, Chief Trader Saunders asked Nind for advice. Nind responded that Howse couldn't be imprisoned since there was as yet no jail, but he could be threatened with dismissal. That solution, replied Saunders, "would be of the same benefit to the Company as plunging a man under water to avoid a shower of rain." He fretted that men could sign up at Red River for service in British Columbia, then desert as soon as they neared the goldfields, without any fear of reprisal.[19]

Indigenous trappers could also find a better source of income working for the packers, and only trapped during the winter. By April, Saunders was so disheartened that he suggested his agreement with the Company be cancelled in the spring of 1862: "My inability to do anything to advance the interests of the Company here, and the knowledge that beyond the place being useful for a station, every expenditure is a loss without any return render my position so unsatisfactory." His resignation was accepted.[20]

Previously, Quesnel Forks had been a supply centre for miners at Keithley Creek and Harvey Creek. It now became a jumping-off place for prospectors heading over the Snowshoe Plateau. A report on July 22 stated there were only about 40 miners at the Forks. All the rest were on the other creeks. Chinese miners had taken over many of the abandoned claims on the North Fork. There were 200 men at Keithley Creek, eight companies at Harvey Creek and four or five companies on Snowshoe. Twenty-one claims at Antler paid as much as $50 to $100 a day. Already, 50 men were working on Williams Creek, which would become the next big strike.

"You can do better up here," Dennis Cain wrote to John McLellan from Antler Creek. "No less than 10 of our Horsefly boys are doing well. You know how I was dead broke last fall; now I have a claim paying from $75 to $100 per day to the hand, a store on the creek, and a pack train carrying goods from Quesnelle City here."[21]

Nicholas Bailey reported from Quesnel Forks:

> I have been prospecting on Swamp River, Harvey's Creek, Goose Creek, as well as several minor streams but on most of them the water was too high. So far as I have yet seen I think very highly of

the Cariboo as a mining country. Some on Antler creek have taken out from $150 to $200 per day to the hand and I hear of some reaching as high as $500. I am down here now for grub. I have taken up a very nice piece of ground on Swamp River for a ranch which I intend cultivating in conjunction with my mining claim and I think I have a good prospect of doing well. Packing is the greatest difficulty here. I packed 75 pounds all the way from here to Cariboo on my first trip which almost used me up, but I am somewhat used to it now. [22]

His "ranch" at Swamp River produced a ton of hay by the end of summer, an important consideration when there were few good pastures for pack trains. Bailey, a native of St. Day, Cornwall, joined in the rush to Williams Creek, then returned to Harvey Creek in 1870.

Governor Douglas reported to Colonial Secretary Newcastle in July 1861:

The latest accounts from Cariboo confirm the former reports of its vast auriferous wealth. About 1500 men are supposed to be congregated in those mines, and the number is continually augmented by the arrival of fresh bodies of Miners. It will be a work of difficulty to keep them supplied with food, a service which now gives employment to about 1200 transport horses and mules, and I am in hopes that the large profits made in that business will lead to its extension. [23]

Acceding to Nind's earlier request, Douglas established a gold escort to assist the miners, and to give "a show of force" to strengthen the hands of the magistrates. Thomas Elwyn left his position as assistant gold commissioner at Lillooet to head the escort, assisted by a sergeant, four men from the Royal Engineers and Thomas Hankin, police constable at Williams Lake. Outfitted in uniforms, and well armed, the mounted escort travelled as far as Quesnel Forks before returning south. Advertised rates were one shilling an ounce to transport gold from Quesnel Forks to New Westminster. Unfortunately, delivery service was slow, with the escort travelling the full distance to New Westminster rather than arranging for an express pickup by steamer from Douglas. Moreover, because the colonial government could not guarantee safe delivery of gold entrusted to the escort, most miners arranged their own transport. The escort was tried for one more year, unsuccessfully, in 1863.

William Barry did not arrive at Quesnel Forks until July, to join his brother Tom and Sam Adler. Already claims at Antler Creek had been recorded in his name on speculation. William's letter to "Friend S" was published in the *British Columbian* in early August:

William Prosper Barry.
(HP4847, BCA)

I arrived here on the 21st July. The trip was a tiresome one. Owing to a scarcity of animals at Thompson River I had to foot it all the way. My brother Tom is at Antler and writes me that this is beyond doubt a second California in '49. I hear of no one making less than $40 a day, and the greater number are making from $100 to $500 per day. The people at Antler and other creeks are in a great state of excitement, and prospecting parties are out in all directions. When a party starts out on a voyage of discovery, merchants agree to furnish the grub free of charge, provided an interest in the claims when found is given them. Every creek yet struck pays big. Provisions are a dollar a pound on the creek. The demand is greater than the supply. A great many will winter here if provisions enough can be got up in the fall. All the trains that arrive here go on to Antler Creek without stopping.[24]

In October William tried to gain a monopoly on the crossings of the Quesnel River by applying for a licence to build a toll bridge eight miles below Quesnel Forks, near the site of John Tow's ferry. The colonial government rejected his application because Tow held a two-year licence.[25]

While the white miners shifted from one site to another, eager to take advantage of the latest strike, the Chinese miners continued to arrive, always ready to take over abandoned claims. Ong Mon staked a claim on Dancing Bill's Bar this year. For the next 25 years the bar would be a lucrative site for Chinese miners; they washed out an estimated $200,000 in gold by 1890.[26] Gradually, other Chinese miners moved up the North Fork to Keithley Creek, working the vacated claims of white miners who had joined the rush to Antler and Williams creeks. A small Chinese settlement developed at Weaver Creek, which flows into Keithley Creek four miles above Cariboo Lake. It was still flourishing in 1902, when the provincial minerologist visited.[27]

The indigenous people were the first placer miners on the Thompson and lower Fraser rivers, but they do not appear to have taken part in Cariboo mining. Intimidation by the white miners, many of whom were pioneers of the California gold rush of 1849-55 could have been a factor. It could also be that packing was a more lucrative occupation. Some Interior Salish men and women from Washington Territory travelled north with Oregon packers,[28] but most of those involved probably came from local communities, when they were available. Nind reported that many natives were absent fishing when they were most needed for packing early in the spring. Smallpox greatly reduced their numbers during the winter of 1862-63.

Native women were resourceful, adaptable and hardy enough to cope with the many difficulties on the trail. A.J. Splawn recalled wintering at the Bonaparte Valley with famous Cariboo packer Red-headed Davis and his native wife. Mrs. Davis was most kind to the young lad, but in a set-to with her husband she didn't hesitate to defend herself with a burning piece of wood from the campfire. When pack trains could get only as far as Beaver Lake during the heavy snows of winter, native women packed up to 100 pounds of supplies on their backs to Quesnel Forks and beyond, receiving $30 to $40 for each trip. Their skills at making snowshoes, moccasins and clothing for the miners brought in additional income. Snowshoes sold for $10 to $25, and moccasins, $3 to $10. Many aboriginal women became partners of men who would be future settlers in the Cariboo, notably Peter Dunlevy, James Sellers and Thomas Moffitt in the Beaver Lake area, and William Pinchbeck at Williams Lake. A vital part of the mining frontier, native women continued to make important contributions throughout the years of the Cariboo gold rush and the later settlement period.

In June, expressman Dan Braley reported that four white women had reached Quesnel Forks. They were probably unaware of the debt they owed their native sisters. The supplies that the latter packed in made conditions bearable and enabled the newcomers to earn a living. Irish-born Catherine "Mother" Lawless gave up managing her large boarding house and restaurant in New Westminster to accompany her son Walter to the goldfields. She stayed long enough at Quesnel Forks to be entered in the 1863 *British Columbia Directory*, and may have had a nearby creek named after her. Johanna McGuire set up a drinking place on Alice Street, and French-speaking Marie Perrin with her lover Armand McHuish operated a restaurant. Perrin and McHuish rented a cabin from James Croft until their modest 14- by 16-foot cabin was built during the winter by a Mr. Caillou. Eliza Baillie was a neighbour.

All these women would follow the gold rush frontier to Williams Creek in the next few years.

By the end of 1861 most of the farming land at the foot of Williams Lake had been preempted. Nind expressed concern to the Colonial Secretary that the remaining good land would probably be taken up by the end of the summer, yet the natives did not have a place of their own. They tended to move about, from the north end of the lake to the south, and to Davidson's ranch. The Colonial Secretary replied that Nind should establish a reserve of 400 to 500 acres, wherever the natives wished, and also a townsite. Although a small reserve was set aside at Soda Creek in the early years, none was legally established at Williams Lake until 1882.[29]

Possibly because of all the established farms at Williams Lake, Nind did not lay out a townsite, either. The earliest settlers were Thomas Davidson, Thomas Meldrum, Dudley Moreland, Thomas Menefee, Marion Woodward and William Pinchbeck. Thomas Elwyn briefly held a one-third interest with Menefee and Woodward in the Mission Ranch (formerly Davidson's) in 1863. Because the trails were so difficult between Williams Lake and Quesnel Forks, packers brought supplies as far as Beaver Lake on mules, then transferred to horses for the last 20 miles to the Forks. Davidson's farm became a dumping ground for worn-out animals and broken cargoes. The cargoes were easily sold to packers who wanted to avoid the long trip to Lytton or Lillooet. At Frank Way's ranch near Mud Lake, a similar situation arose.

Since it took a good month or more to pack goods from New Westminster to the Cariboo, the wisest merchants placed their winter orders in August. Levi wrote to his partner Boas in New Westminster on August 27:

> If you can send up such goods as we want, do so, as I will explain to you it is only 5 or 6 weeks more that pack trains can come in here, and then we can get any price for them, besides which, Spring, when there is a lot of people rushing in, and we the only ones which have goods. You bet I would soak into them. The Country is alright, there is more gold in it as there was in California, dont say nothing to nobody.[30]

Governor Douglas enclosed Levi's letter in his correspondence to the Colonial Office in September, but his reassurance to London that the miners had not suffered from want of food sounded contrived: "The traveller who is prepared to encounter famine in its gauntest forms on his arrival in Cariboo is not a little astonished to find himself in the midst of luxury, sitting down every morning to fresh milk and eggs for breakfast, and to as good a dinner as can be seen in Victoria."[31] Colonial officials were eager to interview Nind when he returned to England in early 1862, to ascertain the truth.

Judge Begbie arrived on his second visit to Quesnel Forks in September, to hold court of assizes. Begbie swore in Charles Seymour as sheriff, then set about finding 24 citizens for a petit jury and a grand jury. Recognizing that it was impossible to find enough British subjects to serve on a jury, Begbie had drafted a proclamation in March 1860 that permitted jurors to be selected "without regard to nationality."[32] Men of different nationalities thus gained an appreciation for British law and order.

In a two-day session, September 5 and 6, Begbie heard his first murder case in the Cariboo, acquitting three Chinese miners, Ah Ho (?), Ah Kum and Ah Fook.[33] He also settled a dispute between Barry, Adler and a packer, Marks, about collecting bridge tolls. Begbie made assize court a serious, if theatrical occasion, attiring himself in full regalia. As he sat bewigged and robed in black, his court clerk called out the formal "Oyez, oyez" opening as in any court in Victoria or London.[34]

Responding to a petition from 32 miners at Antler Creek, Begbie next travelled over the Snowshoe Plateau to deal with cases of larceny, assault and murder, including the murder of a hot-tempered miner, Jeremiah Bulger. His mining partner, Thomas Glennon, had endured four months of Bulger's verbal abuse before stabbing him in the abdomen. All the miners were sympathetic and allowed Glennon to escape. Begbie found 60 to 70 houses at Antler and predicted it would be the centre of the Cariboo in 1862. Since there was neither a jail nor a government building at Antler Creek, Begbie probably held court in a bar-room. (The following year Thomas Elwyn reported the need for a jail at Antler to hold drunk and disorderly cases. All others could be taken to the jail at Quesnel Forks.)[35] While en route back to Williams

Lake, the judge planned to hold a special assize at Beaver Lake on October 11 for an attempted shooting. Once again he was able to locate enough jurymen, but the prisoner, James Connor, escaped just prior to the trial.

On September 25, Begbie wrote a private letter to the Colonial Secretary from Quesnel Forks, describing the mining scene on Antler Creek and reports he had received about Williams Creek (which he did not visit). Douglas quoted the letter in his despatch to London:

> I have no doubt that there is little short of a ton [of gold] lying at the different creeks. I hear that Abbott's and Steele's claims are working better than ever — 30 to 40 pounds a day each. (They reckon rich claims as often by pounds as ounces now; it must be a poor claim that is measured by dollars.)
>
> On many claims the gold is a perfect nuisance, as they have to carry it from their cabins to their claims every morning, and watch it while they work, and carry it back again (sometimes as much as two men can lift) to their cabins at night, and watch it while they sleep. There is no mistake about the gold. Steele is here, he says they took out 370 ounces one day. I was very glad to see the men so quiet and orderly; old Downie looked really almost aghast, he said they told me it was like California in '49, why you would have seen all those fellows roaring drunk, and pistols and knives in every hand. I never saw a Mining Town anything like this. There were some hundreds in Antler, all sober and quiet. It was Sunday afternoon — only a few claims were worked that day. It was as quiet as Victoria.[36]

Before returning south, Begbie took time to draw up plans for the first lockup in Quesnel Forks, a log building 18 by 22 feet with two cells. Even a small lockup greatly enhanced law enforcement in rural British Columbia. Perhaps more than a resident policeman, the bleak accommodation acted as a strong deterrent against crime. Nind had already encouraged William Pinchbeck to build a lockup at Williams Lake during the summer.

Throughout the mining season there had been considerable dissatisfaction with Nind's residing at Williams Lake. Miners resented taking time off to travel 60 to 70 miles over mountains and rough trails to record their claims. Douglas wrote to Nind, asking him to take up quarters at Quesnel Forks. Nind replied from Quesnel Forks, on October 7, that he was not given instructions regarding a government building or residence. Shortly thereafter Nind approved a government reserve at Quesnel Forks and issued specifications for a combined magistrate's residence and jail. D. Lynch's tender was accepted at $1,100. The jail was completed by mid-November and manned through the winter until the following June by constable Napoleon Fitzstubbs. Fitzstubbs and another new recruit, George Gompertz (who spent the winter at Williams Lake) had been hired in New Westminster.

Possibly encouraged by the government construction at Quesnel Forks, a prospector named "Texas" Shones applied to A.C. Elliott at Lillooet for permission to operate a toll ferry south of Quesnel Forks on the Quesnel River at Tow's site. Elliott forwarded Shones' letter to the governor. The name "Texas Ferry" is used locally to this day to mark the point on the Quesnel River where the Little Lake road terminates.

There had been some altercations between residents at Quesnel Forks over the location of their cabins, because the village was developing in an irregular fashion. Nind laid out five streets, two parallel to the South Fork River, two at right angles, and a fifth street bordering the South Fork River. When he suggested that a townsite be surveyed, Colonel Moody refused in a letter to the Colonial Secretary on December 31, 1861:

> It's common rumour that the so called Town of Quesnelle will shift its population in the spring to another site more suitable in the estimation of the miners, packers and store keepers. Antler may possibly follow the same fate. A mining town is in truth for a long while more the character of a prolonged "Fair" than anything else.[37]

The stress from an incredible year of hard work may have contributed to Nind's facial paralysis, the symptoms of which suggest Bell's palsy. Backed by medical recommendations for sick leave from Doctors Wilkinson and Rumsay at Antler Creek, he left Williams Lake in early November, and returned to England in December. He was well enough to marry Elizabeth Frances Sivewright on April 30, 1862, but gained an extension of his leave of absence until the fall. On his return to British Columbia, Nind and his successor, Thomas Elwyn (who served for only the 1862 season as assistant gold commissioner for Cariboo East), supervised a second, but unsuccessful gold escort for the Cariboo in 1863. Their 1863 route did not include Quesnel Forks. It used the new Cariboo Road to Soda Creek and the trail from Quesnelmouth to Williams Creek.

When Begbie returned to New Westminster in November, he wrote several long, detailed letters to Douglas, describing the country and trails of the Cariboo, and setting down his thoughts about future needs for law and order. He reported that the mining population was 2,000 the previous summer, but expected that next year the new, rich diggings at Williams Creek would attract far more people. Possibly three gold commissioners and a similar number of policemen would be required. Although Nind and miner George Harvey had drawn rough maps of the Quesnel Lake area, Begbie prepared the first detailed map of the route to the Cariboo, noting good pastures. Another visitor to Quesnel Forks, Gustavus Epner, drew an interesting map of the Quesnel Lake area, showing Mitchell's bridge and the trail to Cariboo Lake.

Begbie reserved his strongest criticism for the condition of the trails and lack of pasture for animals from Beaver Lake to Quesnel Forks and Antler Creek. The trail was so swampy from Quesnel Forks to Keithley Creek that mules could not be used. Begbie cared greatly for his dogs and horses: on his visit to Quesnel Forks and Antler, he and Nind walked most of the way from Beaver Lake to spare their mounts. A month later, returning from Beaver Lake to Williams Lake via Davidson's new cutoff trail, he took to the woods with a compass because of the travelling conditions. Begbie was most distressed by the fact that out of eight horses taken to the Cariboo in 1861, he returned with only one.

Begbie's negative report on the trails gave support to Governor Douglas' plan for the Cariboo Wagon Road. Both Nind and Elwyn urged Douglas to establish an easier route to Williams Creek. Quesnel Forks had one more year as a major supply depot before the Wagon Road drew miners north to Williams Creek via Soda Creek and Quesnelmouth.

43

The mercury read 18 degrees below zero (F) on December 1, when S.D. Levi of Levi and Boas, left Quesnel Forks for New Westminster. It dropped to 27 below the following day, at Beaver Lake. Three feet of snow made the brigade trail impassable for men and animals, and Levi was forced to take the trail close to the Fraser River, via Alkali Lake to Lillooet. Thus began one of the worst winters in the history of the Cariboo gold rush.

Chapter Four

1862

"This is an awfully miserable, terribly splendid, excellent country. Human beings are reduced to the condition of beasts."[1]

S.G.

THE WINTER OF 1861-62 was long remembered by pioneers for its severity. The Fraser River froze solid past New Westminster, preventing ship access until late February. On the Douglas to Lillooet route, deep snow and frozen lakes delayed pack trains until May. The Quesnel River area escaped the heavy snowfalls, but as a consequence of bad weather farther south, provisions could not be delivered until much later than normal. Quesnel Forks went without mail delivery from Christmas until April. Only two or three *Colonist* newspapers reached the village all winter, barely legible after being handled by so many miners wanting news of the American Civil War.

Some men did not cope well with the isolation. Dr. R. Walker, from England via San Francisco, died in impoverished circumstances in February, having been kept alive by the generosity of the other residents. In March Harry Wolf attempted to shoot storekeeper E.D. Brousson, then made his escape. A special constable, McArthur, was called on to search for Wolf for eleven days, at ten dollars per day.

Other men, like Cornish miner, Johnny Bryant, made the best of the situation. Bryant had worked at Antler Creek the previous summer and wintered over on the North Fork with Harry Coulter. For $100, Steve Leland, clerk at Locke and Hart's store at Quesnel Forks, grubstaked Bryant with supplies. Bryant chose a large quarter of beef at Dick Bennett's butcher shop that provided him with meat all winter. "When I wanted a piece I came down and had a piece sawed off." He spent most of the winter preparing a wing dam on the North Fork, but in early spring, decided his luck would be better at Williams Creek. He left the North Fork in March and went to work on the Cornish Claim on Williams Creek. Bryant's instinct was right, for when breakup came on the North Fork, river ice carried off his winter's work in an hour and piled it under Isaiah Mitchell's bridge. Bryant did well that summer at Williams Creek, selling his interest in the Cornish Claim for $2,000 in the fall of 1862.[2]

Because of a high runoff in 1861, Barry and Adler had the South Fork bridge raised three feet during the winter. In the spring, they advertised it as being "greatly improved and rendered strictly safe for travel." A few months later a new advertisement for the bridge described it as "a short cut to the diggings. Superior accommodations for man and beast may be obtained at all the wayside houses."[3]

By the end of winter, flour was almost more desirable than gold. In January, merchants Levi and Boas had advised that there were 75,000 pounds of flour at the Forks, and 125,000 pounds of other goods. Candles were the only scarce item. Native men and women were again packing goods as far as Antler Creek in the snow, aided by the fact that the North Fork River had frozen to a depth of several feet. Dogs and men could pull toboggans loaded with supplies the 24 miles to Keithley Creek. Several parties were cutting lumber, which sold at $125 per 1,000 feet. Flour sold at $78 a barrel, beans 45¢ a pound, and bacon 68¢ a pound.

Despite the earlier assurances of Levi and Boas, food supplies were giving out rapidly at Quesnel Forks when Samuel Millbury brought in the first pack train of the season in late April. Millbury continued on to Keithley Creek, arriving May 1. He reported that he and his men packed goods to Antler on their backs, through three to ten feet of snow.[4] At Lillooet, Thomas Elwyn was most concerned about the shortage of provisions, claiming that not one pack train had left Lytton or Lillooet by May 2. He estimated that 800 men had gone up to the Cariboo, but there were not five sacks of flour between Lillooet and Williams Lake. Merchants feared that the first pack trains would be attacked by starving men who were penniless. Repeated warnings in the newspapers failed to dampen the miners' enthusiasm.

Ordered to take up headquarters at Quesnel Forks immediately thereafter, Elwyn arrived on May 25. He was accompanied by Chief

Napoleon Fitzstubbs.
(G-01290, BCA)

Constable Charles Seymour who had gained his appointment because he had been acquainted with almost every miner and every claim in the district the previous year. Their journey from Williams Lake to the Forks took five days because they were transporting a heavy metal safe along with their provisions. Finding the jail too small for a magistrate's office, Elwyn rented a house for four pounds a month. When his presence was urgently required at Antler and Williams creeks, he left Napoleon Fitzstubbs in charge, and hurried on. (Elwyn estimated there were now 700 men beyond Quesnel Forks, with 20 to 30 arriving every day). Fitzstubbs was called away to Williams Creek in late June, replaced by a reluctant George Gompertz, who remained until August 1.

Two weeks later, Elwyn reported to the Colonial Secretary from Williams Creek that there were 500 men on Antler creek and claims were paying from $50 to $100 a day. Two hundred men were working on Grouse Creek.

> The yield on this creek [Williams] is something almost incredible, and the rich claims have risen to three times their market value last winter. Only six companies are at present taking out gold but there are between five and six hundred men on the creek sinking shafts, and getting their claims into working order. Cunningham & Co. have been working their claims for the past six weeks and for this last thirty days have been taking out gold at the rate of three thousand dollars every twenty-four hours. In the tunnel owned by this company, the average prospect is thirty-five ounces to the pan.
>
> Messrs. Steel & Co. have been engaged for the last ten days in making flumes but during the previous three weeks their claims yielded two hundred ounces a day. These figures are so startling that I should be afraid to put them on paper in a report for His Excellency's information were I not on the spot and know them to be the exact truth.[5]

The exciting news about Williams Creek reached Keithley Creek at spring freshet time. Just as men were ready to go to work, with wing dams in place, a sudden rise in river levels washed out all their hard

Three assistant gold commissioners who served in the Cariboo: (l. to r.) Peter O'Reilly,
Henry M. Ball, and Thomas Elwyn.
(A-01103, BCA)

work. Many prospectors were forced to seek further credit from the merchants who had tided them over the winter. The Negro owner of the only restaurant at Keithley Creek closed his business because the miners had no money. At Quesnel Forks a number of desperate men broke down the door to Schultz and Trickey's store, forcing Constable Fitzstubbs to use his fists to keep order. Locke and Hart took advantage of the food shortage to sell off goods stored for R.T. Smith. The two merchants contended that a leaking roof had damaged flour, beans, salt, coffee, sugar and other groceries and they were unable to contact Smith. When Smith found out about the sale he sued, claiming £1,800, but the defendants reimbursed him only £280. By June 8 two pack trains had reached Antler Creek, and about a hundred animals were en route from Quesnel Forks.

Elwyn received much criticism for holding over claims for another month, from June 1 to July 3. John Robson, editor of the *British*

Columbian, at New Westminster, pointed out that speculators held most of the good claims in absentia, hoping to sell at high prices to impatient newcomers. The extra month was in their favour. Robson also suggested that speculators may have influenced Elwyn in his decision to hold over claims. But although only 24 years old, and the youngest assistant gold commissioner in British Columbia, Elwyn was sensitive to the needs of the miners. His excuse to the Colonial Secretary was logical: there simply wasn't enough food in the country to support miners who had to be "on the ground" by June 1, to keep their claims for the following year. An excess of litigation would also be avoided.

Speculation in mining claims continued. William and Thomas Barry registered claims at Williams Creek as early as March 1862. Napoleon Fitzstubbs registered three claims: Goose Creek, April 1; Cunningham Creek, April 16; and Williams Creek, April 23. When Elwyn and Begbie were rumoured to be involved in mining at Williams Creek and Cottonwood, the government issued a circular, warning that government officials should not hold claims.

Unfortunately, the delay to July meant that the working time was shortened by another month. Many inexperienced gold seekers returned to Quesnel Forks in June and sold off their equipment, unable to wait a few more weeks for the official opening of mining season. Elwyn noted the number of young Canadians arriving on the creeks:

A great many men, principally Canadians, are returning below. They are, as a rule, entirely ignorant of mining and came up here with a few pounds of provisions on their backs and hardly any money. They have not the least idea where to look for a claim, or how to go about to get one. As an example, I might mention that one man actually thought until he arrived at Keithley's Creek, that gold was found on the top of the ground and was greatly astonished on being told that the bedrock was a more likely place. No man during his first year in British Columbia ought to come to Cariboo before the middle of July unless he has money. By that time the claims are all opened and a green hand can always get good wages.[6]

Some young men went up to the Cariboo and returned sadder but wiser. T.R. Mitchell passed through Quesnel Forks on June 14. He camped 12 miles out from Quesnel Forks on the trail to Keithley Creek, where there was swamp grass for his horses. When he couldn't find work on Keithley Creek he returned to Quesnel Forks to pack goods to Antler Creek. He lost money on this venture and with only $25 in his pocket made his way back to the Forks. Mitchell sold his tent for $12 then returned to Victoria where he found employment for the winter.

Reports from missionary Edward White, who came to Victoria in 1859 with the first group of Wesleyan Methodist missionaries, inspired Doug Bogart to leave Ontario. Bogart wrote home to his family:

> I did feel mad to think that we had to walk five or six hundred miles, and then be fooled. The only consolation I had was nights when we all were tired to sit down and sing to them, "Sad was the day we went away, a hunting of the gold", and one of the Rosses clerks — we had three of them in our Company, would sing, "We did not find it was a sell until we got to Forks of Quesnel. Look away to Cariboo."[7]

James Thompson, resident of Edwardsburgh (Port Elgin) Ontario, and a veteran of the California gold rush, decided to try his luck, also. He left his wife and young family in Ontario and travelled by the Panama route. When he and his companions reached Quesnel Forks on June 14, they found a small community of 30 or 40 houses and 70 or 80 tents. After testing Keithley Creek and Williams Creek, unsuccessfully, they decided to return south. At Maloney's Flat near Grouse Creek they had supper with Jonathan Begg who had also lived in California. Begg now owned a garden nursery on Salt Spring Island, and was on a tour of the mining areas, selling cabbage plants.

During the early years, many returning miners found employment at the ranches at Williams Lake. Thompson and his brother-in-law, Anson Armstrong, worked at Davidson's Lake Valley Ranch, sawing lumber, splitting shingles, and building a baking oven (presumably from mud bricks). Robert Harkness, an overlander from Iroquois, Ontario, passed by the ranch in September. Letters written by Harkness and Thompson to their wives reveal the mixed feelings they had about participating in the Cariboo gold rush. Although they longed to go home to their families, they didn't want to return penniless and be ridiculed.

One correspondent estimated that at least 20% of the miners never got beyond Quesnel Forks. A letter from the village, dated July 2, suggest that conditions had not improved:

> Dear Sir: I arrived here this morning, in good health; but, my God, it is hard work to go to Cariboo. At Williams Lake the little mare gave out — that is, she is lame — so I left her there and had to walk in here, a distance of 64 miles, over a road I cannot describe to you. I will write to you again in a few days, or as soon as I shall be able to form some judgment of matters in general. In the meantime I can only inform you how I found things on my arrival here. Business brisk, but not over 500 pounds provisions in the town. People above are nearly starving, and thousands are rushing back to save them[selves] from famine. The only parties that have anything to sell are Levi & Boas, and they are making a heap of money. Mark's horse train arrived and sold out at immense profits.
>
> This is an awfully splendid, terribly miserable, excellent country. Human beings are reduced to the condition of beasts. No compassion, pity, or mercy, animates the heart of another. Money! money! is all that you hear, and if that fails you, my God! you must starve or steal; for if you beg no one will believe you, because everybody looks like a beggar himself. I have seen some wonderful things in the early times of California and Washoe, but Cariboo is the quintessence of misery on one side, and of the most splendid chances and bright prospects on the other.[8]

After spending three winters in the Cariboo, pioneer miner William Ross Keithley travelled down to New Westminster in June. The *Columbian* reported, "He took bilious fever in March last which has settled in something like dumb-ague accompanied by a distressing cough, giving the premonitory symptoms of consumption." Despite the vast amount of gold attributed to his claims, Keithley neglected to pay Quesnel Forks hotel keepers A.J. Abbott and T.B. Handley £14 ($70) for board at Quesnel Forks and was taken to court. From a notice in the *Columbian*, he appears to have been in trouble with merchants Boas, Levi and Hamburger as well. The advertisement warned the public not to accept a note in their names from Keithley, worth $2,400. On May 27, 1862, Keithley had sold half of his interest in the Peter Company at Williams Creek to the three merchants for $3,000. Keithley escaped to Oregon in October after stabbing Jane Milner, alias Ashmore, on Esquimalt Road in Victoria (the woman recovered). He was not heard from again until he wrote to the *B.C. Mining Journal* in 1900 from a home for destitute men in Butte, Montana.

Unlike the white miners who preferred the all-or-nothing challenge of prospecting, Chinese labourers were willing to work on the Cariboo Road for small wages. Road contractor G.B. Wright advertised that men would be hired for not less than two months, and paid in cash at the end of their work period. In July, 500 Chinese were employed at $40 a month on the road between Pavilion and Williams Lake. Many of these Chinese probably retired from roadwork to placer-mining in the vicinity of Quesnel Forks. One report mentioned that 300 to 400 Chinese miners were working on the North Fork River, but this may be exaggerated. As the Chinese prospected the area between the South Fork River and Horsefly, they found copper deposits that are only now being mined, more than 130 years later.

The most unusual method of packing supplies to the Cariboo was introduced in the summer of 1862. Initially, bactrian (two-humped) camels had been imported from Manchuria to San Francisco, and used for packing at mines in Idaho and Montana. Entrepreneurs operated on the theory that camels could carry more than mules or horses, and did not need to eat as frequently. Cariboo merchant Frank Lauermeister purchased 23 of the animals (including a pregnant female) in San Francisco and had them shipped to Victoria in April, with a case of leather shoes to protect their feet. The camels were first employed briefly on the Seton Portage. While en route to the Cariboo in June one died on Pavilion Mountain. They carried goods on both the Quesnelmouth and Quesnel Forks routes to Williams Creek, and at the end of the season were turned out to feed at the Forks (probably at Little Lake).

This was the one and only year that camels were used as pack animals, principally because their strange appearance frightened mules and horses, and their feet were not made to wade through swamps and deep mudholes, or traverse the sharp rocks on the mountains. Various unproven stories relate that one animal was mistakenly shot for a bear at Beaver Valley, and another served up for dinner by Barry and Adler when they later owned the 150 Mile stopping house. On their tour of the goldfields in 1863, Milton and Cheadle saw a camel near Clinton. The last animal is supposed to have lived until 1905, on a ranch east of Kamloops. The Camelsfoot Range in the southern Cariboo honours a unique and daring enterprise to maintain a supply line to Quesnel Forks and Williams Creek in 1862.

Because of the intense mining developments on Williams Creek and other sites on the north side of the Snowshoe Plateau, this year the Alexandria District was divided into Cariboo East and Cariboo West. Cariboo East included Mud Lake, Quesnel Forks, Keithley Creek, Antler Creek and Williams Creek, under the administration of Thomas Elwyn. Cariboo West, which became the responsibility of Peter O'Reilly, extended from Lightning Creek west to Quesnelmouth.

In June, the colonial government transferred Peter O'Reilly from Hope to the Cariboo as its second assistant gold commissioner. En route to Williams Creek via Quesnel Forks he took the wrong trail from Little Lake and ended up at Tow's ferry, ten miles below the Forks. O'Reilly backtracked, arriving at the Forks on the evening of June 26. Here he found George Gompertz "all down." He went for an evening stroll on the South Fork bridge, later noting in his diary that the village was a "wretched hole." O'Reilly wrote from Quesnel Forks on June 28, 1862, that he had passed 300 to 400 head of cattle on the trail and that 1,200 more were coming from Kamloops. Provisions were expensive and in short supply. A freshly caught, ten-pound trout sold for ten dollars. An estimated 400 men had returned from the mines.[9]

Obviously concerned with the threatened increase in lawlessness, Judge Begbie also arrived in the Cariboo in June. He made his way to the new centre of the gold rush, Williams Creek, via the Beaver Lake trail. By late July he was at Cottonwood, suffering from rheumatism, when one of the most notorious murders in Cariboo history occurred near Quesnel Forks. On the evening of July 26, two Jewish

Looking west, down the North Fork (Cariboo) River and the route taken by the two Jewish merchants in 1862. The gold rush trail crossed Isaiah Mitchell's bridge, built where the river makes a large curve, at the centre of the photo.
(A3665.37, NAC)

merchants, David Sokolosky and Harris "Herman" Lewin, and their French Canadian packer, Charles Rouchier, were shot to death and robbed on the upper trail between Isaiah Mitchell's toll bridge and the Forks. Sokolosky and Lewin had traded in the Cariboo the previous year but dissolved their partnership in March 1862.

William Tompkins Collinson never forgot this gold rush tragedy. As a young husband and father seeking adventure, he found more than he bargained for. Collinson left his small holding at Sumas Prairie in the Fraser Valley in June, travelling as far as Antler Creek. While returning to Keithley Creek he met up with the three men, and helped carry their gold to Cariboo Lake. Collinson journeyed on alone to Quesnel Forks where he learned that the men had not yet arrived. A search party from Quesnel Forks found the bodies of the victims dragged off the trail, five miles from the village. Sokolosky's body bore evidence of a violent struggle with their assailant(s). Not only the gold they were carrying, but their watches and even their hats were stolen. The value of the missing gold was estimated at $10,000 to $12,000.[10]

Methodist minister Arthur Browning arrived at the Forks just as the bodies of the murdered men were brought in. He found Philip Coote, the resident policeman, drunk, and Thomas Elwyn, the assistant gold commissioner, was 50 miles away, engaged in registering claims at Williams Creek. At a public meeting on July 29, residents of Quesnel Forks elected Browning as Chairman, and Samuel Goldstone, a travelling merchant from Victoria, as secretary. Browning selected two committees. One group, composed of James McLaughlin, John Boas and William Kirkman, proposed the following resolutions that were passed:

> Resolved, That as a dreadful highway robbery and murder of three of our valuable citizens has been committed in the vicinity of the town of the Forks of Quesnelle, your Committee appointed to report feel it incumbent upon them to censure, in the most emphatic terms, the course that the Government of the Colony of British Columbia have deemed proper to pursue in leaving the citizens of the town of the Forks of Quesnelle and vicinity without a resident magistrate.
>
> Resolved, That we the citizens of the town of the Forks of Quesnelle have reason to believe that the murderers of Mr. H. Lewin, Mr. D. Sokolosky, and Mr. Rouchier are making their escape and are on their way out of the country and in the absence of any officer of the law, deem it advisable to take the responsibility upon ourselves to arrest all suspicious persons, and call upon the Government to bear us out in our acts, and to defray whatever expenses may be incurred.[11]

The second committee, composed of Edward Griffin, Moses Harris and John Peterson, proposed that a four-man posse be dispatched, and a reward of $3,000 offered for the capture of the murderers. Thomas Barry served on the coroner's jury with William H. Grey, foreman; James McLaughlin, John Boas, Moses Harris, Charles Allwin, William Carlyle, John Peterson, Samuel Goldstone, Henry Davidson, William Richman and John Wolfe. Browning served as acting coroner. Edward Griffin left immediately to alert all police constables on the route south. When he arrived in New Westminster he was to "lay the matter before the Governor."[12]

Elwyn arrived at Quesnel Forks six days after the murders, having received an express notice from Philip Coote. He reported to the Colonial Secretary:

> I am informed that at a public meeting held here prior to my arrival from above, great indignation was expressed on account of my non-residence at this place. I beg to submit that since the 6th of June I have never been able to remain over five days at any one place and have been constantly and incessantly at work. Even my present temporary absence works a great hardship on those persons whose cases I have been obliged to postpone. The season is so short and provisions so high that few men can afford to be idle for a fortnight, not knowing whether they own a claim or not. I mentioned in a former letter my continued absence from Head Quarters and recommended the formation of a third and southern district. The late sad occurrence has, I would respectfully submit, rendered still more necessary some such step as I then ventured to advocate.[13]

John Robson, in the *British Columbian*, criticized Governor Douglas for neglecting the lives of the miners, making it necessary for the citizens of Quesnel Forks to form their own vigilance committee. At Lillooet, Assistant Gold Commissioner Andrew C. Elliott posted a $1,000 reward and sent a native messenger to notify Ball at Lytton to be on the alert for the culprits. To assist with the manhunt, former police constable Flynn was detained from going to the Cariboo, and miners using the Lillooet ferry were searched. Although several men were arrested and jailed at Douglas and at Victoria, no one was ever convicted of the murders. A second $1,000 reward, posted by Braverman and Lewin for the arrest of the murderer(s) of Herman Lewin, apparently went unclaimed.

A myth developed around Boone Helm, a notorious American outlaw who was in the Cariboo at the time of the murders. Victoria police kept Helm under arrest briefly in October, before he left for the United States. When he returned to British Columbia a year later, presumably to recover the buried loot, he was arrested a second time and deported. Just before being hanged in Virginia City, Nevada Territory, on January 14, 1864, for unrelated crimes, he was supposed to have confessed to the deeds, but this has never been verified. There were other murders during the Cariboo gold rush that were every bit as ruthless, but most were solved. The brutal killing of two well-known Jewish merchants and their packer in the prime of life, and with no one brought to justice, was remembered by Cariboo pioneers as an exceptional tragedy.

Arthur Browning was not the only minister to visit Quesnel Forks in 1862. At the time of the three murders, Anglican ministers Reverend John Sheepshanks and R.J. Dundas also passed through, en route to Williams Creek. Sheepshanks recalled seeing the bodies of the victims in an outside shed. (At the same time, Bishop George Hills and Reverend Christopher Knipe journeyed to Barkerville via Williams Lake and Quesnelmouth, on the new trail.)

George Weaver was one of the early pioneers who turned his energies to opening up new routes. He tried to interest Thomas Elwyn in hiring him to establish a trail from Quesnelmouth to Lightning Creek, but Elwyn chose Samuel Kyse to do the work. Earlier in the year, Weaver promoted access to the mines via Bella Coola, claiming that the Chilcotin could be crossed in five days in good weather. Nind's suggestion to Douglas in 1860, for an alternate route to the goldfields from Bella Coola, was now taken seriously.

Colonel Moody of the Royal Engineers dispatched Lieutenant Henry Spencer Palmer north to Bella Coola in July, with orders to travel across the Chilcotin Plateau to Williams Creek to ascertain the viability of the Bella Coola route. Palmer overcame a series of difficult challenges as he made his way out of the Bella Coola Valley and across the plateau, but he carried out his orders efficiently. He arrived at Dunlevy's stopping house in Beaver Valley in mid-September, returning from Williams Creek via the Snowshoe Plateau and Quesnel Forks. In his report to Moody he described Quesnel Forks as "a cheerless cluster of some fifty wooden houses and cabins."[14] Palmer discouraged miners from using the Chilcotin route, but a few packers and miners persisted until the Chilcotin uprising in May 1864 curtailed all non-native activity in that region for almost three decades.

The 1862 mining season was hampered not only by a late spring but by an early winter. In late September a snowstorm on the

Snowshoe Plateau caught packers unprepared. At 5,000 to 6,000 feet elevation, familiar landmarks disappeared under a low cloud ceiling and deep snow drifts. Within ten days 400 to 500 pack animals perished, valued at $50,000. Packers Dan Shafer, Armstrong and John Clugston lost 40 to 50 animals each. Saloon operators closed down and set off for the lower country as did Thomas Elwyn. Elwyn chose the new trail via Cottonwood to Quesnelmouth, but he sent his government records with two men who used the trail via the Snowshoe Plateau. When they got into deep snow, one packer, "Big George," hung the bag of records on a tree limb, planning to retrieve it in better weather. Serious doubts were expressed that it could ever be located, but fortunately for historians, the papers were rescued safely. The gold commissioner's records for the Cariboo are one of the most complete sets of mining records still extant.

During this same storm the J.D. Cusheon family were members of a party of 30 rescued on the Snowshoe Plateau by Moses C. Ireland. And in a separate mishap, Johanna McGuire, on her way to winter quarters at Quesnel Forks, went missing temporarily. Many pioneer miners first knew of Johanna at Yale during the Fraser River gold rush. At first she was reported murdered on the Swift River trail, and that $3,000 in gold had been stolen. Later information confirmed that she had merely lost her way, and she eventually reached Quesnel Forks safely. (Two years later, Johanna died in Victoria, apparently after a severe beating by another Cariboo pioneer, Ned Whitney. Whitney was not charged and he departed for the United States.)

Some of the richest merchants and miners on Williams Creek passed through Quesnel Forks with their season's earnings. William Cunningham brought down $40,000, Steel, $35,000, Goldstone, $15,000 and Levi of Levi and Boas, $20,000. Although their profits were considerably less by comparison, Tom Barry and Sam Adler had a good year, too. They reached Victoria with $10,000. While waiting for the California steamer they applied to W.A.G. Young, Colonial Secretary, for continuation of their bridge charter. They had been given a five-year charter in 1861, but this reapplication was necessary because the centre span of the South Fork bridge had collapsed on July 30. Elwyn issued a ferry licence to Barry and Adler for the interim.

By December, the warehouses at Quesnel Forks were well stocked with food for the winter. Constable Philip Coote prepared to supervise the jail with 14 pounds of candles on hand, while some 25 men and five women settled into their cabins to wait out the cold weather. With good gravel drainage and two rivers for fresh water, Quesnel Forks was a healthy place to spend the winter months. Unlike the steep valley at Williams Creek where multiple privies contaminated the groundwater, the Forks never suffered outbreaks of mountain (typhoid) fever and dysentery.

Smallpox was another matter. The natives of New Caledonia had suffered through an outbreak as recently as 1849. The dreaded disease was introduced to Victoria residents in the spring of 1862, claiming miners and especially aboriginals. It appears to have reached Quesnel Forks in a round-about way, via Bella Coola. En route to Fort Alexandria, infected miners left a deadly legacy when they stopped for care at native villages in the Bella Coola Valley or at Nancootlin (Anahim Lake) on the Chilcotin Plateau. When smallpox reached East Cariboo, 60 natives died at Williams Lake and 50 at Beaver Valley. Several natives died at Quesnel Forks in December, as well as hotel owner Andrew Jackson Abbott, age 27, a native of Massachusetts.[15] The only medical doctor was at Williams Creek, too far away to be of assistance. At Lillooet, smallpox claimed another pioneer of the Cariboo gold rush, Hi Robinson, who had recently arrived from Beaver Valley.

The brief mining season and the smallpox epidemic had caused much unhappiness in 1862. Ever hopeful, the miners looked forward to greater success in the New Year.

CHAPTER FIVE

1863-1870 — STAYING ON

"Where I am, the altitude is over 4,000 feet above
Sea Level & 54 North Latitude. I am about 400 miles
from the sea by the trail road."[1]

Robert Scott, Little Snowshoe Creek

Despite THE CONTINUING smallpox epidemic, 1863 was the
finest year of the Cariboo gold rush. Cariboo miners recovered most of
the $4,000,000 in placer gold reported for British Columbia. This
amount would never be equalled. By fall the Cariboo Road was
completed as far as Soda Creek where passage could be taken on the
little sternwheeler *Enterprise* up the Fraser River to Quesnelmouth.
However, the final section of the journey to Williams Creek from
Quesnelmouth was still a rough, 100-mile trail, and many packers
and miners continued to use the familiar pack trail via Quesnel Forks.
During the winter it was easier to bring merchandise as far as Beaver
Lake, then transport it over the Snowshoe Plateau by sleigh and individual packers. In the summer there was abundant grass on the
plateau for pack animals.

The most sensational event by far was the transportation of Sophia Cameron's body from Williams Creek to Victoria in February, 1863. Sophia had died of typhoid fever the previous October, but her husband, John A. "Cariboo" Cameron, was determined to carry out her wish that final interment would be near her home in Ontario. Native packers, hauling toboggan loads of supplies from Quesnel Forks to Antler and William creeks, had kept the trail open most of the winter, and thus Cameron, with help from friends, was able to travel in cold weather. When he reached Victoria at the beginning of March, he had his wife's coffin temporarily buried in the Pioneer Cemetery at Victoria. He returned to the Cariboo to work on his claim during the active mining season, then took Sophia's body to Ontario in the fall.

Although the Cariboo winter had begun in September, it was considerably milder than 1861-62, and plenty of provisions were packed in. The *Colonist* reported that a Mr. Harris of Harris Brothers, Quesnel Forks, had brought down $11,000 in gold in February. Flour was 38¢ a pound and beans 75¢. In the spring, the trail to Quesnel

Sophia Cameron.
(D-07952, BCA)

62

Forks and over the Snowshoe Plateau was just as bad as ever. George Hargreaves, a young English surveyor, described his visit to the Cariboo in June:

> Left Deep Creek on Friday the 5th [of June], branched off, intending to go by the Forks of Quesnelle, which road I would not go to Cariboo by again if there was another, however far round it might be. It is considered the nearest but it certainly is the roughest, over the tops of high mountains and through swamps to the end of the journey. Camped at a place called Big Lake. On the following day passed the grave of a young man from Devonshire, the place being marked with a post, who had died and was buried far from any human habitation, in a wild, desolate country, with miles of burnt stumps around from which cause our attention was directed to his grave post which was newly cut and squared.
>
> Thursday 12th reached Snowshoe Creek where we stopped eight days to prospect, one of our party having a claim there. Nothing good on the creek. Very few men working there. Left there on the 20th, followed up the west branch of the creek and when we got on the north side of the mountain we found the snow very deep and not hard enough in many places to bear our weight. The consequence was we fell through and so for about four hours we were rolling and tossing about. The difficulty was to get out. When you are down on good ground it is not easy to get up with a heavy pack on, but to be buried in snow and first get on your legs and then mount the snow again is anything but fun. I know you are laughing. So did we at first but when we found it to continue and we lost our only guide as to which was the way — which was a small cut in the bark of a tree here and there — we began to look blue. However we reached a place called Sawmill Flat near Antler Creek by 8:30 pm, after the hardest day we had had since leaving Victoria.[2]

The toll-bridge operators, Isaiah Mitchell and William Barry, worked hard to entice road traffic their way. Mitchell cleared out trails from his bridge to Quesnel Forks (eight miles), and to Davis' crossing on Keithley Creek (14 miles). In September, he took advantage of the fact that the Cariboo Wagon Road had just been completed past Lac La Hache, by opening the route first discussed with Nind two years previously, from 108 Mile via Horsefly to Quesnel Lake. This work required $2,500 to $3,000 of Mitchell's personal funds, and a $3,000 grant from the colonial government. Mitchell built a steamer to carry passengers across the lake to Cedar Creek where a trail led over Spanish Mountain to his bridge. Mitchell advertised that by taking this route miners could save 45 miles — at least two days' travelling. The government granted him a charter so he could collect tolls. Because the trail made escape easy for law breakers, it became known as the Skedaddle Trail, or Murphy's Cutoff — it ended south of Murphy's ranch on the Cariboo Road.

Reports in the *Colonist* such as the following were now suspect, because Mitchell wanted to direct miners away from the Cariboo Road:

> A party of Canadians who have been hunting and trapping in the Horsefly District, report having struck gold in paying quantities on the South Fork Lake. Most of the travel for Keithleys Antler and Cunninghan Creeks is expected to go by the Horsefly trail, branching off at Horsehoe Lake in the coming season.[3]

One young man who arrived via the 108 Mile trail and remained in East Cariboo was Jimmy Adams. Jimmy mined on Keithley Creek and the Snowshoe Plateau for the next 50 years. When interviewed in later life he claimed that he never left Keithley Creek until 1921 when he returned south to live with a partner, William Adams, at Lillooet.

Not to be outdone by Mitchell, William Barry erected a bridge across the North Fork, one and a half miles above Quesnel Forks, that was 250 feet long, eight feet wide, and supported by two piers. He secured a charter to charge tolls for three years. The trail on the north side of the bridge connected with the Snowshoe, and was supposed to have plenty of grass.

Following their appeal to the colonial government the previous November, Barry and Adler were able to renew their bridge charter over the South Fork for three years from August 1, 1863. They paid £80 rent annually, on a half-yearly basis. Toll rates were: foot passengers one shilling; loaded animals four shillings, unloaded animals, pigs, sheep, oxen two shillings. They advertised their bridge as shortest route to the mines; cattle did not have to swim rivers, and there was good accommodation along the route.

Judge Begbie chose the new route to the Cariboo, via Soda Creek, this year, and except for fishing expeditions to Keithley Creek, he does not appear to have visited Quesnel Forks again. Thereafter, any civil or criminal cases involving residents of East Cariboo were heard at the Richfield courthouse. There were three cases in 1863. In a murder case, again involving Chinese at Quesnel Forks, Begbie found the accused not guilty.

The second case involved the packer Redheaded Davis, Lucius Loucks, and hay. Next to gold and flour, hay was the most imporant commodity, worth $150 per ton. In order to feed 100 animals using the Snowshoe Plateau route, Davis purchased six tons of Swamp River hay from Loucks at Cariboo House, Keithley Creek. Loucks clamed he was not paid in full and laid a complaint. Begbie ordered Davis to pay Loucks $512.[4]

The third case involved Marie Perrin and Caillou, a carpenter who built her a house at Quesnel Forks during the winter of 1862-63. Caillou claimed he was not paid for his work and eventually won a decision from Begbie.[5]

In the spring of 1863, Philip Nind returned from England with his bride, Elizabeth. He took over command of the gold escort, resurrected for the 1863 mining season. Nind estimated that five trips to Barkerville would cost $2,000 each. He counted on $1,000,000 worth of gold being shipped, on which the escort fee would be 1.5%. Oliver Hare, customs collector at Douglas, joined Nind on the first trip to the Cariboo. They reached Barkerville in early July, but Nind could only collect $40,000 in gold for transport. He was too late for the winter gold which had been taken south, and too early for summer production.[6] To make matters worse, when Nind took ill in August, his assistant did not keep the accounts in order. The *British Columbian* heavily criticized the project because it did not generate the revenue expected to cover its expenses. The escort disbanded amidst considerable controversy, and Nind replaced John Boles Gaggin as assistant gold commissioner at Douglas in December. Nind was moved to Lytton in May 1865, when Ball was transferred to Quesnelmouth.

Interestingly, Nind did not think highly of his fellow commissioners, Ball and Elwyn. Within a year after leaving British Columbia for Queensland, Australia, in 1866, he wrote to his friend Peter O'Reilly: "if faces give any clue to character both Ball & Elwyn will one day stand on trial for their lives in a criminal dock."[7] Nevertheless, from 1860 to 1865, the four administrators struggled as best they could with the demands of settling mining disputes, the abuse of natives and Chinese, and Lands and Works responsibilities such as establishing trails and wagon roads, erecting government buildings and auctioning Crown Land. Nind initially received £300 per annum plus £100 for expenses, later increased to £450. The treasury minutely scrutinized all expense accounts — even the smallest deficit had to be repaid. Forced to make decisions without immediate contact with colonial officials in Victoria, these "men on the spot" sometimes corresponded for a year or more before receiving government reimbursement for their outlays for food, shelter and horse transportation. Until a circular from James Douglas requested "the entire and undivided services of its officers," all of the assistant gold commissioners and some of their constables speculated in land or mining claims. However, their transgressions were outweighed by a strong sense of loyalty to the Crown that kept them at their stations during the most turbulent years in the mainland colony's history.

Although three toll bridges now served miners in the vicinity of Quesnel Forks, 1863 ended on a less optimistic note. Most miners knew that the surface diggings on the major creeks were giving out. Large amounts of capital and numbers of skilled workers were needed to mine the deposits on bedrock, 30 to 50 feet below the surface, or to timber the tunnels into dry diggings. A great many Chinese miners moved in to tidy up the discovery claims, as a winnowing out of the pioneers took place. The hardiest or foolhardiest men remained, determined to at least break even if they couldn't make a fortune.

As the chaff separated and departed for fresh mining ventures, the residue settled in to make the best of their locations. Better transportation meant that there were ample provisions at reasonable prices throughout the Cariboo. No longer did miners have to make ten dollars a day merely to survive. There was time now to enjoy a less frantic pace, to revisit the old claims, to be satisfied with smaller paystreaks. Harvey, Keithley, Goose, and a few unworked creeks on the south side of the Snowshoe Plateau received more thorough attention.

William Barry gave up the struggle to secure traffic for his toll bridges and joined brother Tom, and Sam and Moses Adler at Barkerville. Besides saloon businesses the four men invested in mining claims, either separately or together. In July 1868, they held interests in the Blue Dick Company on Rich Gulch.[8] William Barry must have spent part of each year at the Forks between 1864 and 1869, because he took every opportunity to request government aid for trails in the vicinity.

On the positive side, most miners who stayed on in the Cariboo were old friends by now. They joined together to register claims on a new strike, and when that played out they regrouped for yet another location. Their contributions to the settlement and development of the region during the next four decades ensured stability and continuity not only for the mining industry but for agriculture. When gold recoveries declined, many pioneers established farms on the eastern Chilcotin plateau, and on the arable benches and valleys east of the Fraser River.

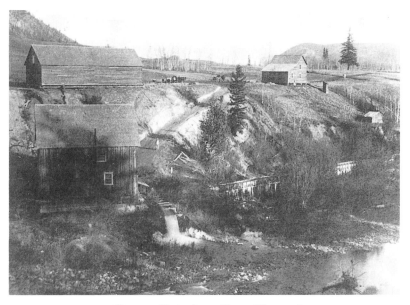

William Pinchbeck's flour mill at Williams Lake.
(A-02596, BCA)

They included James Sellers and Peter Dunlevy at Soda Creek, William Pinchbeck and Tom Menefee at Williams Lake, Alex Porter at Chimney Creek, and Timoleon Love, Daniel Nordenberg, William Riskie and Samuel Withrow at Riskie Creek. Native cooperation and assistance were vital to the success of these ranching operations.

The dedication of government officials such as Henry Maynard Ball and John Bowron at Williams Creek, Oliver Hare and, later, William Stephenson, at Quesnel Forks must also be mentioned as important stabilizing factors. Their many years of service and their intimate knowledge of mining claims and miners ensured that the administration of mining laws went smoothly, and litigation was kept to a minimum. The miners went about their business confidently, knowing they had reliable, trustworthy friends in charge.

Ball moved from Quesnelmouth to Barkerville in 1870, replacing Chartres Brew after his untimely death. Ball was popular with the miners and administered the mining laws fairly, but as the years went by he grew more and more unhappy with his situation and government parsimony. Claiming health problems after 14 years in the Cariboo, he retired to San Francisco in 1881.[9]

John Bowron arrived in Barkerville in 1863, and commenced public service as postmaster in Richfield. He served as a police constable, court clerk and government agent, and became gold commissioner in 1882, following Ball's resignation. He had studied law in Quebec before travelling west with a group of Overlanders in 1862. His even-handed interpretation of the Mining Act, combined with extensive knowledge of the Cariboo region and the miners themselves, made him irreplaceable. The provincial government kept Bowron at Barkerville, despite numerous requests for a transfer after his wife became terminally ill with breast cancer. He died shortly after retirement, in 1906.[10]

Oliver Hare's connection with Quesnel Forks began in 1866 when he held an interest in a claim at Cedar Creek. A native of Devonshire, England, he first emigrated to Australia, and then came to British Columbia in 1858. Hare filled various positions: customs collector at Douglas, second in command of the gold escort in 1863, and Supreme Court Registrar in New Westminster and Barkerville, where he was well regarded by Judge Begbie. He spent the last three years of his life as the first government agent at Quesnel Forks, or as Begbie teased, "King of Quesnelle at the Forks." They were not happy years because he suffered from ill health and was miserably lonely during the winters. Hare died of heart disease in Victoria on December 26, 1876, at the age of 53.[11] His replacement, William Stephenson, a native of Saint John, New Brunswick, would serve East Cariboo for the next 30 years.

While Bowron, Ball, Hare and Stephenson carried out their duties conscientiously, the pioneer miners who stayed on were every bit as tenacious. In 1861, Aurora Jack Edwards, a former sea captain, had one of the earliest and richest claims on Williams Creek. John Bowron estimated final production was worth $850,000, which was $50,000

Mining flume and bridge construction near Quesnel Forks.
(D-07983, BCA)

more than the second richest, the Cameron claim. In 1866 Edwards prospected two creeks near the foot of Quesnel Lake, which he named Coquette (now called Poquette) and Cedar. He staked discovery claims on Cedar Creek, 13 miles above Quesnel Forks, with partners George Devoe and John King Barker. News of the gold find, published in the *Cariboo Sentinel* and the *British Columbian*, created a minor rush. More than 60 miners registered claims adjacent to Edwards' Discovery Company: familiar names such as William Hazeltine, John Polmere, Duncan McMartin, Isaiah Mitchell, Peter Dunlevy, and Oliver Hare. The Aurora company built a flume 1,800 feet long, washing out $7,000 during the first year. Another group of miners worked all winter on Coquette Creek, running a tunnel. There were enough miners to support several stores, and William Barry reopened the trail from Quesnel Forks at a cost of $1,500. He also secured government assistance to clear out the trail from Deep Creek to Quesnel Forks, by paying half the $800 cost.

The Cedar Creek rush lasted about two years. It was only one of many mining adventures for Aurora Jack Edwards and John King Barker to boast about as they lived on to old age in the Quesnel Forks area. Edwards invested his earnings in a farm on southern Vancouver Island in 1880s, but he couldn't stay away from East Cariboo for long. Barker joined Peter Dunlevy on a trip to the Cassiar in 1871, and assisted Marcus Smith in railway surveys. In the 1890s he became well known for his involvement in the Bullion Pit mine, near Dancing Bill's Gulch.

Harvey and Keithley creeks attracted oldtimers as well. There were butcher shops and stores at both locations, and a population large enough to warrant polling stations on election day. Based at 150 Mile House, Edward Toomey supplied cattle and packed in provisions. Samuel Smith opened stores at Harvey Creek and Keithley Creek. Nicholas Bailey returned from Williams Creek to Harvey Creek and worked there until his untimely death at age 38 in 1872. During the early years of the Cariboo gold rush, three-quarters of a mile of the lower portion of Harvey Creek had been worked. The high gravel banks farther up the creek were now tunnelled, with good results. At the time of his death, Bailey's Perseverance Mining Company had been doing well. His 5/6 interest was auctioned off to Donald Rankin and James Turley for $850.

During the first years of the gold rush, Nind reported that William Keithley and others had made hoses from canvas and were washing gravel off the high banks of the creek. Men operating sluices at the bottom of the banks had processed the loose gravel, which was then dumped into the rushing waters of Keithley Creek. The oldtimers began mining these gravel banks again, based on the theory that they had been part of a creek bed established at a higher level. It was now infilled with gravel which might contain gold toward the bottom of the deposit. This supposed creek bed ran parallel to Keithley Creek on the left bank. There were a number of successful mines, based on this theory, most notably the Onward and Kitchener, and the Grotto tunnel.

Timoleon Love returned from the Cassiar to work claims on Black Bear Creek in 1867 and Keithley Creek in 1869. His partners on Black Bear Creek included Peter Dunlevy, James Sellers, William Morehead and Oliver Hare. Charles Ettershank managed to talk the colonial government into providing food for a five-man exploration party into the mountains at Horsefly Lake in 1865. He wangled further aid the following year, even though Peter O'Reilly warned the Colonial Secretary that he was unreliable. Ettershank and his famous partner, Billy Barker, were still at Horsefly ten years later.

THE SNOWSHOE BOYS

Among the most interesting groups of miners who stayed on after the gold rush were the men who established themselves on upper Keithley Creek, Snowshoe Creek and Little Snowshoe Creek. Unwilling to give up the search for gold as long as they could "turn a creek" or build a penstock, their claims were located close to one of the mother lodes, the quartz reefs of Yanks Peak and the Snowshoe Plateau. The tantalizing possibility of a good paystreak kept them in semi-isolation, 4,000 feet up on a mountainside, for the rest of their lives.

The importance of the quartz outcrops had been noted when the area was first explored. Thomas Hayward travelled down to Victoria in 1863 to request a special government grant for quartz mining. His partners were E. Jeffray and C.L. Miller. Hayward's request forced the authorities to create regulations for simple mining partnerships.

Rapidly descending 2,000 feet in ten miles, Keithley Creek slices through hundreds of feet of gravel overburden, from Barr Creek

Meadows to Cariboo Lake. Even in late summer it carries a good supply of water. It is fed by a number of tributaries draining off the Snowshoe Plateau: Luce Creek, Little Snowshoe Creek, French Snowshoe Creek, Snowshoe Creek, Rabbit Creek, and Weaver Creek.

The Snowshoe Boys established claims on their banks and built sturdy cabins that could withstand extremely cold temperatures and snow to the depth of ten feet or more: William Pearce and William Polmere on Keithley Creek, Robert Scott on Snowshoe Creek, James Strain, Joseph Rawley, Robert Barr and Thomas Hayward on Little Snowshoe Creek, and William Luce on Luce Creek. When they required extra labourers during the working season, most of them could afford to hire Chinese miners living at the Weaver Creek Chinatown farther down Keithley Creek. Luce, Scott and Hayward were resourceful enough to remain in their cabins throughout the long winters and deep snow. As they visited back and forth and tended

Looking east, across Little Cariboo Lake to the Keithley Creek delta, Vieth and Borland's ranch, and Cariboo Lake. The Cariboo River commences, lower right.
(1-61028, BCA)

John Polmere, one of the Snowshoe Boys.
(HP6880, BCA)

their traplines on snowshoes, they helped keep the trails open. The other men spent the coldest months at Barkerville or at Vieth and Borland's Willow Ranch at the mouth of Keithley Creek.

Over the years to 1900, oldtimers came and went on the Snowshoe. Jimmy Adams of the Great Snowshoe Company worked for five years on Little Snowshoe Creek, excavating a 3,800 foot tunnel on bedrock, beneath 80 feet of gravel overburden.[12] The fact that he found only a short-lived paystreak in no way lessened Adams' enthusiasm for mining. He was still prospecting on Little Snowshoe with Robert Borland in 1913. In 1901 George Vieth, Robert Barr and Jimmy Sivewright worked the Golden Gate and James Strain leases on Little Snowshoe Creek. In 1903 the mining inspector found Aurora Jack Edwards labouring alone on a claim a short distance above Weaver Creek. He had held the claim for many years. Timoleon Love, Hizer Newell, Kansas John Metz, John Polmere, and Samuel Kyse also owned claims at various times.

It was important to keep the trail open to the Snowshoe Plateau and Barkerville, not only for transporting food and mining equipment, but also for mail delivery and medical emergencies. The Royal Cariboo Hospital at Marysville (on Williams Creek) was the only medical facility in the Cariboo until the infirmary at the Bullion Pit mine was established about 1895. There were few disasters, but when they happened, the closely knit community was deeply involved. Snow avalanches killed Edward Kimball at 5 Mile Creek in late January 1874, and John Morris at Harvey Creek in May 1887, and as many miners as possible turned out to help search for the bodies.

Chinese miners were also taken to the Royal Cariboo Hospital. When a bank cave-in on Keithley Creek seriously injured Ah Sou in August 1875, there was no doctor available at Quesnel Forks, and no medicine at Davis's Crossing. Ei Tie sent a message to Barkerville for a doctor, and a Chinese resident returned to assist in bringing the injured man to hospital, but Ah Sou died near Grouse Creek, still ten miles away from medical care.

Over the years, residents of East Cariboo submitted many petitions to the Department of Lands and Works in Victoria, demanding more attention to the trail from 150 Mile House on the Cariboo Road to Quesnel Forks, Keithley Creek, and Little Snowshoe Creek. A typical petition in 1885 claimed that 400 men required 400,000 pounds of supplies annually. (Maintenance of the trail on the other side of the Snowshoe Plateau was the responsibility of the gold commissioner at Barkerville.)

There were enough miners working in the area to support a subsidiary store established by Vieth and Borland near the mouth of Little Snowshoe Creek. It was staffed by Robert McNab, a native of Renfrew, Ontario, and a partner in the V&B company. Supplies could also be bought from Chinese stores at Weaver Creek, or from V&B headquarters, at the mouth of Keithley Creek. The miners made payments in gold and, in winter, with furs they had trapped. The furs were sent to the Hudson's Bay store at Barkerville until it closed in the 1870s. (Marten were worth $2.50 to $3.50 per pelt; beaver 50¢ to 75¢ a pound, and mink 75¢ each in 1869.)[13] Although credit was given generously, Vieth and Borland often held mortgages on the Snowshoe miners' claims, acquiring some of them after the death of their owners.

One of the most enterprising miners, Robert M. Scott, from Belmont, Ontario, made and repaired snowshoes. This was a vital service in an area where snow remained on the ground for six months of the year. Like many others, he set traps for marten in the winter. His location near the Antler Creek trail, and his culinary talents made his cabin a popular stopping house. Visitors would be treated to donuts, berry pies, coffee and beer. A vegetable garden augmented supplies ordered in November from Vieth and Borland. A typical winter order included 20 pounds of oatmeal, ten pounds of bacon,18 tins of canned milk, 30 pounds of butter, 30 pounds of beans, 20 pounds of apples, 25 pounds of dried peaches, three tins of yeast powder, 250 pounds of flour and a side of beef which he salted down.

Scott liked to boast about his location, 4,000 feet in altitude, and 400 miles from the ocean, in letters to his family. Despite this semi-isolation, he rarely spent days alone, even in the dead of winter. His cabin filled with friends at Christmas and New Year's, no doubt because of his good cooking. The *Colonist Weekly*, *Star* and *Empire* magazines, and varied correspondence with relatives in California, North Dakota, and Ontario, kept him in touch with the outside world. His mail, including medicine from a brother-in-law in Ontario, was delivered to his door by the expressman from Barkerville.[14]

Scott's diaries cover most years from 1863 until his death in 1892. For the first few years he spent November to February in Victoria, stopping to mine a claim near Pavilion as he came and went. Major events such as the great forest fire of 1869, the deaths of Edward Kimball, William Luce and other friends are noted, along with the names of visitors, and how much gold was recovered for the week. In a separate notebook he kept a record of the weather, taking recordings morning, noon and night. Scott was raised in a Methodist family in Ontario, and rarely worked on Sundays. The few brief lines in copper-plate handwriting each day reveal the tenacity and resourcefulness of one oldtimer and his friends, as they stayed on to the end.

Scott died at the Willow Ranch in 1892, and was buried in the Keithley Creek cemetery. With all his years of mining, a niece felt certain that Scott was wealthy, and she wrote to William Stephenson for particulars. Stephenson informed her that her uncle had been indebted to Vieth and Borland's store; there was no inheritance.

Scott's neighbour, William "the Live Yank" Luce, was a native of Martha's Vineyard, Massachusetts. He had taken part in the California gold rush with a younger brother, Edmund who succumbed to typhoid fever in 1851. Edmund's body was buried on the outskirts of San Francisco, but a few years later the rapidly developing city preempted the cemetery, and Edmund's remains, along with many others, were reinterred in a new location. Luce sent money to have his brother's new grave properly marked. After Luce died, on May 28, 1881, another brother, Presbury, at North Tisbury, Massachusetts, requested that his grave also be properly cared for.

The story of Luce's headboard forms another part of Cariboo folklore. Johnny Knott at Barkerville carved the headboard, and Fred

William "the Live Yank" Luce.
(H-06359, BCA)

Littler was to deliver it. Fred supposedly grew tired of his load, and tossed the board into the woods short of its destination. It was found in the 1930s and brought to Luce's upper cabin site on the Snowshoe Plateau, where it was tied to a tree. Doris Lee found the board while pasturing sheep in the 1950s, and repainted the now raised lettering. Lead paint had protected the letters for a hundred years while the rest of the wood had eroded about an eighth of an inch. The board has been placed in the Williams Lake Museum for safekeeping. Luce was not buried on the plateau, but in the small cemetery at Little Snowshoe Creek.

Luce probably gained his nickname from his first claim in the Cariboo, "the Live Yank" at Harvey Creek. He registered a claim on Little Snowshoe Creek in 1863, where he mined in partnership with Thomas Hayward for some years, then operated on his own. He was the only one in the Snowshoe area to take advantage of the Gold Mining Amendment Act in 1873 that for a brief period allowed individual miners to acquire a Crown Grant for their mining claim, plus further acreage. After registering his 14-acre claim, Luce had to hold it for two years, and spend ten dollars an acre.[15] Luce's claim was the uppermost mining operation, at 4,500 feet. To visit it today, one must climb through mossy woods cut by old flumes, and scramble over a creek bed filled in with tailings piled ten feet high. The foundations for his cabin are small, but still visible.

Luce is supposed to have rescued a lost Jewish peddlar after finding him huddled beneath a tree in the snow, and brought him back to his cabin. Restored to good health, the grateful traveller presented Luce with the only possession he had, a sack full of mirrors. Luce and the peddlar are commemorated by the westernmost mountain on the Snowshoe Plateau, Yanks Peak, and a cirque on its northeastern side named Jew's Hollow. In May 1863, a Jewish peddlar named Zerchosky was lost for 13 days on the Snowshoe Plateau. He died at Quesnel Forks in June but it isn't known if he was carrying mirrors.

The small cemetery at Little Snowshoe Creek became the final resting place for at least four of the Snowshoe Boys. Although they got their fair share of exercise, hiking up and down the mountain, and working on their claims, most them died in their 60s and early 70s. There were two deaths from mining accidents: Joseph Rawley and

John Polmere. Luce's former partner, Thomas Hayward, cared for Luce for ten days until he died from heart failure at age 61 in May 1881. Hayward died on Snowshoe Creek in 1891.

In 1869 George Vieth and Robert Borland formed a strong partnership that would last until Vieth's death in 1906. Both were shrewd businessmen, born and educated in eastern Canada. Borland came from Port Hope, Ontario, and Vieth from a well-known family in Halifax, Nova Scotia. With a third partner, Robert McNab, they built up their holdings in East Cariboo during the next three decades. Facilities at the Willow Ranch included a post office and hotel. By

Martha Hutch using a rocker at Keithley Creek.
(PN3433, RBCM)

Mary Vieth, wife of George Vieth, Keithley Creek.
(Courtesy Dale Hunchak)

1900 the hotel had a bar, storeroom, dining room, kitchen and ten bedrooms. At the height of the hydraulic boom in the 1890s, Vieth's brother, Henry, managed a store and hotel at Quesnel Forks. Today, the log cabin post office at Keithley Creek remains intact.

Vieth and Borland speculated in mining all their lives, either by developing their own claims, lending money to "starved-out" miners, or buying up claims from estates. Borland claimed that $2,000,000 had passed through his hands during his years at Keithley Creek. About 1890 they purchased the 150 Mile stopping house from Gavin Hamilton which they operated until 1899. As a sideline, they also owned a pack train of mules which transported goods to Hazelton and further north for the Hudson's Bay Company.[16]

For 50 years, a native women, Martha Hutch, provided much needed domestic help at Willow Ranch. She was a handsome, strongly built woman from Sechelt, given the nickname (affectionately) "Saltchuck." Martha bore three children of three different husbands: Agnes Lamont, James Hutch[inson?] and Mary Saunders. Mary bore George Vieth a son and two daughters: Edward, Nellie and Jennie.

George sent the children to Halifax, to be educated under the care of a spinster sister, Ann. Although George Vieth hoped his son would become a mining engineer, Edward returned to the Cariboo and worked in the area for the rest of his life, latterly for the Department of Highways at Williams Lake. Martha spent her final days at the ranch and is one of the few pioneer women buried in the Keithley Creek cemetery.

* * * * *

For the first few years of the Cariboo gold rush, James Douglas supervised all legislation for the new colony of British Columbia. Petitioning for representative government began in 1860. The signatures of 300 British citizens collected at New Westminster, Hope and Douglas in the spring of 1860 include many of the future settlers and pioneers of the Cariboo: William Barker, John Butson, Peter Toy, William Pinchbeck, Oliver Hare, Jean Caux (Cataline). In response to the petition, which was submitted to the Colonial Office in London, Douglas pointed out that the population of the new colony was too unstable for this form of administration. The Duke of Newcastle in London accepted his explanation but after four more petitions, he thought it was time for a Legislative Council, and Douglas was requested to set up the council, which would be partially representative. One-third of the 15 councillors should be magistrates from the various districts, one-third members of the Executive Council, and one-third elected. Election for representatives from East and West Cariboo took place in October 1863; James Orr won for Cariboo East, and Dr. A.W.S. Black for Cariboo West.

By the spring of 1867 there were 200 Chinese miners on the North Fork.[17] Some of these men may have arrived from the worked-out sites at Wild Horse Creek and Big Bend in the Kootenays, from Rock Creek, and from completed sections of the Cariboo Road. The increase in the Chinese population in the Quesnel Forks area later provided the opportunity for Oliver Hare to become a tax collector and government agent.

As always, there were problems keeping routes open from the Cariboo Road to the Snowshoe Plateau. Isaiah Mitchell's bridge badly needed repairs by 1867. Ever willing to grasp an opportunity, William Barry proposed a new bridge seven miles farther up the North Fork, near the mouth of Spanish Creek, but the government approved repairs to Mitchell's bridge by packer John G. Jennings.[18] Interestingly, once the bridge was restored, Mitchell managed to renew his charter to operate for another three years, from June 1868. He advertised in the *Cariboo Sentinel* that the route to 108 Mile on the Cariboo Road from Barkerville via Quesnel Lake was only 117 miles. He provided a horse boat at the lake, charging one dollar for passengers and two dollars for horses.

In August 1868 the trail between Quesnel Forks and Mitchell's bridge became "quite impassable" according to Chartres Brew. Jennings lost a horse and pack worth $150 and a Chinese packer lost a horse and merchandise worth $300. Brew estimated that 1,000 people used the trail. Clearly, a more reliable route was needed between Quesnel Forks and Keithley Creek and this would be accomplished in 1869.

The tangled masses of blackened forests that confronted the earliest gold miners bore mute evidence that nature and man were vulnerable to forest fires. Domestic use of fire now complicated the unpredictable combination of dry summers and lightning strikes. In September 1868 Thomas Barry and Sam Adler were operating the Fashion Saloon at Barkerville — "the largest in B.C." The late summer had been hot and most of the buildings tinder dry. When fire broke out in the roof of their saloon, the flames spread quickly to other establishments. Within a few hours almost the entire village of Barkerville, 93 houses and 23 cabins, burned to the ground. Barry and Adler estimated their loss at $18,000. William Barry, who operated a saloon with William Stirling, claimed that he lost all his investment, too. Chartres Brew reported Stirling's saloon as a $10,000 loss and his house at $2,000.[19] When William Barry and Stirling dissolved their partnership in May 1869, Barry returned to live permanently at Quesnel Forks.

In June 1869, forest fires raged on both sides of the Swift River, and they may have been the source of the fire that eventually threatened Quesnel Forks on July 20. The conflagration spread from Twenty Mile Creek up the Quesnel River, crossing below Little Lake. All the residents of Quesnel Forks turned out to save the village. Fortunately for the small band of firefighters, the fire veered around the Forks, consuming only the lockup. The open fields were vulnerable on the opposite side of the North Fork, and William Barry lost his hay crop. Although the fire burned itself out before reaching Keithley Creek, the wind blew enough smoke and ashes towards Barkerville to blacken the sky at 4:00 P.M. Weary miners emerging from underground wondered if they had worked too long; others thought the world was coming to an end. A dense cloud of smoke hanging over the Fraser River from Quesnelmouth to Soda Creek made Captain Wright afraid to risk a trip down river with the new steamer *Victoria*.

At Little Lake John King Barker, Duncan McMartin and James Johnson saved their lives by taking refuge in an old section of burned-over timber. Other men survived by submerging themselves in streams and lakes.

Out of approximately 150 Chinese miners working in the burning area, the death toll amounted to 11. The unfortunate men, employees of the Kwong Lee Company at Quesnelmouth, had been caught by the fire near Twenty Mile Creek. Coroner F. Valentine Lee came from Barkerville to conduct an inquest. The bodies were taken to Quesnelmouth for burial, in coffins hastily made from sluice boxes.[20]

The fire destroyed an estimated $8,000 worth of tools and provisions. Burned and fallen trees blocked 43 miles of trail from Quesnel Forks to the Cariboo Wagon Road, and this route had to be reopened as soon as possible. William Barry proposed to supervise the work at a personal cost of $150 to $200, but packers quickly cut out the downed timber. Fortunately, there was time to replenish food supplies at the Forks before winter weather caused further transportation problems.

The Lands and Works Department reinstated William Barry's charter for bridges over the North and South Forks in October 1869, but before Barry gained permission to charge tolls again, on the South Fork bridge only, the government insisted that he open a new trail, the Duck Creek trail, to connect his North Fork bridge to Keithley Creek; this would ensure an alternate route to the old trail via Mitchell's bridge. (The North Fork bridge near Quesnel Forks was no longer a toll bridge because Barry abandoned the terms of his charter in 1864, when he moved to Williams Creek.)

While William Barry once again took up residence and community leadership at Quesnel Forks, his brother Tom and Sam Adler searched for new business opportunities. They left Barkerville in 1869 and purchased the 150 Mile House and property (previously known as the Lake Valley Ranch) from Edward Toomey. With yet another brother, John Barry, they briefly operated the stopping house and ranch before selling and moving on to the Omineca and Cassiar gold rushes. These gold rushes in northern British Columbia drew many pioneers, both white and Chinese, away from the Quesnel Forks and Keithley Creek areas, including Kansas John Metz, Duncan McMartin and James May.

At the request of the provincial government, a census was made of the Cariboo in 1869. In an area of 80,000 square miles there were:

919 white males, 69 females

720 chinese males, 6 females

27 colored males, 4 females

700-1,000 Indians

with 125 people in agriculture, 1,447 mining, 19 manufacturing, and 75 in trades. During that year there had been eight births, 13 deaths, and three marriages. A decade after the first rush to the Cariboo, the region was holding its own.

CHAPTER SIX

1870-1880 — THE CHINESE TAKE OVER

"The Chinese have it all their own way. The white miner seems to have set his face against this part of the country."[1]

Oliver Hare, Forks of Quesnelle

DURING THE NEXT decade, while British Columbia joined Confederation, and worked out the difficulties of gaining a railroad, the Keithley Creek/Quesnel Forks area became a Chinese province. The increase in population led to the establishment of a government agent and the necessary amenities of a post office and jail.

In 1870 approximately 200 Chinese miners contributed $2,000 annually in licence fees. The white population numbered only 100 and these people were located east of Quesnel Forks in the Keithley Creek and Snowshoe Creek areas. By 1881 the Chinese population had doubled to 413 while the white population remained steady at 102. Barkerville had a similar distribution between white miners and

Chinese, as did Quesnelmouth. Increased pressures placed on the Chinese in Victoria and New Westminster by provincial legislation encouraged them to seek refuge in rural areas where they could avoid harassment, yet earn a living. Many of the Chinese at Quesnel Forks came from the Four Counties region of Kwangtung Province, South China. Kinship and shared home-county origins offered security and friendship in a harsh, foreign environment.[2]

In the 1880s, many Chinese belonged to the Chee Kung Tong association. This association provided help in times of need, and assistance with employment, and meted out discipline. While the association isolated the Chinese from integration, its main purpose was social welfare. Generally, the Chinese were peaceable, but when pressured they could defend themselves against white racism.

Inequities between white and Chinese residents covered everything from wages to vital statistics. White mine labourers earned six dollars per day, the Chinese three dollars to $3.50. The Chinese had to submit to government demands for payment of taxes and mining claims, yet they couldn't vote. The Qualification and Registration of Voters Amendment Act of 1872 stated, "Nothing in this Act shall be construed to extend to or include or apply to Chinese or Indians." After 1883 an enumerator could be fined up to $50 if he placed a Chinese or Indian name on the voters list.[3] In 1884 the provincial government passed another law preventing Chinese from purchasing Crown Land and from exhuming their dead in order to send the bones back to China. When the provincial legislation on registering births, deaths and marriages came into effect in 1872, Chinese and Indians were excluded. A change in legislation in 1897 finally permitted registration but this was rescinded in 1899. Permission to register Chinese, Japanese and aboriginals was not reinstated until 1917.[4]

Confederation in 1871 brought neither roaring prosperity nor the promised railroad. Dr. John Helmcken, Joseph Trutch, and Cariboo MLA Dr. Robert Carrall formed the delegation that went to Ottawa to effect Confederation. Elections for a Member of Parliament were slated for December 1871. Earlier in the year, the editor of the *Cariboo Sentinel*, J.S. Thompson, was urged by mining friends to represent the Cariboo at both the provincial and federal levels. He did not poll enough votes to win a seat in the provincial election, but as the only nominee, he easily gained the federal position. Supporting better mail service and the transcontinental railway, Thompson represented the Cariboo until his death in 1880.

A tremendous amount of effort went into surveys through the mountains of British Columbia to tidewater, for the promised railroad. The first survey considered a terminus at Waddington's favoured site, Bute Inlet. A bridge to Vancouver Island and a railway to Victoria would ensure that the city could once again play the lead role, now usurped by New Westminster, as the main port of entry for the province. While Mahood searched for a route from the Thompson River through to Lac La Hache, Thomas Elwyn returned to the Cariboo to assist B Company survey crew on the Fraser River. James Reid optimistically named his grocery store at Quesnelmouth the Canadian Pacific Railway Terminal.

Work on the section to Bute Inlet, supervised by Marcus Smith, involved well-known surveyors Otto Tiedemann and Edgar Dewdney. Smith strongly favoured a Bute Inlet terminus via Fort George and Pine Pass. He investigated a connecting link across Seymour Narrows to Vancouver Island, and south to Nanaimo in December 1872. One of his surveyors who supported this route was former Cariboo MLA, Joseph Hunter. Smith took the completed report to Ottawa in April 1873. The federal government took its time. When Hunter returned to the Horsefly area the following summer, with another surveying company, he was accompanied by George Hargreaves, the young Englishman who grew discouraged after a difficult ascent of the Snowshoe Plateau in 1863. Smith gave Hargreaves the responsibility of surveying the Chilcotin and Blackwater areas in the spring of 1875.

J.S. Thompson made a passionate speech in Ottawa in 1874, urging the government to get on with building the railway. British Columbia Premier George Walkem, who held one of the three provincial seats for the Cariboo, travelled to Ottawa and then to London, England, to demand that the federal government honour its commitments. Walkem was treated like a hero on his return to Victoria, but his efforts proved fruitless. Because of a change in government in Ottawa, and an international depression, a decision on the final route was not made until July 1878. By then, seven routes had been more or less checked out, and the route through the Fraser Canyon to Burrard

Inlet won official approval over the Bute Inlet proposal. Quesnel Forks did not figure in any railroad survey until 1886.

With a railway just a golden dream, rural communities in British Columbia struggled along as best they could during the 1870s. Government officials like Oliver Hare, and community-minded residents like William Barry and Ah Ching provided the backbone, for village life at Quesnel Forks and many other rural areas. In the Cariboo a delicate balance had to be maintained between the white residents and the Chinese miners who outnumbered them four to one. As before, instructions for recording gold output and collecting taxes, formulated at polished mahogany desks in Victoria, were carried out with a good dose of common sense 400 miles away, on the rugged creeks of the Cariboo.

Despite its small population, Quesnel Forks was a lively place during the next decade. Among the few white residents remaining in Quesnel Forks, William Barry was the leader. Literate and business-minded, he was always ready to take on a road contract. The ongoing problem of maintaining trails and bridges required government expenditure annually. As the Chinese population doubled, law and order became another concern. Fearing an increase in crime after the Omineca gold rush died down, Barry led a petition for a police constable and a jail at the Forks. Thereafter he served on many coroner's juries, and assisted the government agent, Oliver Hare, as much as possible. Hare needed support because he seemed to have an ingrained dislike for the Chinese miners whom he called "brutes."

In June 1870, Barry's bridge on the North Fork was carried away by the spring freshet.[5] He rebuilt it by the end of December at a cost of $1,175. The bridge was a single span, 250 feet long and eight feet wide. Barry spent a further $760 improving the Duck Creek trail from the North Fork bridge to the mouth of Keithley Creek, employing six men for six weeks. For this work the colonial government granted him an extension of the charter for the South Fork bridge for another three years, effective March 25, 1871. For clearing out the trail from Quesnel Forks to the other side of Little Lake, a distance of eight miles, plus 216 feet of corduroy (logs laid horizontally across a swampy or muddy section of road) Barry received an additional $100.

In November 1870, Barry was concerned that a large bulkhead on the South Fork might break away during spring freshet and injure his bridge. He wrote to gold commissioner Henry Maynard Ball at Williams Creek:

> A company of Chinamen are about taking water out of the South Fork River at a point known as "the falls" and situated about one half a mile above my bridge at this place. Their object is to bring water on the benches along the South Fork River for mining purposes. To accomplish this object they are to put in a very large bulkhead as they have to raise the water a very great height from the river to get it on the bench. They propose putting in the bulkhead at the falls and if the said bulkhead should be taken away by the spring freshet it would be a very great injury to my bridge here. ... It would be very hard on me if I was to lose this bridge by such an undertaking. I therefore appeal to Your Honour for some redress in this case and hope that it is in your power to render it to me and at as early a time as may be convenient to Your Honour."[6]

The Chinese, Ah Mi, Ah Chac, Ah Fou, Ah Pack, and Ah Tye, members of the Hing Ching Company, defended themselves:

> We think that mining rights are paramount to bridge privileges in the country and that an enterprise in which about $800 has already been spent, in good faith, by working men should not be stopped because one man imagines that in the event of a very high freshet it might be detrimental to him.[7]

In spring of 1871 there was a stabbing incident between two Chinese residents of the Forks, Ah Tak and Ah Tip. Ah Tak was tried at Barkerville and sentenced to five years in prison. Many residents of the Cariboo grew concerned that a large number of Chinese miners returning from the Omineca would create further problems. A jail had been built at Quesnelmouth, and William Barry organized a petition to the government for a constable at Quesnel Forks. He expected that 250 to 300 Chinese miners would winter there.

Oliver Hare acted temporarily as tax collector and police constable for Quesnel Forks in the summer of 1871. It was a pleasant season, with lots of fish in the river, and fresh beef supplied by Captain Charles F. Houghton from the Okanagan Valley. Hare appears to have had a financial interest in providing meat for Quesnel Forks. Besides registering claims and dealing with taxes, Hare collected $50 from Kwong Lee for an opium licence.

On October 24, 1871, Hare was summoned to the Forks to investigate the murder of an Indian woman, Mary, who had been living with George Cook. He reported to Ball at Barkerville:

> On my arrival I found to my surprise the whole of the Chinese population eager to give me assistance; before I came some of the leading Chinese (Ching and others) had taken a regular census of the population of the town, by going to each house to find if anyone was missing. It soon became known to them that a man named "Le Noui" had absconded. I offered on behalf of the Govt. $200 for his conviction. I then took upon me to hold a meeting of inquiry, knowing the great length of time it would take for the coroner to come and hold an inquest, especially at this time of the year, and fearing it might defeat justice, and also acting on your suggestion with regard to Ah Tip, should he have died. I accordingly summoned all the white population, and Ching, on the jury. My reason for getting the latter was, I wished someone to be able to watch the interpreter.
>
> While in the midst of our inquiry a report was brought us that Le Noui was in a cabin near the falls. All hands started off in pursuit, and in a very short time he was brought in a prisoner. Somehow (which has not been clearly shown) he managed to take what we suppose to be a strong dose of opium to destroy himself, rather than be hung, as he confessed he had committed the deed. We got a Chinaman who was said to understand such cases to do all he could to recover him, but he died in the course of an hour.
>
> I was then informed that one of the Chinamen who arrested him had been seen to give him the dose. I at once made him a prisoner, and this morning held another inquiry concerning the cause of death. We have just concluded the meeting and the jury have

cleared the prisoner from giving the deceased opium as a poison, but as a stimulant, and gave the verdict that the deceased committed suicide.

I hope what I have done will give you satisfaction. There ought to be a place here to lock a man up in. The population of Chinese this morning exceeded 150.[8]

Hare was appointed constable and coroner in May 1872, just before a difficult situation arose. He wrote to Ball June 26, 1872, about another Chinese murder:

I have to inform you that "Chew Ying" the Chinaman who was wounded in the shooting affray, died yesterday. Knowing an inquest on the body was requisite, I took upon me to act as coroner; and as there has been a bitter feeling here among the different tribes of Chinese on the subject, I made up my mind it would not do to have one on the jury; and as Mr. Barry was the only white man here I have to send to the nearest claims, (9 miles off) for four more who kindly gave me their assistance. I have sent all particulars to Dr. Bell the coroner for Cariboo, who I hope will be pleased to have escaped the journey. On examining the body we found his wounded thigh in a frightful state, withered to the bone. How he has survived as long is a mystery. The verdict is wilful murder against Li Chen; Ah Tye; Ah Chock and Ah Lock. The three latter are no doubt gone to Peace River as one of them has a claim there.

Acting on your instruction I have had a substantial bridge made over Morehead Creek and a long length of corduroy repaired. The price asked was $175 — but I got it done by Barry for $150. The trail is much encumbered by windfalls, but as the packers manage to get round them and you can only allow $200 for the route, I have thought it best to reserve the remaining $50 for obstructions that may occur.

Some of the travellers over the trail have been using logs from the bridges and corduroy for firewood. I have therefore posted up notices cautioning them of the penalty if caught. We suppose it to have been done by Chinese packers. The Chinamen in this district are inclined to give a deal of trouble and I am obliged to deal strictly with them.[9]

In August 1872 the Department of Lands and Works approved $600 for a lockup at the Forks. On October 11, 1872, Hare reported to Ball about his residence at Quesnel Forks and the ongoing problems with the North Fork bridge. It appears the bridge was once again washed out.

I have the honour to inform you on my return to the Forks of Quesnelle I purchased on behalf of the Government of B.C. a log building of E. Tye & Co. situated at the end of the bridge and have converted it into a substantial lockup and residence. I have built two strong cells with 2 inch planks and iron fastenings, a suitable room for an office, a living room & kitchen, also a large convenient back yard. Altogether it is the best premises in town.

I have not been able to get the bridge over the North Fork contracted for yet, as the old cribbing turns out to be too much decayed to build on. Therefore, Lamont and other parties I have spoken to on the matter will not undertake the job for $300. I hope to get sufficient subscribed in the district to make up what may be required to build a substantial bridge on new cribbing and will make the best terms I can.[10]

Barry managed to renew his right to charge tolls on the South Fork bridge until 1883. In 1874, Thomas Spence used the fact that Barry had been granted three renewals to request a further term of three years for Spence's Bridge. He claimed that Barry's operation was, "about two thirds more in proportion to the original and other expenditures of the Thompson River Bridge."[11]

One of the most unsung occupations in East Cariboo was that of the mail carrier. In summer he delivered mail weekly from Barkerville to Harvey Creek, Keithley Creek and Quesnel Forks. In winter, he delivered fortnightly, despite snowstorms and the difficult trek over the Swift River trail on snowshoes. Incredible as it may seem, isolated miners on upper Keithley Creek, 30 miles from Barkerville, received door-to-door delivery in mid-winter. After the storms of winter and the thawing in spring, the trails were muddy and blocked by windfalls. And still the mail got through.

These hardy expressmen had many adventures as they made their 120-mile circuit, but none so tragic as that of Edward Kimball, a native of Massachusetts, and the brother of Charles Kimball, of Cook and Kimball, well-known forwarding merchants at Lytton. Kimball was a popular figure on both sides of the Snowshoe Plateau. He held interests in a variety of claims in the Snowshoe Creek area and owned a store at Keithley Creek. On January 27, 1874, he collected Oliver Hare's mail at Quesnel Forks and left for Keithley Creek on his return journey to Barkerville. Two days later, as he travelled on snowshoes through the Five Mile Canyon on the Swift River trail, an avalanche roared down. It buried Kimball, missing his travelling companion, Kansas John Metz, by only a few feet. Miners from Antler Creek, the Snowshoe Plateau and as far away as Barkerville turned out because it was known that Kimball was carrying gold as well as the mail. The men worked for 48 hours, digging a trench 80 yards square, in snow five to 15 feet deep.

Kimball's body was interred with full honours in the Camerontown cemetery. The following spring his friends marked his grave with a

The South Fork bridge at high water. The section of bank behind the centre span slid into the river in September 1898.
(HP74112, BCA)

headstone and a picket-fence enclosure. When his store at Keithley Creek was advertised for sale, William Barry at Quesnel Forks, and A.S. Bates at 150 Mile House posted copies of the inventory of merchandise, on which prospective buyers could place tenders. Several topographical features in the Cariboo were later named for this popular mailman.

Kimball's replacement, Fred Littler, did not have anything named in his honour, yet he was every bit as popular and resourceful as Kimball. A wiry Englishman, Littler boxed in various sporting events at Barkerville in the early years. His pugnacity led him into the claim jumping altercation known as the "Grouse Creek War," and with a number of other miners he spent 24 hours in the Richfield jail in 1867. (After much legal wrangling, the contest between the Canadian Company and the Grouse Creek Bed Rock Flume Company was settled by Justice Needham, a month before claims were laid over for the winter.)

While carrying out his mail contract, Littler used a small cabin at the halfway point of his route, Antler Creek, as an overnight stopping place. "Littler's cabin" shows up on maps and remained a landmark until the early 1900s. Since he was literate and knew the miners and most of the area intimately, he acted as poll clerk on election days, and conducted the 1881 and 1891 censuses for the Keithley Creek/Quesnel Forks district. He invested in numerous claims along his mail route, although he must have had little time to do any active mining.

With dependable expressmen available, who were willing to work in all weather, William Barry led a petition for a post office at Quesnel Forks in November 1871. This was established on July 1, 1873, with Barry as postmaster, and he held the position until his death in 1877.

British Columbia's admission into Confederation posed some problems for the administration of the law in rural areas. In May 1873 Oliver Hare prohibited Isaiah Mitchell from fishing during spawning season. Upon receiving Mitchell's letter of complaint, the *Colonist* took Hare to task:

What is Isaiah to do? There is not a month in the whole twelve during which some species do not spawn. To obey Hare's dictum is not to fish at all; and not to fish is to starve! But the worst feature

93

of the case is that Hare himself fishes, catching five to Isaiah's one. He also enjoys a monopoly of the trade in beef in that locality; and Isaiah reasons thus: "The fewer fish I have to sell the more beef and fish will Oliver sell. But is it fair that he should have his annual salary from the public purse and enjoy a monopoly of the beef and fish trade, while a poor pioneer of fifteen years may not be permitted to catch a fish?" And he with the Scriptural name, having asked Oliver to show him the law on the point, and having been gruffly told to go to Victoria for it, writes to us to know how the law stands. We will tell Isaiah. The Dominion law regulating the taking of fish has not yet been extended to British Columbia and, in all probability, will not for some years to come. In the absence, therefore, of any law on the subject, Oliver is wrong, and Isaiah may catch away.[12]

Isaiah Mitchell's name disappears from public records in three years. Presumably, he returned home to New England to spend the latter part of his life.

Hare had more problems collecting rent from the Chinese miners. He wrote to Bowron on June 18, 1873:

I have two or three questions to trouble you about. First, have the China ranch men paid you any rent this year? [In margin: How much is the rent for the China ranch? I have never collected it.] I cannot find out from them; when I ask them they "No Sabe." They are a [indecipherable] lot. All I have collected from them is a trade licence.

Next, has E. Tie or Ching applied to rent plot of ground here formerly held by "Peter" an old Frenchman? Ching applied to preempt 2 years ago. Capt. Ball wrote me he could not grant it, but they could have it by paying the rent, or something to this effect. Same week they had the fence repaired and told the Chinamen it belonged to them (E. Tie & Ching) but when I ___to them about it they denied having said so. It may be they have made it all right at your end. If not, I wish you to ask Capt. Ball what I am to do in the matter.[13]

On July 8, 1873, Hare conducted another inquest. Ing Com had disappeared while returning from Keithley Crossing to Quesnel Forks.

Ah Tye reported to the jury that he had seen some tobacco and a hat alongside the trail and thought something was wrong. Two adult bears and three cubs came out of the scrub and chased after him. One caught him by the boot, but he was on horseback and managed to get away. On the same day bears chased away Ah Ching at the same spot.

The jury consisting of William Barry, John King Barker, Hugh Doak and two Chinese, E. Tie and Sing Hen, concluded that Ing Com had met his death by being attacked by bears. This is the only fatality involving bears known for the Quesnel Forks area, for the period 1859 to 1900.

On December 30, 1873, Hare reported to Ball:

> Most of the Chinamen are now busy preparing their wingdams. There are not so many in progress as last year, but I hope they will meet better success as the weather is so much more favorable. The prospects on Keithley Creek are greatly improving, several claims are turning out good pay; but Harvey Creek does not appear very encouraging. I have my accounts ready to forward to the subacct. I find my collection exclusive of Road Tax amts. to $2,419.50 which considering the reduction of fees for recording is the best I ever made.[14]

For his lonely position, year after year, collecting taxes and maintaining the trails, Hare was paid $1,500 annually. He reported to the gold commissioner at Barkerville concerning trails, but they were supervised by John Saul, at Clinton. On July 1, 1874, Hare wrote to John Bowron:

> I have just been informed that Mr. Saul has gone down country sick which makes matters awkward as regards to trails from here to the 150 Mile House. I wrote him last mail saying I had put on a man to clear the fallen timber. I went to Beaver Lake to inspect the work. Found it well done. The trail had never been so badly blocked before, in fact it was quite impassable. I found Beaver Lake bridge only half made and yesterday received notice that it is broke down. The contractors had put in unsound timber for the stringers. I was writing Mr. Saul for instructions as to what can be done in the

matter when I heard from Mr. Borland he has gone down and that you were acting for him. The Beaver Lake men have offered to rebuild the bridge in a substantial manner for $100 which is a low price as it has to be shifted to a spot lower down the creek or it never will stand. The cribs and abutments were filled with gravel which have all been undermined and washed out. These parties will make a good job of it for their own sake. There must not be any time lost as the travel will soon be great with pack trains. The creek is now too high to ford.

Please write me as soon as possible about the bridge if you have the power to order the work to be done; if not please acquaint Mr. Saul of the affair.[15]

Within the month Hare had other problems. He wrote to Ball on July 30:

A short time since Barry lost one of his dogs evidently poisoned by strychnine; and a Siwash also had one die the same way. The poor fellow had set great value on him and had been offered $100 for him several times. It was near being a more serious matter for I am informed a Clootchman found the piece of meat which poisoned their dog and she was about to eat it herself but for the interferance [sic] of her husband. There is no doubt but the poison has been carelessly used by trappers. Is there any law to prevent such fellows doing so near settlements? I am particularly requested by Barry to write you on the matter. He is in a great way about the loss of his dog.[16]

Hare made his usual rounds collecting taxes during the summer. His report to Bowron in September underscored the difficulties faced by government agents in rural areas when carrying out orders made in Victoria.

Herewith I send my accts for July & August which I hope you will find correct. While I was collecting on Keithley I had sent a man down the main river instead of going myself, which will account for using two books as you will perceive by the numbers.

96

He succeeded pretty well. There are not as many Chinamen on the river as there has been in former years. I have had a deal of trouble in collecting on all the creeks. Have been obliged to go twice on some & on Keithley three times. The brutes find out when I am on the way & hide til I have passed. Some of them ought to be punished but I never get any encouragement for doing it.

It is ridiculous to suppose the miners are going to supply us with correct information. I have tried to collect what information I could while at the claims. Most of my questions would be answered satisfactorily but when I came to those yields per pan, etc., I was either snubbed or laughed at — and as for knowing what the Chinese are doing, it is simply preposterous.[17]

In 1874 there were 120 Chinese on North and South Fork rivers and a further 79 on Keithley, Harvey and Snowshoe creeks. Ever hopeful of another rich strike, Aurora Jack Edwards and Angus Lamont set out on a six-week expedition to the head of Swamp Creek. Another pioneer, Billy Barker, sank a shaft to 142 feet at Horsefly, in the summer of 1873. The following year Billy's friends generated a petition to the provincial government, requesting $800 to $1,000 to assist him in developing the potential of the Horsefly placers. Charles Ettershank, who had bilked the government out of provisions to explore at Horsefly in 1863, was involved in this venture as well.[18]

In July 1875 heavy rainfall and high river levels caused Hare more concerns. He wrote to Bowron:

In the middle of June, owing to incessant rains, the main trail to Keithley via Mitchell's bridge became impassible by mud slides and fallen timber, and as two trains and some cattle were daily expected I had to get the abandoned trail on the opposite side of the North Fork cleared.

The both rivers have been many feet higher than ever known before. Mitchell's and Barry's bridges have had a narrow escape owing to the great quantity of drift logs floating down; both are more or less damaged, but to what extent of course will not be known till the water has fallen. The South Fork is at the present moment up to within a foot of its highest stage for the last 7 or 8 years.[19]

On Dominion Day at Keithley Creek, the morning was "dull and unpromising" but the afternoon proved fine as the miners celebrated with sports and horse races. They divided more than $250 in prize money. Angus Lamont won ten dollars for standing jump; William Polleys ten dollars for hop, step and jump; and John Malcolm, ten dollars for running jump. The report in the *Cariboo Sentinel* also described who won the horse races:

> Twelve o'clock arrived, when a salute of 21 guns was fired. Dinner was then announced, and justice was done to the good things Veith [*sic*] and Borland had provided. At 1 o'clock Messrs. McNab and Polleys, the starters, marshalled the horses for the Keithley Derby, heats 2 in 3, for a purse of $100. Three entries — Weasel, Dan O'Rourke and Billy. Won with great ease by Daniel O'Rourke.[20]

A provincial election in the fall of 1875 brought candidates Walkem, Davie, Pearson and Walker to Keithley Creek for a meeting at Vieth and Borland's ranch. Robert McNab was appointed chairman and William Polleys, secretary. When the candidates had finished addressing the miners, Fred Littler, George Vieth, Aurora Jack Edwards, and William Polleys had a few words to say. Maintenance of trails and the utility of Crown Grants had been topics on the agenda at other meetings in the Cariboo. Under the Qualification and Registration of Voters Act, 1875, miners in gold mining towns and camps could vote if they had held a Free Miner's Certificate or a Licence for three months prior to sending in their claim to vote. Elsewhere in the province the time period was six months.

Hare submitted his report on the 1875 mining season in September.

> As will be seen there are no white men engaged in mining, either on the Quesnelle River or Forks; therefore the Chinese have it all their own way, and will find pay, remunerative enough for them for many years to come. On the whole, I have found the Chinese more peaceable this year than usual, but to require the same amount of

hunting up on the licence question as ever; many of them try every scheme to avoid payment.

There are three well fitted up stores at the Forks, two of which are licensed to sell opium, and all for spirits. Judging from the vast quantity of goods brought in by pack-trains, they must do a large business. There are also two butcher shops. On Keithley Creek there are four stores, three kept by white men, the other Chinese; two of the former are licensed to sell spirits.[21]

The Chinese population continued to increase as the decade wore on. Possible contributions were anti-Chinese legislation in California, and the low fee charged for registering a group of claims. More cabins were built at Quesnel Forks, with scant regard for streets or property lines. Hare submitted one more annual report in September 1876, and described a new method of recovering gold from the Quesnel River.

A Chinese cabin at Quesnel Forks, with fish drying on upper front of building.
(A-04981, BCA)

Owing to the severe cold the river fell unusually low in February and March last, giving the Chinese a good chance for working among reefs and shoals to advantage. They also adopted a new style of mining in the south fork; rafts of logs were moored in the stream, on which were generally three Celestials, two of whom had shovels and picks with handles eight to ten feet in length, for scooping up the dirt from the bottom of the river, which the third person passed through his rocker; although a tedious process, they managed to get from three to four dollars per man per diem in only a few hours. I saw nearly every day's proceeds, therefore feel quite safe in stating that at least $3,000 can be added to the estimated yield of the claims. ... Many persons suppose that a Chinaman can afford to work for less wages because his style of living is so much cheaper, but let me tell those persons that John is as fond of good living as they are. When I go to a Chinese cabin I can tell nearly at a glance if the claim pays by the number of oyster, lobster and sardine tins, also China wine and Hennessy brandy bottles lying around their domicile. [22]

In 1876 there were 156 Chinese miners compared to 28 white miners in the Keithley Creek/Quesnel Forks area.

When Hare's health began to deteriorate at the end of the summer, he requested a leave of absence, pleading that, "another winter here would certainly kill me." He travelled to Victoria in October, but continued to fail, and died on December 27, 1876. Many important government officials attended his funeral. Hare was described in his obituary as a man who "retained throughout his life a childlike simplicity and frankness of character and a tenderness of heart that endeared him to all who knew him."[23]

Fred Littler acted temporarily as police constable and tax collector until William Stephenson arrived in May 1877 to begin his new position as the second government agent at Quesnel Forks.

CHAPTER SEVEN

A NEW ERA

"Was 9 1/2 hours from Keithley home. Got very wet and have been laid up with rheumatism ever since I got home. I think my bones will ache for the next month."[1]

William Stephenson

W ILLIAM STEPHENSON REPRESENTED a new era in government administration in the Cariboo. Gone were the Anglo-Irish commissioners who had looked after the miners so well during the early years: Thomas Elwyn, Philip Nind, Oliver Hare, Peter O'Reilly, William Cox and Chartres Brew.[2] The last British-born commissioner, Henry Maynard Ball, would resign in 1881. After two decades of British administration, it was time for Canadians to take over.

Stephenson, a native of New Brunswick, initially reported to Ball and then to his successor, John Bowron, at Barkerville. George Tunstall, born in Michigan but educated at Lower Canada College, Montreal, shared the overland journey with Bowron. After a career as a miner, Tunstall left Barkerville in 1879 to become assistant gold commissioner at Kamloops. He replaced John Ussher who was murdered by the McLean brothers.[3] On Bowron's recommendation, another native of Quebec, Joseph St. Laurent, of Barkerville, was chosen as tax collector and road superintendent for the Quesnel Division in 1882. St. Laurent looked after road maintenance as far away as the Chilcotin, and also carried out some police duties.[4] The new group of government administrators got along well with each other and with the miners. Just as strict military training had prepared Ball, Brew and Cox for the rigours of gold rush administration, 15 years of placer mining and voluntary community work prepared the Canadians for government service during the settlement years from 1875 to 1910.

Stephenson's first decade at Quesnel Forks tested his stamina and resourcefulness to the limit. He was responsible for collecting taxes from white and Chinese miners in the Keithley Creek and Williams Lake divisions, ranging from Harvey Creek and Horsefly in the east to Hanceville in the west, and from Alexandria in the north to 141 Mile House in the south, roughly 10,000 square miles. Until a wagon road replaced the pack trail from Quesnel Forks to 150 Mile House in 1894, he travelled on foot, by horseback or canoe in summer, and on snowshoes in winter.

For a short time prior to Joseph St. Laurent taking over at Quesnelmouth, Stephenson also collected taxes for the Quesnel Division.[5] The new premier of the province, Andrew Charles Elliott, levied income, real estate and school taxes when he replaced George Anthony Walkem in 1876.[6] Elliott was so desperate to improve the government's financial situation that he even tried, unsuccessfully, to reimpose road tolls on the Cariboo Road. (The tolls had been abolished in 1871.)[7]

As the Chinese population of the Quesnel Forks/Keithley Creek area doubled within a decade, Stephenson relied on his own judgment more than had his predecessor, Oliver Hare. Hare's previous employment as customs collector and court clerk in British Columbia had placed him on friendly terms with government officials, especially Judge Begbie. He also had a strong-minded, articulate friend in William Barry to assist him in looking after the needs of Quesnel Forks between 1873 and 1877. Barry wrote the letters and petitions that gained a new jail and postal service for the village. Most importantly, he was instrumental in obtaining the position of police constable and government agent for Hare.

Stephenson was not so fortunate. He had not been closely associated with members of the provincial government, and George Vieth, the community activist equivalent to William Barry, lived at Keithley Creek, 20 miles away. Vieth wrote petitions regularly to Lands and Works, demanding trail and bridge improvements. In his travels as mailman, Fred Littler garnered the necessary signatures from local miners. For general assistance, Stephenson relied on gold rush pioneers John King Barker, Kansas John Metz and Hizer Newell, the few white men residing at Quesnel Forks. Because they had mined and trapped over most of the East Cariboo, Metz and Newell were especially helpful in locating lost miners.

In his 1877 mining report for the Keithley Creek/Quesnel Forks area Stephenson listed only 37 white males, but 209 Chinese males, nine Chinese women, and four Chinese children. The one white woman and child listed were his wife Jennie and son Allen. Two years later, when he reported on Chinese in the Cariboo, the numbers had grown to 375 males and ten females. Of the men, 305 were miners, 12 merchants, seven cooks, six butchers, and 35 subsisted "chiefly by gambling or any other rascality." They paid a total amount of $1,205 in taxes annually.[8]

Little is known about Stephenson until he arrived in the Cariboo with his younger brother, John, in 1863, at the height of the Cariboo gold rush. Both men were born in Westfield, a suburb of Saint John, New Brunswick. They apparently did well as miners because they stayed on in the Barkerville area after the gold rush died down, becoming members of the Williams Creek Fire Brigade, and the Cariboo Chapter of the Free and Associated Masons. Their friends included John Bowron, Joseph St. Laurent and George Tunstall.

William returned to Saint John to marry Sarah Jane "Jennie" Gillespie in December 1870. The newlyweds spent the winter in the Maritimes, travelling west by railway to San Francisco in April 1871.[9] The journey by train, steamer and stagecoach to Barkerville must have been arduous for Jennie. She then had to make the difficult adjustment from life in a century-old seaport to frontier society in a mountain village that was struggling to survive in the face of dwindling mining resources. During the following year, William was injured twice in mining accidents. His active mining career ended in 1872 when he was badly crushed by machinery in the shaft house of the McPherson claim. In 1873, a cave-in on Lightning Creek killed his brother, John, at age 26.[10]

John Bowron recommended Stephenson for the position of tax collector for the Barkerville area in 1876. The experience William gained there was an advantage a year later when he applied for and was granted the government agent position at Quesnel Forks. He and Jennie, now pregnant with their first child, moved to their new home in May 1877. Stephenson lost no time in getting things in order. He wrote to the Chief Commissioner of Lands and Works on June 9:

> Upon my arriving at this place I find that during the absence of any Government Agent here last winter the Chinese have partially obstructed some of the passages leading from the river and I would recommend the opening of one good thoroughfare from the bridge by the removal of one house owned by Mr. W.P. Barry, which if done would be of great benefit to the place, and especially to the Govt. building in case of fire. Hoping you will call Mr. W.A. Johnston's attention to the matter.[11]

It was not possible to move the house before Barry died on July 6, 1877, at age 38, from inflammation of the bowels and stomach. He had suffered from an inguinal hernia for five years. Coroner Dr. John K. Bell went to Quesnel Forks to take charge of Barry's effects, assisted by Aurora Jack Edwards and Angus Lamont of Keithley Creek. They found only $45 in the house — enough to cover funeral expenses.

Barry died in straitened circumstances. In order to raise money to upgrade the South Fork bridge, he had mortgaged the North and South Fork bridges for $1,500, the previous December, to Hugh Ross at Barkerville. Ross transferred the mortgage to William Manson who wanted to sell the property following Barry's death. The Barry family closed ranks. Brother Michael Barry obtained Letters of Administration in September 1877, and Thomas Barry and Sam Adler, now operating a saloon in the Cassiar, loaned $800 to help pay off the mortgage.

Michael Barry next dealt with toll evasion. Quesnel Forks merchants Ei Tie and Kwong Lee tried to circumvent paying tolls on the South Fork bridge by ferrying goods across the river, but they did use the North Fork Bridge (a non-toll bridge) and the connecting road between the two, maintained by Barry. In February 1878, Judge Begbie ruled in Barry's favour: he could recover the South Fork bridge tolls evaded by the defendants, and court costs.

Possibly as a result of Begbie's decision, in August 1878, Vieth and Borland, backed by local miners and Chinese merchants Ei Tie and Kwong Lee, agitated for an end to bridge tolls. Their petition promised a subscription of $1,527.50 if a trail from 108 Mile to Quesnel Lake (presumably Isaiah Mitchell's original route) and a toll-free bridge at Quesnel Forks were constructed. Vieth and Borland, Ei Tie and Kwong Lee pledged $500 each, Kwong Lee later rescinding the offer.[12] The government did not act on this petition. Fifteen years later, the trail from 108 Mile was opened up as far as Horsefly in 1894, by the Horsefly Hydraulic Company, in order to bring in mining equipment.

In January 1880 Michael Barry sent a petition to Lands and Works, requesting that the provincial government purchase the South Fork bridge from William Barry's estate. Michael asked Sam Adler, who was spending the winter in Victoria, to provide the government with information, but it was not interested. After a few years, the Barry family grew impatient with Michael's management, and Sam Adler returned to Quesnel Forks to sort matters out. He wrote to his wife, Mary, in Victoria, asking her to secure family support for ousting Michael, but Michael resisted. The outcome is not clear. Possibly Michael left the Forks once the charter on the South Fork bridge expired in the spring of 1884. Believing they had paid enough tolls over the years, miners and merchants of the Keithley Creek and Quesnel Forks area submitted yet another petition to the provincial government, requesting that the charter not be renewed. Michael eventually settled in Brownville, on the south bank of the Fraser River, opposite New Westminster, where he managed a hotel and post office.

Having lost the charter, Sam Adler went on to dabble in various projects. He invested in property near Salmon Arm during Canadian Pacific Railway construction in 1884, and took a pack train of supplies to the Granite Creek gold rush, near Princeton, in 1885. He applied for a liquor licence in June 1891, at Port Essington, at the mouth of the Skeena River, but three years later he was manager of the Globe Hotel at Lytton and a member of the Yale and Lytton Pioneer Association. Whether by accident or carelessness, Adler had suffered losses by fire at Sacramento, California, in 1852, and at Barkerville in 1868. For a third time fire affected his life, destroying the Globe Hotel about 1897. Adler next managed the Kootenay Hotel at Golden in 1898 and another hotel in Grand Forks in 1900. He checked out the rush to Atlin in 1900, returning to the Cariboo to reconnoitre the brief gold rush in the eastern Horsefly region in 1901. Nothing is known of him after 1903, but he left a unique sentiment. He boasted that he found the gold for his wife's wedding ring in the Cariboo, for his daughter's wedding ring at Granite Creek, and for his granddaughter at Atlin. Sam may have retired to California, like his business partner, Thomas Barry. After their Cassiar venture, Tom operated the Cold Tea Saloon in Victoria in 1881, then moved to Los Angeles, where he died in 1886.[13]

The contribution to the early development of British Columbia by the Barry and Adler families is noteworthy for their entrepreneurship and perseverance in the face of difficult odds. With their business skills, they could have lived in the safety and comfort of Victoria or New Westminster, but they preferred to be on the front lines of the gold rushes to the Fraser River, the Cariboo, Granite Creek, Omineca, and the Cassiar. Barry and Adler's South Fork toll bridge may have been a risky venture, but because they invested their personal funds, it also represented an immigrant's faith in the future of the Cariboo and British Columbia.

* * * * *

Besides collecting taxes, William Stephenson's many other responsibilities included assisting gold commissioners Henry Maynard Ball and (later) John Bowron, acting as clerk at Court of Revision, supervising road and bridge maintenance, and acting as justice of the peace, coroner and police constable. Perhaps his most important role was as an unofficial social worker, caring for the sick, insane and destitute. In later years, when his mining friends grew old and feeble, Stephenson ensured that they reached hospital or the Provincial Home for Men at Kamloops.

Caring for men and women who became insane was the most difficult challenge because of the great distance to the asylum at New Westminster. Stephenson's first case occurred in March 1878. He accompanied a Chinese man from Quesnel Forks to Clinton where government agent Michael O'Connor took over. This errand of mercy covered 320 miles, and kept Stephenson away from Quesnel Forks for 14 days. He wrote to John Bowron on April 8, 1878:

> I would have sent in my monthly a/c if there had been any money to send you but the trouble is there is not a cent in the office and very little bis doing. My trip with the infernal crazy Chinaman has left me with a pile of vouchers and no cash. I went as far as Clinton, handed him over to the Govt. Agent there. He sent him right on down. I then had to get a horse to get back home as there was no use waiting for the stage as they would not promise me a passage. So I had to ride horse back to Soda Creek and from there get home the best I could. I got here on the 3rd after an absence 14 days. Will come over to Barkerville as soon as horses can travel, but not before as I have had enough walking on this last trip to last me for a while.[14]

In June 1880 Stephenson had to look after a Chinese woman with a mania for setting fires. She was alone because her husband or owner had died. Stephenson planned to send her south with a Chinese pack train as soon as possible, but in the meantime he placed her in a cabin at the edge of the village where there would be less danger. The poor woman was probably well out of the way when fire destroyed Quesnel Forks on October 12, 1880. It broke out in an unoccupied house belonging to Kwong Lee. Lee lost $5,000, Ei Tie $5,000, and Michael Barry $3,000. In fighting the fire Barry burned his arm and hand. Only the government agent's house was saved because Stephenson, a veteran of the Barkerville Fire Brigade, kept filled water barrels on the roof. A Chinese neighbour made liberal use of the water supply to extinguish small fires as they broke out on the roof. Stephenson wanted to reward him with $15 or $20.[15]

On the day of the fire Jennie Stephenson was on her own with her son Allen, a new baby, Gillespie, and a teenage nursemaid, Mary Coutts. This frightening incident was one of many that combined to affect Jennie's mental health. She witnessed two other major fires that destroyed parts of the village in 1883 and 1887.

A special request from Lands and Works sent Stephenson to 150 Mile House in July 1880, to determine the best site for a school house.

> Acting under the instructions of Mr. Bowron, I have the honour to report in regard to the most available material for a school house for the Williams Lake School. I find the site chosen by the trustees here a most eligible one with the exception of a China house of ill fame, which is built upon Govt. land without leave to build and close to the site chosen. Said house not paying any rent to Govt. except a Trade Licence issued by A. Barlow and bearing date 1st July 1880. The house has the reputation of being an opium den and place of prostitution and which it would be needful to supress if the Govt. built a school house upon the proposed site or upon the nearest eligible site to 150 Mile Post.[16]

Gavin Hamilton, owner of the 150 Mile stopping house, was willing to renovate one of his houses for a school with the provision that most of the improvements would be given over to a new school if and when it was built. There were personal reasons for his keen interest in education. Gavin and his wife Margaret had 12 sons and four daughters of school age.

A year later, in late November 1881, Stephenson was called out on another errand of mercy. Samuel F. Anderson, formerly a mining partner with Billy Barker at Horsefly, was a victim of frost bite. Usually, Stephenson recovered his travelling expenses from the government, but in this particular case he was unsure of reimbursement, even though he had no choice of action. He reported to John Bowron on December 2:

> Herewith enclosed find vouchers amounting to $55.10, being the amount I had to pay out for food for men and horses while conveying from this place to the Cariboo Hospital a man named S.

F. Anderson who had both of his feet badly frozen while going from this place to Beaver Lake. Anderson left here at noon November 14. On the afternoon of the 16th word was brought to me that he was lying in the woods 11 miles from here. The two white men that were here, J.K. Barker and John Metz, at once started off with me. We found Anderson and got him on a horse and brought him to this place.

After doing all we could for him here, I came to the conclusion that to save his life it was necessary to get him to the hospital where he could be cared for and have proper medical treatment. On the morning of the 19th he then being strong enough to set on a horse for a few hours at a time, I started with him for Barkerville via Keithley, Snowshoe and Antler Creek, knowing I could get help when needed at any of those places. The snow lay about 2 1/2 feet deep along our route but with the help of horses and men we got him through. The help was all voluntary and I also had the use of the horses free of charge. The amounts paid out by me for which I send in the voucher was unavoidable expense for food for men and horses while on this trip. It took 4 days to get him over and three days for us to return.

If I have done wrong in going to the expense of taking the man to the Hospital and the vouchers cannot be allowed, please return the vouchers to me.[17]

Anderson had both feet amputated at the Royal Cariboo Hospital. Mining friends took up a collection and the provincial government provided emergency funding to send him to Toronto for prostheses. Despite Stephenson's apprehension, the provincial government reimbursed his expenses.

* * * * *

Quesnel Forks had barely recovered from the fire of 1880 when another one occurred on March 28, 1883. Stephenson wrote to Bowron:

We have had another fire. E. Tie and Co.s fine new store value $6000 with a loss of goods of about $2000. The fire broke out about 1/4 past 8 yesterday morning. In twenty minutes after the fire was discovered the roof was in flames from one end to the other. A few minutes after that the Barry house caught and away it went. About that time I thought our old house was called but we weathered the storm, although I would not have given $2.50 for the chance as there were only 2 Chinamen would stick to us. Barker and Littler were here. Fortunately there was no wind at the time.[18]

Despite losing $8,000, Ei Tie remained in business because more Chinese were moving to the area as a result of Canadian Pacific Railway construction. Between 1882 and 1885 over 17,000 Chinese labourers entered the province. Seven thousand came from the United States where they had completed the transcontinental Union Pacific Railroad, and 10,000 directly from China. When construction of the Fraser Canyon portion of the railway ended during the winter of 1883-84, hundreds of Chinese labourers were left to fend for themselves. At Ashcroft, Henry P. Cornwall reported to the Provincial Secretary in December 1883 that 2,000 labourers were camping along the banks of the Thompson River for 35 miles. Many of these men, no doubt, headed north to the Cariboo, swelling the population of Quesnel Forks. The Chee Kung Tong Society at Quesnel Forks assisted them by providing lodging and introductions to local miners.[19]

In the 19th century, secret fraternal organizations formed an important part of South China society. Chinese immigrants introduced these societies to California during the 1850s and a decade later, Chinese miners from California established the first Zhigongtang (Chee Kung Tong) lodges in British Columbia.[20] The CKT Society, formed in 1882 at Quesnel Forks, played an important role in looking after transient men.

New members of the Chee Kung Tong had to be sponsored. Their ages varied from 21 to 50 years, suggesting that some men were pioneers of the first wave of gold seekers from California, in 1860.[21] The society built a two-storey building containing a shrine on the main floor, and sleeping accommodation on the second floor. Its mandate addressed the needs of merchants (Huashang) and labourers (Huagong):

The purpose in forming the Cheekungtong is to maintain a friendly relationship among our countrymen and to accumulate wealth through proper business methods for the benefit of all members. Thus, those who do mental work and those who do physical work are devoting their strength to this common goal.

The constitution of the society contained 24 clauses. Among them were the following:

6. When new businesses are opened by the Society and helpers are needed, only members who have paid dues and have seniority in the Society are qualified for these posts. Any competition or struggle for these posts among members will not be permitted.

14. Members must follow a policy of first come, first served when selling or buying businesses or mines. Anyone who does not follow this regulation will be punished in accordance with the regulations if a complaint is made and evidence presented.

20. Any dispute or mutual suspicion among members should be settled in the Society in accordance with reason. Those who persist in quarrelling with one another or who appeal to the courts either create more trouble and expense or damage friendships.[22]

Self regulation saved a good deal of time and money, since the provincial court was held 60 miles away at 150 Mile House.

The hostel provided food and staples such as candles, with the cost divided among the boarders each week. The rules for the hostel included, "All those who stay in this hostel should look after each other. ... Friendly relations and kindness among lodgers are most precious." Lodgers were not expected to stay longer than a week.[23]

The Chee Kung Tong kept careful record of donations for funerals, important ceremonies, and political causes. Subscription lists for members of the society, with names, birthdates and amounts paid[24] suggest that the Chinese residents of Quesnel Forks were carefully monitored and highly visible to their own community even though they wanted to remain as invisible as possible to white government authority.[25] Whereas Barkerville had more than one society, it appears that no other society except the Chee Kung Tong was permitted in Quesnel Forks.

The Chee Kung Tong Society provided solace against the discriminating legislation introduced by the government of British Columbia in the 1880s.[26] In 1884, Bill 14, the Chinese Regulation Act, created problems for government agents in rural districts. It required every Chinese miner to pay $15 for an annual licence, whereas white miners paid five dollars. All Chinese males 14 years and older were to pay an annual head tax of ten dollars. Furthermore, graveyards could not be desecrated (thus preventing the removal of Chinese dead for return to China) and the use of opium was restricted. Stephenson, St. Laurent, and Sam Rogers at Barkerville found the regulations onerous. In December 1885, Stephenson wrote to Attorney General Alex E.B. Davie:

> There is a Chinaman here by the name of Ching, belonging to firm of E. Tie & Co. He is a naturalized subject; he holds considerable mining property in his name; can he get a mining licence as a subject, or will he be considered by the Act as a Chinaman and have to pay fifteen dollars for it?

To which Davie replied,

> In answer to your inquiry, does a Chinaman becoming a naturalized subject come to be considered a "Chinese" within the meaning of the "Chinese Regulation Act, 1884," I have the honour to say that the term "Chinese" is defined in sec. 2 of the Act, and that the naturalization of a Chinaman does not make him any the less "a native of China."[27]

After much correspondence by government agents and tax collectors, and challenges by Chinese at Barkerville and Victoria, the Act was disallowed.

In the face of growing discrimination against Chinese in British Columbia, the Dominion Government established the Royal Commission on Chinese Immigration in 1884. There were 51 witnesses, including some who participated by supplying written answers to a list of 27 questions provided by the commission. The written responses of Judge Begbie and William Stephenson were published in the final report made by the Commission. For the Chinese census Stephenson reported (at Quesnel Forks) two merchants, 128 farm labourers and miners, two butchers, two prostitutes, four store employees, one doctor and two barbers. To several questions he indicated a grudging admiration for Chinese endeavour. To question 4, "Are they industrious, sober, economical and law-abiding, or are they lazy, drunken, extravagant or turbulent?", Stephenson replied, "As a class they are industrious, sober, and economical. They are not lazy, drunken, extravagant, or turbulent; they do not openly violate the laws, but they will evade them in every possible way without bringing themselves into actual contact with the law. They are inveterate gamblers — men, women and children."[28]

Suicides, mining accidents, and murders claimed the lives of the Quesnel Forks Chinese. More than 30 men and women were buried in the central portion of the Quesnel Forks cemetery. In the summertime, wildflowers fill in the shallow depressions where their bones were removed and returned to China. Because Cantonese custom presumed that the soul would not rest until the bones of the dead were returned to their homeland, approved agents from as far away as San Francisco travelled to rural British Columbia cemeteries, to disinter the dead after seven to ten years of burial. They cleaned and packaged the bones with appropriate identification, paid the government agent ten dollars for each individual's remains, and transported the containers to Victoria where they were stored at Harling Point. At intervals a consignment would be shipped to the Tung Wah Hospital in Hong Kong, which was the distribution point for various home counties.

Chinese merchants dominated Quesnel Forks. By 1889 there were five local stores: Yee Wo, Fook Sang Lung, Wo Sang, Kin Fung and Kwong Lee. Their shelves were stocked with a wide variety of goods. Staples of rice, peanut oil, Chinese mushrooms, dried bean curd (foo jook), pumpkin seeds, sunflower seeds, rice noodles, preserved vegetables (chung choy), and red dates were augmented by joss candles, ink sticks and tobacco. The Fook Sang Lung company had opened a hotel and general merchant business in 1884, and theirs was the only hotel in Quesnel Forks until 1892. When they renewed their liquor licence in 1899, their holdings included five lots with buildings and improvements and a stock of liquor valued at more than $4,500. They could accommodate 75 men and ten horses.[29] Only merchants could save enough money and maintain the right contacts in China to acquire wives, and they were favoured by immigration regulations that permitted relatives of merchants to enter British Columbia. Sadly, the thousands of young Chinese men in British Columbia who held menial jobs could never afford to marry and have families.

A major event for the Quesnel Forks Chinese community in 1886 was the arrival of a young Chinese girl from China to marry merchant Wong Kim. Kim was 43 and Quie (or Quey) Young was only 15. Because her feet were bound, she most likely came from a merchant-class family. She was a handsome woman who appears to have adjusted well to her unique position. Mrs. Yee May Kim, as she came to be known, lived until 1948 and had nine children, five daughters and four sons.[30] Her first two daughters were sent back to China to marry, but her youngest daughter, Wong Ting How, nicknamed "Topsy," married and lived in Quesnel. All but one son moved away.

Yee May Kim (Mrs. Kim) with daughter Wong Ting How, at Quesnel Forks.
(Courtesy June Wall)

114

After her husband died, Mrs. Kim supported herself by baking bread for the Bullion Pit miners. According to one local historian, she also received a pension from the Chee Kung Tong Society because her husband had been the head man. Wong Kuey Kim looked after his mother at Quesnel Forks until her death.[31]

* * * * *

Stephenson's annual mining report for 1885 discussed the local economic situation and the influence of the Canadian Pacific Railway:

> In the face of all the cry about hard times and no money, the traders seem to ship as heavy as usual and the money must come out to pay for the goods, as I do not believe the traders give all their goods away. A few years ago the traders made an outcry about high freights and a Toll Bridge at this place. Well, that bridge has been free for the last season; freights also have been moderate to this place, but the price of goods are quite up to former years.
>
> The construction of the CPR has made a boom in the lower country but so far has acted adversely to the mining industry of Cariboo, as by its employment of Teams and Pack Trains up to this last season it has kept freights high to Cariboo. Also, when men that were mining become discouraged or doubtful of their claim they had Rail Road work to fall back upon, and away they went. But now that the CPR is about finished we may look for cheap freights so that living will be much cheaper than heretofore, and also Cariboo may yet [get] a share of the influx of people which the CPR is bound to bring into the Province and Cariboo may soon see better time than the present.[32]

Because his report was strictly about mining, Stephenson could not include the agricultural statistics he had gathered that year. At 150 Mile, Vieth and Borland produced 23,000 pounds of barley, and Gavin Hamilton, 75,000 pounds. On the Sugar Cane Indian Reserve the natives raised 65 acres of wheat and 37 acres of barley. Sitkum Lake Jim raised eight acres of wheat, amounting to 10,000 pounds. St. Joseph's Mission cultivated thirty acres of wheat, ten acres of oats, and six acres of barley. At Soda Creek, and across the Fraser River at the Salmon, Withrow, Hance, Riskie and Doc English ranches, the yield was also favourable. L.W. Riskie had 100 acres in wheat, Withrow, 60 acres, and O.T. Hance 25 acres.

It was time now for Stephenson to build a new house; the sill logs were rotting away on the 1861 structure that Oliver Hare had bought from Ei Tie in 1873. Stephenson chose a prime location just across the road from the old building, at the head of the South Fork bridge. It was completed in 1886, and survived another major fire at Quesnel Forks, in June 1887, as Stephenson reported to Bowron:

> Here we are again; this unfortunate place had another good scorch yesterday and burned down about one half of the houses in the place, 1 store, King Tie co., 2 blacksmith shops, a storehouse with about $2000.00 worth of goods, and some 9 or 10 dwelling houses. The nearest house to the Govt. house was burned. It was only about 25 feet from our woodshed. How we escaped I don't yet know. As usual I was away. Had left about 10 minutes when the fire broke out; had only gone up the North Fork for a few hours. Mrs. Stephenson was alone. She says the Chinamen helped her first rate. Between her and them they tore away the fencing and everything they could to keep the fire from our house. In fact they gave her such good help the house was saved, but Mrs. S. is now quite ill after the excitement and the work. We are about in going order again and I intend to go up to Keithley Crk. tomorrow to see about starting that cussed Snowshoe Bridge Trail before I go out to the road. This scrape will put me a few days behind time in getting away.[33]

Up until 1886 the provincial government had been willing to grub-stake one or two groups of prospectors each year to explore new territory in the Cariboo, but this program had brought little, if any, results. The provincial government and the miners now felt that the development of quartz or hardrock mining offered the best plan for the future. The government abandoned grubstaking in 1886 and entered a 50/50 shared venture with the federal government for a geological survey of the Cariboo. Mining engineer Amos Bowman of the Geological Survey of Canada was hired in 1886 and 1887 to survey and map the Cariboo mining areas.

Bowman arrived via Quesnel Forks with an assistant, James McEvoy, and a guide, pioneer miner Alex Porter. They first surveyed the Cariboo Lake area and the Snowshoe Plateau, then the Barkerville area. Bowman came at the right time, while James Porter could introduce him to the Snowshoe Boys, John Bowron, William Stephenson and other gold rush pioneers who were still alive. Bowman recorded many of the original discovery claims on his maps, as well as the miners' cabins, and even a mailbox on the Keithley Creek trail.

At the same time that the provincial government helped finance Bowman's survey, it offered a loan of $20,000 for the establishment of a quartz mill. Quartz milling developed in California in 1852, once placer mining slowed down. This form of lode mining eventually depended on stamp mills, costing $50,000 to $100,000, that could only be financed by stock companies. The stamps were heavy pieces of iron mounted on the bottom of vertical shafts, geared to rise and fall vertically. Once the quartz was crushed, the gold was separated and captured by various devices. Despite the fact that only one out of ten mills succeeded in California, there were high hopes for a boost to the economy for the Cariboo. (Ten years earlier, the provincial government had offered a loan of $15,000 to establish a ten-stamp mill north of the Quesnel River, under the Quartz Act of 1877). Peter Dunlevy took advantage of the latest offer, but very little work was done at Barkerville. The provincial government repaid the loan to the Bank of British Columbia.

In addition to the survey and the quartz mill, Lands and Works superintendent Forbes George Vernon requested a civil engineer, John Bell, to examine the feasibility of a railway from the Bonaparte Valley to Barkerville. Bell visited the area in November and December 1886. He arrived at Quesnel Forks "with a dilapidated following and camp outfit," and praised Stephenson for his assistance in getting him on the way again towards Barkerville. When Bell compared mileage and costs with an alternate line from the North Thompson River to Barkerville, the route from Bonaparte Valley worked out as the cheapest, at $7,500,000. In his report he referred frequently to the survey made by Marcus Smith in 1873, which went as far as Beaver

Valley. Bell favoured laying track through Beaver Valley, crossing the Quesnel River near Quesnel Forks, following the North Fork to Keithley Creek, ascending to the McMartin Creek/Swift River trail, and thence to Antler Creek, Cunningham Pass and Barkerville.

Freighters grumbled that a railway would take away their livelihood, but they needn't have feared competition. Although a number of railway companies were incorporated during the next decade they did not carry out any development. (Members of the Cariboo Railway included Vancouver mayor David Oppenheimer, and Canadian Pacific Railway executives Harold Abbott and J.M. Browning.[34]) The railway was supported in principle, if not financially, by John Bowron and local entrepreneur Ithiel Blake Nason at Barkerville. It was not until three decades later the first Pacific Great Eastern train made its way from Squamish to Williams Lake, in January 1919.

If the gravel deposits of East Cariboo could be likened to a giant casino, sometimes paying off, but most often not, William Stephenson's position as mining recorder made him the pit boss. He knew where all the best "shows" were taking place, and he was tempted to try his luck occasionally. In 1888 he complained to Bowron, "my prospecting has got me in the usual fix: 'hard up'. And it looks as if it would keep me so for some time to come. I had to quit whiskey so as to be able to prospect. Guess I will have to quit prospecting if I am ever to get out of debt."[35]

A year later, Stephenson's many years of mining experience finally paid off. With members of his South Fork Hydraulic Company, including John King Barker, George Vieth, and a number of other local miners, Stephenson registered a claim on the South Fork, next to the Hop E. Tong claim at Dancing Bill's Gulch. By analyzing boring samples he concluded rightly that an ancient river bed had been filled in with gold-bearing gravel and till. This deposit ran parallel to the South Fork River for two miles, but was separated from it by a wall of intrusive rock called a "stock." The placer gold at Hop E. Tong's claim, eroded from the larger deposit, had been worked by Chinese miners since 1861. The gold in Stephenson's claim was found mostly in two layers of the gravel, one halfway down and one near bedrock. The deposit was 300 feet deep, and a tremendous amount of overburden had to be removed first. This removal could only be achieved by using dynamite and the most advanced form of hydraulic mining.

Hydraulic mining and stamp mills had been introduced in California by 1860. The gentle topography of the goldfields in eastern California permitted relatively easy delivery of heavy iron machinery from the foundries in San Francisco. However, this advanced form of mining could not be implemented on a large scale in the Cariboo until a railway was built through Ashcroft, and the pack trails leading from the Cariboo Road to East Cariboo mines were upgraded to wagon roads. When hydraulic mining shut down in California in 1884, there was further incentive for developing it in the Cariboo.

Given his long experience in mining, William Stephenson was aware of the growing demand for hydraulic mining properties emanating from California, and the interests of financiers, especially directors of the CPR, in developing mining and railroads. The South Fork Hydraulic Company commenced test pits in 1889. John King Barker took charge of locating a reliable water supply, and surveying the necessary ditch routes from Polleys Lake. At the same time, R.T. Ward was developing the Harper lease on the Horsefly River, and five miles downstream Dan McCallum worked another placer claim. Hydraulic mining ushered in a new mining boom in East Cariboo.

CHAPTER EIGHT

THE ROARING '90S

"A church or almost any kind of an institution
cannot possibly affect the morals of this place. It
might possibly do a little good, but it cannot make it
any worse than it is."[1]

William Stephenson

Despite renewed interest in placer deposits in the Quesnel Forks area, the population, both white and Chinese, had dropped by 1891. There were only 212 Chinese and 66 white residents in the Keithley Creek/Quesnel Forks area. This all changed in a few years as large capital investments supported modern methods of hydraulic mining. In 1895 and 1896, hundreds of itinerant labourers made their way up the Cariboo Road, then over the rough wagon road to Quesnel Forks, to work on the Golden Quesnelle Dam, the Bullion Pit site and at many new claims being developed on the Quesnel River and the North Fork. As it had been in the Cariboo gold rush, once again Quesnel Forks was a familiar name to residents of Victoria and

New Westminster. Stephenson's mining report for 1891 noted the growing importance of hydraulic mining:

> Our old mines in the creek bottoms and along the shallow
> benches are getting about worked out, and it is to hydraulic mining
> that we will chiefly have to look for our output of gold in placer
> mining for the future, and there is every reason to believe that the
> immense gravel deposits which are to be found along the rivers and
> creeks in this section of Cariboo will amply repay those who have
> the capital and enterprise to invest in hydraulic mining. So far,
> every hydraulic mine that has been opened in this section has
> proved good paying property.[2]

The Chinese ceased mining gravel with ten-foot-long shovels from rafts anchored in the South Fork River. Digging ditches was a more lucrative occupation. The Victoria Hydraulic Mining Company employed 50 Chinese and ten white labourers to complete seven miles of ditch, bringing water from Spanish Lake to their claim on Coquette Creek. Stephenson's South Fork Hydraulic Company employed ten white and 35 Chinese labourers to complete five miles of ditch.

From the very beginning of the Cariboo gold rush, East Cariboo had strong ties with California. Many of the first prospectors into the area were veterans of the California gold rush, and the Chinese, Jewish and white merchants at Quesnel Forks relied on suppliers in San Francisco. The hydraulic boom in the 1890s forged another important link when mining engineers and labourers in California found employment in the poorly legislated mining areas of the Cariboo, and large manufacturers of mining equipment, such as the Joshua Hendy Company of San Francisco, gained a new source of customers.

The first major environmental legislation in the United States was directly related to the damage caused by hydraulic mining in the foothills of the Sierra Nevada Mountains of California. For more than two decades, gravel and mud from hydraulic mining operations washed downstream, filling in the main river channels. As a result, major flooding wreaked havoc in the Sacramento Valley each year. By the 1880s, 39,000 acres of California farmland lay buried under debris. The mining industry was countered by a strong agricultural sector that demanded environmental protection. Their persistent lobbying brought results in January 1884, when new "anti-debris" laws effectively shut down hydraulic mining in California. The closures represented an investment loss of $100,000,000, and the depression that ensued left investors, mining engineers and foundries seeking new fields of endeavour.

The British Columbia Department of Mines totally ignored the lessons to be learned from California's mining disaster. For example, Williams Creek, choked with mine tailings, overflowed the bulkhead at Barkerville many times, flooding the townsite. The provincial government did not bring in any new regulations to control the dumping of gravel into rivers and lakes in British Columbia. Neither the Placer Mining Act, nor the Water Rights Act addressed this looming problem, thus giving former California mining engineer John Hobson and a non-professional, R.T. Ward, a clear field in which to operate.[3]

HORSEFLY GOLD MINING COMPANY

Harper's Camp gained its name from Thaddeus Harper and a tragic episode in Cariboo history. Thaddeus and his brother Jerome, from Virginia, had arrived in British Columbia at the time of the Fraser River gold rush. Through hard work and the wise lending of money, they quickly became wealthy pioneer stock raisers and flour mill owners. They had begun with a sawmill at Yale during the Fraser River gold rush, then acquired herds of cattle which they pastured on the west side of the Fraser River. Their operations formed the basis of the famous Gang Ranch in the Chilcotin. Mills at Clinton (moved later to the Bonaparte River) and Soda Creek, supervised by a nephew, R.T. Ward, produced a good quality of flour that was sold at Barkerville. Jerome was the astute business manager. In 1862 he sold his interest in a claim on Williams Creek for $10,000. As the gold rush diminished, however, he chose not to invest further in mining speculations, concentrating on mills and the development of the Gang Ranch. Unfortunately, Jerome died insane, at age 42, in 1874. After a period of litigation Thaddeus inherited the bulk of the estate, valued at $176,000. Free of his brother's influence, he invested in any scheme that took his fancy, and he became a vulnerable target for unscrupulous developers. The old Blue Lead claim at Horsefly caught his attention.

For more than a decade, Hong King and other Chinese miners had worked the Blue Lead claim. Following the death of Hong King, white miners took a renewed interest. In 1878, the five-member Water Witch Company staked claims next to the Hong King site, selling an 11/12 interest to Peter Dunlevy, 2 1/12 to R.T. Ward, and two whole interests to Harper. Harper purchased all interests in the company, and obtained a ten-year lease from the gold commissioner in 1884. With the lease went the rights to an unspecified amount of water from Moffat (also known as Mussel) Creek.

About this time, tertiary syphilis began to affect Harper's reasoning. The disease was exacerbated in July 1884, when a horse kicked him in the face at the Gang Ranch. Once Harper recovered physically (but not mentally) from the accident, he proceeded to spend over $40,000 on a 40-mile road from 150 Mile House to the Horsefly River. He brought in a sawmill, a 40-horsepower engine and other equipment for his mine, and he opened a store at the site, that was called Harper's Camp. He then became involved in a second mining operation on Lightning Creek, with John Cameron (not "Cariboo" Cameron) in 1888, creating a debt of $50,000. When Cameron pressed Harper for payment of the promissory note in 1889, maliciously encouraging other debtors to follow suit, the Harper estate went into receivership. Within 15 years after his brother's death, Thaddeus had spent the fortune they worked so hard to amass. After a series of court cases, Harper finally obtained judgment against Cameron in 1892, to the effect that he was insane when he agreed to the Lightning Creek mining lease. While Harper's estate was in receivership, Ward obtained the Horsefly lease in 1891, with the approval of the courts. Nevertheless, Harper continued to visit the mine for at least a few more years, hoping to gain it back.[4]

William Stephenson did not think highly of Ward. In a private letter to Bowron he expressed the opinion that Ward was using Harper's money, and only remained at Horsefly as long as Harper would pay the bills. Intent on protecting his water-right interests on Moffat Creek, especially when the Harper lease came up for renewal in 1894, Ward became the proverbial "thorn in the side" of John Hobson and the Horsefly Hydraulic Mining Company which applied for water rights on the creek, too.

In his fight with the company, Ward was supported by R.P. Rithet, one of the trustees who administered Thaddeus Harper's estate from 1884 to 1885, following the Gang Ranch accident. Rithet was a partner in the prosperous Rithet and Welch Company with offices in Victoria and San Francisco. Ward sold his interest in the Harper lease to the Horsefly Gold Mining Company in 1894, in which Rithet held stock, but retained his position as manager and secretary of the company. In 1897 the value of the company was reported as $1,000,000 in ten-dollar shares.[5] Up the Cariboo Road, from Ashcroft to Horsefly, freighters hauled four hydraulic elevators and material for 14,525 feet of hydraulic steel pipe. The pipe was manufactured on site at a cost of $5,500. Ward's 1896 mining report showed that the company had assets of $180,985 and expenditures of $180,032. Provincial mining reports estimate that only $500,000 was recovered by 1910.

Harper's mining interests at Horsefly had encouraged other local miners such as Dan McCallum to explore gravel resources farther down the Horsefly River. Ward claimed that while California mining engineer John Spaulding was visiting his mining site, he was asked by Canadian Pacific Railway executives for the name of another California mining engineer who could help them develop gold mining in the Cariboo. Spaulding suggested John Hobson.

HORSEFLY HYDRAULIC MINING COMPANY

John Beauregard Hobson's fondness for Irish whiskey came naturally. He was born in Ireland and educated in mining engineering in California. The "anti debris" legislation in 1884 closed 33 hydraulic operations in the Iowa Hill area of Placer County, where Hobson was a partner in three mines.[6] Hobson subsequently found work with the California State Mining Bureau and he also helped to organize the California Miners' Association which lobbied Congress for better mining conditions. When a branch line to the Cariboo from Canadian Pacific Railway stations at either Ashcroft or Kamloops seemed imminent in the early 1890s, CPR President William Van Horne and a consortium of CPR businessmen, in a private initiative, invited Hobson to investigate mining possibilities in the Horsefly and Quesnel Forks areas.

John Beauregard Hobson with a black bear.
(ZZ-95373, BCA)

CPR General Superintendent Harold Abbott was the most active member of the group. He apprised Premier John Robson of his Cariboo interests in a private letter in February 1892. With the letter, he enclosed a report made by A.F. Stewart, in September 1891, on an exploration survey from Bridge Creek via Clearwater and Quesnel Lake. Stewart included excerpts from Marcus Smith's 1873 survey report on the Horsefly and Beaver valleys, and emphasized the fact that the route was close to placer mines at Horsefly and to the Hepburn claim near Quesnel Forks.

At the same time, Cariboo residents assisted the CPR interests. Peter Dunlevy and J.F Hawks of Soda Creek and Charles Dupont of

Victoria were quick to act as brokers in acquiring Dan McCallum's mining claim on the Horsefly River. In 1884, Dunlevy, Hawks and Dupont had invested in the Coal Harbour Land Syndicate that helped establish Vancouver over Port Moody as the terminus for the CPR. (Hence, Hawks and Dunlevy streets in Vancouver; Pender Street was originally called Dupont Street.) More recently Dupont had been involved in the Nelson-Fort Shepherd Railway in the Kootenays and with Dunlevy in the Island Mountain quartz mine near Barkerville. Hawks, Dunlevy and Dupont were part of the "old boys network" of speculators that included CPR executives Abbott, John M. Browning and J. D. Townley. Once Dunlevy and Dupont acquired McCallum's discovery claim, they transferred it to the private company formed by CPR executives, with Hobson as mining engineer. Prominent among the executives were W.D. Matthews of Toronto, and Abbott and Browning of Vancouver.

Eventually, there were 19 mining leases. The claims stretched along the Horsefly River, covering 2,100 acres, five miles down river from James Moore's 1859 Blue Lead claim at Harper's Camp. The Horsefly Hydraulic Company was established by an Act in 1894, granting mining privileges for 25 years for an annual rent of $550. Not less than $5,000 per year had to be spent on development. Water rights for 2,000 miner's inches from Moffat Creek were granted, at the same time that R.T. Ward applied for 3,000 miner's inches for the Horsefly Gold Mining Company. These two grants of water proved to be a subject of contention for several years. The Act also stipulated that the lease should contain a covenant prohibiting the employment of Chinese or Japanese persons. Hobson ignored the covenant, bringing in experienced crews from his former mining operations at Iowa Hill, California, to open up the mine, and hiring Chinese and Japanese labourers to build a 13-mile ditch from Moffat Falls to Rat Lake. With no regard for the annual salmon migration, thousands of tons of gravel (with mercury) were dumped into the Horsefly River.

Since it was important to get equipment into the mining site as quickly as possible, Abbott undertook the building of a sleigh road from 108 Mile to Horsefly in the fall of 1893, following the route blazed by Isaiah Mitchell in 1863. Abbott persuaded the government to pay $3,000 for its cost and for the upgrading to a wagon road the

A Japanese miner at the Horsefly Hydraulic mine.
(D-07743, BCA)

following spring. The final amount, by special vote, came to
$5,907.34. In comparison, the vote for all the road maintenance in
the Cariboo was only slightly more, at $7,096.60.[7]

Between 1894 and 1896, the mine recovered $92,426, or 12.3
cents per cubic yard. After initial success, however, the richest gold
sources were thought to be in cemented gravel. Having encountered
similar conditions in California, Hobson brought in a ten-stamp mill,
capable of crushing 190 tons in 24 hours. An adit, or horizontal
tunnel, was run from the hydraulic pit for 1,350 feet. The yield per
ton of crushed gravel ranged from only 99¢ to $1.78 per ton, with

127

The Horsefly Hydraulic Mining Company stamp mill on Horsefly Creek. The penstock, lower right, delivered water to the mill.
(HP 100011, BCA)

operating costs of $1.40 per ton. The cemented placer deposits were low grade, and after further drifting in 1899 and 1900 the mine was shut down.

The mining activity on the Horsefly River encouraged Alex Meiss and Harry Walters to build hotels at Harper's Camp. When Minnie Walters was born in 1896, the miners at the Horsefly Hydraulic Mine contributed to a gift for the first white child born at the camp. Perhaps someone today still cherishes this heart-shaped locket made of gold, with a W outlined in five rubies, five diamonds and four sapphires.

CARIBOO HYDRAULIC (BULLION PIT) MINE

At the same time that Ward was challenging Hobson to water rights at Horsefly, Hobson investigated William Stephenson's South Fork Hydraulic claim for the CPR syndicate in 1893. By this time Stephenson had acquired a second lease adjacent to the first one, and had a crew washing gravel on Black Jack Gulch. Water supplies, however, were giving out, an important incentive for the Chinese hydraulic operation on Dancing Bill's Gulch, and the South Fork Hydraulic Company at Black Jack Gulch, to sell to the CPR syndicate. Harold Abbott supervised the purchase of the South Fork Hydraulic, paying off the original owners with stock and money to the value of $64,500. The largest stakeholders were CPR officials, many from eastern Canada. Within the next decade, most of the original local investors eventually sold their stock, with the exception of Stephenson and John King Barker. A second Act in May 1894 created the Cariboo Hydraulic Mining Company, and its mining properties consisted of six leases, covering 277 acres.

The company increased stock in 1896 from $3,000,000 to $5,000,000. In 1898, a reorganized company, now called Consolidated Cariboo Hydraulic Mining Company Limited, made a

John King Barker and a gold ingot cast at the Bullion Pit mine.
(VPL914)

129

call, or a demand for payment, of five dollars per share. With 800,000 shares in distribution, $4,000,000 was raised for further development. Directors of the Company were President, W.D. Matthews, Toronto, Vice President H.C. Hammond, Secretary, James L. Lovell, Toronto, R.B. Angus, Montreal, T.G. Shaughnessy, Montreal, John Cassils, Montreal, G.F. Hartt, Montreal, E.B. Osler, Toronto. Major shareholders in 1898 were Sir William Van Horne, 59,160 shares, T.G. Shaughnessy, 59,960, and R.B. Angus, 59,070. Local stockholders included John B. Hobson with 6,576 shares, William Stephenson, 7,209, John King Barker, 4,296, and James Bain, 856.

By 1899, the CCMC consisted of 34 placer mining leases, covering 2,584 acres, plus 320 acres of pasture land. Within this area was supposed to lie ten miles of an ancient, gold-bearing river system, extending from Black Jack Gulch to the mouth of Morehead Creek. With an estimated recovery of 20¢ per cubic yard, the total value of gold in the gravel was thought to be $100,000,000. Annual payment for leases amounted to $2,002.75.

After many years of experience in the California mining industry, John Hobson knew how to set up a major hydraulic operation and how to lobby the government for change. He was also familiar with the hydraulic mining method of sinking shafts to bedrock, then running tunnels out to river banks. Auriferous gravel was thus washed down the shaft and out over riffles that trapped the gold. (Immediately prior to being shut down in 1882, large California mining operations washed 12,000,000 parts of gravel to recover one part of gold. Mines such as the Bloomington required over 150 miles of flumes and reservoirs. The Eureka Lake and Yuba Canal Company installed 300 miles of flume.)

The water system for the Bullion mine was not nearly as extensive as the Bloomington, but it nevertheless impressive. Hobson inherited a 17-mile ditch system, from Stephenson's Cariboo Hydraulic Company, that brought water from Polleys and Boot Jack lakes. It provided sufficient water for hydraulicking in the spring and summer, but Hobson needed a further supply to finish off the season, in September and October. At a cost of $25,000, he built a dam 35 feet high and 410 feet long across Morehead Creek, and additional flumes increased the water system to 33 miles. At the start of the mining season in 1899, the canals could deliver 5,000 miner's inches of water under a head of 420 feet. Eventually, water was collected from over 60 square miles. One visitor to Polleys Lake was amazed to see the gate-tender's son put a catch of trout in a box and send it floating down ten miles of flume to the cook at the Bullion mine.

Hobson spared no expense in equipping the Bullion Pit mine. His 1899 report included the following description:

> The mine equipment consists of a portable hydraulic plant of four lines of thirty-inch and twenty-two inch riveted steel pipes, aggregating six thousand feet; six No. 8 hydraulic giants, with deflecting nozzles; varying from six to ten inches in diameter; one steam power hoisting and pumping engine for sinking shafts for bank blasting; one fire-proof magazine for dynamite; one magazine for bank blasting powder; one dynamite thawing house; one fuse-cutting and detonator-priming house in each of the hydraulic pits [there were two]; one general blacksmithing shop for general forging, waggon work and horseshoeing; one pipe making shop fitted with rolls and other appliances for making and repairing hydraulic pipe; one steam-powered sawmill, having a capacity for cutting daily about four thousand feet of lumber. This mill is also supplied with a planing and matching machine, boring and framing machines.[8]

The mining crews were treated well, with good accommodation, and medical care. Between 1897 and 1905 there was a doctor in residence at Bullion, and an infirmary.[9] Hobson tried unsuccessfully to obtain government support for a hospital but only the doctor was subsidized. Ten camp buildings housed 124 miners. When the camp was relocated in 1901, to allow for expansion of the Bullion Pit, Hobson had many of the buildings wired for electricity. Oriental and white miners were housed separately, with dietary differences between Japanese and Chinese respected. For example, Japanese miners preferred long-grain rice; and the Chinese, short-grain rice. Hobson continued to use experienced miners from his former mines in California to form the nucleus of his crews, hiring men locally as needed for installing miles of flumes and working at the face of the mine.[10]

Hobson prided himself in running a safe mine. An average mining season used 75,000 pounds of dyamite and an equal amount of black blasting powder.[11] Given the amount of dynamiting that took place, and the 300-foot depth of the face, the fatality rate from accidents at the Bullion Pit was surprisingly low. There were only three mining deaths in 12 years. In one serious accident, a Japanese miner fell into the large flume, was carried 150 yards and dropped 40 feet onto the tailings dump. He survived because the mine's resident doctor, Dr. McKechnie, provided immediate medical care. There were two murders: a Chinese cook in 1906 and a Japanese miner in 1907.

Gold production for the Bullion mine reached its peak in 1900. After 62 days of washing, the mine recovered 510 pounds of gold, valued at $135,275. Hobson had it melted into a cylinder, which was displayed at the Domion Express office at Ashcroft before being shipped to Toronto. Between 1902 and 1905 a series of dry summers seriously reduced water supplies for hydraulicking. There was enough water for 30 days of washing in 1906 but it couldn't be used because part of the South Fork ditch had been cut in preparation for the new Spanish Lake water supply. Hobson reported the amount of gold recovered from June 1, 1894, to June 22, 1905, as $1,233,936.51. Gold recovery involved large expenses for dynamite and mercury. For example, in 1897, $19,300 was spent on explosives, and $1,116.00 for 23 flasks of mercury. One dynamite blast used 560 kegs of black powder.

THE GOLDEN RIVER QUESNELLE DAM

The dream of 1860s expressman, James Batterton, to dam the Quesnel River and mine the river bed became a reality in 1896. Fifteen years earlier, by a special Act, the provincial government permitted John Adair, Jr., and Joseph Hunter to form the Quesnelle Lake Dam Company, in March 1881. They gained the exclusive right to build a dam and to mine the bed of the South Fork River on a ten-year lease, providing they spent $30,000 before the end of 1883. They had to also spend $15,000 annually until the dam was completed, and pay annual rent of $350 from 1884. This was a speculative venture, for neither Hunter nor Adair had the personal finances required to build the dam. In 1882 Hunter tried to interest English investors in the scheme. The Act was amended to less stringent terms in 1883 but the dam was not built. When the ten-year lease expired in 1891, William Baines of Victoria acquired a 20-year lease and attempted to float a limited company in London, the Quesnelle River Gold Working Syndicate of British Columbia.[12] He was not successful and Hunter regained control.

The international depression of the early 1890s abated somewhat by 1895, allowing developers with the right contacts, to obtain money in England for foreign projects. In 1896 the Golden River Quesnelle Limited Company formed in London, with British Columbia Agent General Forbes George Vernon as chairman. With seemingly a "finger in every pie," Charles Dupont was involved in this mining venture also. Hunter and Dupont had been speculating in real estate since 1878.[13] Holding power of attorney, Dupont sold Hunter's interest in claims on nine miles of the South Fork to the GRQ for £270,000. Of that amount, Hunter received £23,000 in cash and £247,00 in ordinary shares. Total capital was £350,000, of which £80,000 was paid up (actually realized). Hunter became chief engineer of the project, with Dupont as manager. Keeping operations "all in the family," Dupont's brother, Arthur, residing with Peter Dunlevy at Soda Creek, became the accountant.

Trained as a surveyor and civil engineer in Scotland, Hunter was an ambitious man. On first arriving in British Columbia, in 1862, he mined in the Cariboo for seven years. He represented the Cariboo in the provincial legislature during the 1870s, and would do so again in 1900. During the 1870s, as District Surveyor General for the Canadian Pacific Railway, he spent considerable time surveying a route through the Cariboo for the proposed railway. He married Premier John Robson's daughter, Frances Ellen, in 1878, and at the time of his involvement with the GRQ dam, represented the Comox area as MLA, and was General Superintendent of the Esquimalt and Nanaimo Railway. In the winter, he would leave Quesnel Forks on Friday morning at 4:00 A.M., travel by sleigh all day Saturday, catch the train at Ashcroft on Sunday for New Westminster, and arrive in Victoria on Monday, in time for the afternoon session of the legislature.

Construction costs for the dam were estimated at $250,000. The company executives did not like the fact that Dupont and Hunter personally supervised all aspects of the project. However, given the great distance between London headquarters and the dam site, they could only rely on an advisory board in British Columbia, consisting of Sir Henry P.P. Crease, Charles E. Pooley, F.B. Pemberton — and Joseph Hunter. Excavation began in the fall of 1896, and continued all winter with three shifts of men. Of the 209 labourers employed in December 1896, 66 were Chinese. The company built bunkhouses for the men and constructed two roads to service the dam site: a sleigh road from the Bullion Pit mine to the south bank of Quesnel Lake, and a wagon road between Quesnel Forks and the dam site on the north side of the South Fork River. The dam was built 18 feet high, in a curve, with a radius of 460 feet. At the north end, nine 12-foot discharge gates

Joseph Hunter.
(HP3109, BCA)

The Golden River Quesnelle dam and nine gates, built at the foot of Quesnel Lake in 1896-98. Note fishway at centre.
(D-07990, BCA)

controlled the raceway. It was an impressive feat of engineering for which Hunter received considerable praise and publicity.

Once the nine gates to the GRQ dam were closed, mining operations on the South Fork began in September 1898 at French Bar. Instead of using dynamite, the company purchased a steam derrick with a 100-foot boom to remove the boulders in the river bed. A representative from the Joshua Hendy Company supervised installation of the machine. The original plans called for mining all ten miles of the South Fork River down to Quesnel Forks, but gravel sluiced from the Bullion Pit operation blocked the last few miles to the Forks. (The Mining Act of 1891 allowed placer-mining companies to discharge tailings into nearby rivers.) Because of heavy runoff in the summer of 1898, and delays in the transport of machinery, the derrick was only employed for two weeks. In 1899, dredging did not commence until after spring freshet because of a scarcity of funds for labourers.

The results were disappointing. The only gold found was underneath large boulders. As the oldtimers had predicted, during patient years of wing damming and mining from rafts, the Chinese had already worked over most of the river bed. The GRQ folded in 1900. It was subsequently purchased by Hobson's Consolidated Cariboo Hydraulic Mining Company, which allowed Chinese miners to once again work the river bed in their old ways.

Development of the the Bullion Pit mine and the GRQ dam caused additional headaches for Stephenson. More law enforcement was required, trails and bridges needed upgrading, and a rush on mining claims meant careful recording procedures had to be followed. Developers could importune government officials in Victoria and John Bowron in Barkerville, leaving Stephenson, isolated in Quesnel Forks, to ascertain the legality of a mining claim. Beginning in 1893, mining brokers staked claims on every possible site along the Quesnel River and on the North Fork. Stephenson cursed the "wild cat lot" that kept him up late at night registering claims and preparing maps.

Quesnel Forks, 1896. William Stephenson's house is located inside the fenced-in enclosure at the head of the South Fork bridge. The jail is behind the house, in the corner. The first government agent's house is across the road, on the right.
(HP 10494, BCA)

Andrew Burrill.
(G-8283, BCA)

He quickly saw the need to survey Quesnel Forks into lots because stores and hotels would be required. (Vieth and Borland had already built a store in 1892.[14]) Most importantly, the old pack trail from 150 Mile House to Quesnel Forks was no longer adequate; a wagon road was needed in order to bring in heavy hydraulic equipment. The provincial government provided $5,000 for a wagon road, and $3,000 to upgrade the South Fork bridge to withstand heavier loads. The bridge was completed by the spring of 1895. Stephenson contracted Andrew Burrill to build a new jail with leftover lumber, on a corner of the government reserve, near his house. Stephenson also built a summer kitchen at his own expense.

With the ground still covered in snow, Stephenson and James Champion began laying out the townsite of Quesnel Forks in February

1892. Stephenson's report to Bowron reveals the prevailing negative attitude toward Chinese ownership of property:

> I have had Mr. Champion at work for two days laying out town site here. I have been helping him but the snow is so deep that we can only get around on snowshoes and as there is considerable measuring to be done to get through the part that is already built upon and the ground is frozen so that it is almost impossible to get stakes correctly placed. Champion thinks it best to let the work stand for a while now as we have settled a base to work from and laid off a few lots where Mr. Vieth wants to build, and for the time have stopped the Chinamen from building in where the street will come.
>
> I would not be surprised if you get an application for an order to let Chinamen build a wing on what they call their Mason house. Said wing will project into the street about 3 feet and I have warned them not to build it. Champion tells me they have asked him [to] write to you for an order to let them build or for him to move the stakes of the street just a little so that they can build where they want to. As you know there is lots of room for all and plenty to spare but these high binders think they can have their own way. I have put the price of lots 50 x 100 ft at $100.00 and the principal reason is to prevent Chinese from getting whites to buy and then sell them to the Chinese which if lots were $50.00 they would do. $100.00 per lot will not stop any one that wants to build, while I think it will prevent the best lots from falling into the hands of Chinese. As I understand the law the Govt will not sell to Chinese but I do not know how to prevent a white man from selling to them after he has got his title. I think it is a mistake that a white man can turn around and sell to Chinese. Please instruct me as to selling lots how to proceed & etc. ... I would like to be able to keep the celestials paying their $2.50 per month ground rent. It counts up.[15]

It took several years before the survey plan for Quesnel Forks was finally approved by the Department of Lands and Works. In his first plan, Champion laid out the townsite in 300-foot-square blocks, with 60-foot-wide streets. Three of the streets were named for prominent men in Barkerville, Ithiel Blake Nason, Joe Mason and Samuel

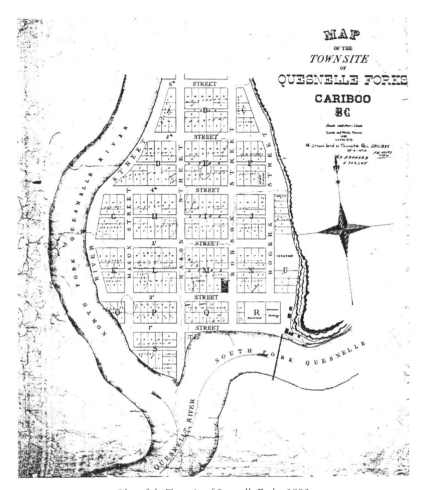

Plan of the Townsite of Quesnelle Forks, 1893.

Rogers, and the fourth street for Premier John Robson.[16] The lots were 50 by 100 feet. Lands and Works rejected the plan because there was not enough access to the North and South Fork rivers. They suggested that 20-foot alleys bisect each block. Once Champion made these corrections, Stephenson auctioned the lots at the upset price of $100 on April 29, 1895. Unfortunately, one of the would-be purchasers, George Vieth, had already built a store on "his" lot, which made him vulnerable to any mischievous person in the audience who might bid the price up unnecessarily. Vieth wanted to buy two lots adjoining one

139

another, and complained bitterly to Lands and Works when the price of the second lot was bid higher by a competitor:

> Over two years ago about the time Messrs. Stephenson and Champion was staking out the flats for a town sight we applied to Mr. Stephenson for a lot to build a store. The one picked out was 50 by 100 feet and now shown on the government plan as Lot 1. We built our store on it in a way that if we wanted Lot No. 2 to enlarge our building we could buy it. Eight months ago we applied to Mr. Stephenson for joining Lot 2. He verbally agreed that we should have it at the same price $100.00 each. At the same time we asked him what about the payments for these lots. His answer was as soon as the other lots comes into market I want the money. A few days before the sale we understood from other persons that our lots was to be sold at auction the same as others. We asked Mr. Stephenson. He told us such was the case. We protested against it but no avail. At the day of sale he started to sell other lots. When he came to our Lot 2 Mr. John Hepburn wanted this lot. We bid it up to $125.00. He got the lot. We could not go any higher. Mr. Hepburn had us in the doing for the next lot sold was ours with the building on and he could run that up to a high price to get even with us. He run it up to $150.00. All other lots apart from these was sold at $100.00.
>
> We contend Mr. Stephenson did not treat us right that he misled us about securing those lots two years ago. We had put every confidence in him and put our building up in a way to join on to it from No. 2 lot. Otherwise we would have applied to the head office in Victoria and not of been deprived our right and thrown with the hand of speculators.[17]

When Lands and Works questioned Stephenson on the matter, he insisted that he had made no promises to Vieth; he intended to follow the law concerning the selling of lots. Despite having to pay more for their property, Vieth and Borland remained at the Forks. By 1901 their hotel featured a bar-room, storeroom, dining room, kitchen, sitting room and seven bedrooms. A barn stabled 12 horses. When the store burned down in 1902, it was rebuilt immediately.

Other lot purchasers included John McRae, formerly of Vancouver, who built a hotel in partnership with his brother Angus. A year later they added a storehouse with a large, second-storey room for meetings. When applying for a liquor licence in 1900, McRae described his hotel as "sixty feet long, forty feet wide, containing a bar-room, sitting room, dining room, store-room, kitchen, and twenty bed rooms, with stabling for twenty horses." Hans Helgesen, whose wife and family resided in Metchosin, near Victoria, also built a hotel. Pioneer miners Andrew Burrill, William Polleys, and Kansas John Metz, and two women, Luella Walsh (a.k.a. Luella Runyon or MacKenzie) and Annie Lynne acquired lots. Stephenson did not auction any of the property in the Chinese section of the village. He advised Lands and Works, "I would not sell any lots upon which the Chinese stores stand although some parties wanted to buy those lots. My reason for not selling was to keep out of trouble until I could [see] Mr. Bowron and consult him re the matter. And as those people (the Chinese traders) are paying the Govt. $2.30 per month ground rent there is nothing lost."[18]

On receiving an application for a town lot from the Presbyterian Church, Stephenson passed it on to Bowron, with the dour comment, "A church or almost any kind of institution cannot possibly affect the morals of this place. It might possibly do a little good, but it cannot make it any worse than it is."[19] Stephenson reserved a lot for the church, but it was never utilized and reverted to the Crown.

As the Bullion Pit mine began recovering gold, several notorious characters arrived in the Cariboo, bent on stagecoach robbery. The first to cause trouble was Samuel Bankley, who pulled a gunnysack over his head before carrying out his heist. The camouflage, which bore the name "Pinchbeck," was easily traced to 150 Mile House. The Cariboo region was a large, sparsely populated area, and strangers bent on mischief often forgot that because of the small population, most people knew one another. A newcomer, especially one who didn't "fit in," was quickly spotted and kept under surveillance. Police Superintendent Hussey came up from Victoria during the manhunt, and personally escorted Bankley to the Kamloops jail to begin his sentence of ten years.

On the evening of June 7, 1894, two Chinese miners sat smoking their pipes in front of their cabin, near where Morehead Creek flows into the Quesnel River. They might have been mulling over their terrible experience of the week before, when a stranger with a gun had forced them to hand over their gold. The robber tried to return it when he saw the small amount, but the miners, too frightened to comprehend his intentions, refused the offer. The robber warned them not to report the incident, but the minute he left they hurried up river to Quesnel Forks, to notify William Stephenson.[20] So now suddenly, out of the shadows stepped the same man again. Enraged because he had botched a stage holdup near Morehead Lake earlier that day, and because he had just learned that the Chinese miners had contacted Stephenson, he deliberately shot both men to death. It is believed that he set their bodies adrift in their boat, because, months later, other Chinese miners found two badly decomposed bodies and the smashed boat caught in a drift pile, 20 miles below the Forks. Unaware of the tragic circumstances, they presumed that the men had drowned. On the basis of their evidence, Stephenson ordered the bodies buried at Quesnel Forks without an inquest. In 1898 Harry Brown, behind prison bars for the Morehead stage robbery, provided most of the above scenario in a written confession. Brown died, insane, in Kingston Prison, Ontario, without coming to trial for the murders, and the names of the victims are unknown.[21]

Stephenson's report to John Bowron at the time of the stage robberies and murders reveals how stressful it was for him. He had travelled 50 miles by a rough trail to the telegraph office at 150 Mile House, only to find the telegraph system out of order. Frustrated at not being able to contact E.H. Fletcher, the Post Office Inspector in Victoria, or Bowron at Barkerville, he resorted to writing to Bowron:

Hell to pay generally with me just now. First I am crippled with inflammatory rheumatism in my knee and cannot get around as I need to do just now. Mail robbed 11 miles from Forks and trouble with contractors, men on Horsefly re paying mining licences. Here all day yesterday trying to wire but can get nothing up or down. Have three men following robber. They saw him next day after he robbed the mail. Had it been a bear or anything to be caught by a bullet from a rifle we would have had him fixed and buried before now, but unfortunately my men could not do as we wished (shoot).

The robber is well armed. Could I get authority to put more men in woods we might yet corrall him, but although Mr. Fletcher was wired to on the 9th no reply yet. It makes me sick. Tried yesterday to get message to you but no go. So don't know what to do.[22]

The following year there were more difficulties. Increased activity on the Bullion Pit mine and the completion of the wagon road to Quesnel Forks in 1895 attracted hundreds of job seekers. Stephenson urged Superintendent Hussey to send him leg irons and handcuffs:

I think some of the worst vags. on the coast have been run out of the towns there to get clear of them, and now we have them in this out of the way place. They have not a cent, but manage to get drunk or pretend to be drunk, abusive and disorderly. There are now four locked up with the prospect of more before the night is through. I have only one pair of handcuffs to do all the work. I think only a chain gang will put a stop to some of those fellows here. Of course, I cannot go just that far, but when I am forced to give them a short term it would be well to be able to make them work, do something. Some steps must be taken to clear the toughs out of this place as soon as possible.[23]

Stephenson initially hired William Parker as police constable. A native of Minnesota, Parker owned a large, thriving farm at Big Lake where Stephenson wintered his horse. Unfortunately, Parker had a serious hearing disability that affected his duties as a policeman. When a trip to Victoria to consult with doctors failed to help Parker, Stephenson reluctantly sought a replacement. The new constable, James Bain, was not popular with the Chinese miners. They didn't like his overbearing manner when collecting taxes, and he quickly put them in jail if they gave him any trouble. His temper got so out of hand on one occasion that he castrated a horse that had escaped from a stable in Quesnel Forks, causing its death.[24]

In late July 1895, Stephenson received information from R.H. Hall, at the Hudson's Bay store in Quesnelmouth, that the Hudson's Bay agent at Fort George, Ernest S. Peters, and several other white miners were being terrorized by drunken natives. Because Joseph St. Laurent was occupied with annual road maintenance, Stephenson recruited William Parker. Using two canoes, Parker left Quesnelmouth for Fort George with four special constables, two natives, and provisions for three weeks. As the days passed by Stephenson waited anxiously for word of the expedition. Eventually, Parker returned to Big Lake safely, after bringing the culprits before a justice of the peace at Quesnelmouth. This native/white clash led to the installation of David Anderson as police constable at Quesnelmouth in 1896.[25]

While en route to 150 Mile House for news of Parker in August, Stephenson got caught up in another affray. He reported to Superintendent Hussey from his destination:

I got here this morning from Beaver Lake near which place we were yesterday hunting a Chinaman. I had committed the fellow for trial. Bain caught him in the act of breaking into Vieth & Borland's store at Quesnelle Forks on the night of 21st Aug. last, and we had him in the gaol at Quesnelle Forks awaiting the Assizes. On the night of the 30th Aug. he managed somehow to cut his way out of the cell and escape. He took Bain's revolver, a hatchet and other things out of the gaol. Bain discovered the escape and after finding which way he went, started after him. Got up to and ahead of him (by making a circuit). About 1/2 past 2 a.m. it was rather a dark night, when Bain went up to him to arrest him. He shot at Bain almost point blank with Bain's own revolver. Bain says he had a close call, and unexpected. Before Bain recovered himself the Chinaman was in the brush and in the darkness he managed to elude Bain. ... We then got between him and Beaver Lake, at a point that we thought he would make. It was a bridge on the road. It was now 2 p.m. I stationed Bain there to guard that point and then went on to Beaver Lake to get men to guard other places, and was to have been back with Bain before dark.

About two hours after I left Bain the Chinaman came to the place. Bain jumped into the road and called on him to stop. He, the Chinaman, at once pulled out the revolver. Bain had a Winchester. When he saw the Chinaman pulling his pistol. Bain fired a shot over his head, thinking to intimidate him, but the Chinaman levelled the pistol at Bain. Then to save his own skin Bain fired at him and dropped him. The wound in my opinion is not serious as the bullet passed through the thigh, a little below the hip. He lost considerable blood in getting him to Beaver Lake, where we now have him.[26]

After receiving complaints from the Chinese at Quesnel Forks, Hussey expressed concern for Bain's safety. Stephenson reassured him, "when they see that they cannot run him out of this [place], they will then have a wholesome respect for him."[27]

Bain was rough not only with the Chinese residents; he made the local liquor sellers, Luella MacKenzie and Dollie Gilbert (also known as Florence Walker) extremely unhappy. Dollie Gilbert decided to leave Quesnel Forks in 1896, and requested Hussey to write to Bain concerning his ill-treatment. Stephenson replied to Hussey's query:

Your letter of 12th inst. re one Florence Walker alias Dollie Gilbert, duly to hand, with enclosure. Dollie's story of course is very good on her side, but here we know her better. Why does she not state that she was convicted for selling whiskey and fined for same? Also that her house was a rendezvous for drunken men. Constable Bain told me several times that he had warned her that if she did not do better he would close her house, which he finally had to do with my approval. It is true that there are two other females of the same brand as Dollie who have houses here. One of them (known in Vancouver as Mrs. Dr. Runion) goes here by the name of Mrs. A.L. Welsh. Her I have also had up convicted and fined for selling whiskey, but she has managed lately to keep a quieter place. The other I have not caught yet but hope to before she quits. We have a rough lot to deal with and I endeavour to do the best I can, and be as just as it is possible to be. As for Florence Walker, alias Dollie Gilbert, rightly Maggie McCan, this is a good place for her to keep away from. I have made no investigations re this matter. It is too familiar to me.[28]

Dollie did not return, but Luella refused to give in. Nicknamed "Calamity Jane," she was highly temperamental and many people were afraid of her. The government agent at Williams Lake claimed she was suspected of causing the death of a Chinese girl. She lived at Quesnel Forks and then at Likely until the last few years of her life. Stephenson's son, Allen, was one of the few people who could get along with her, and there seems to have been a friendly, if not intimate, relationship between them.[29]

The other women at Quesnel Forks kept a lower profile. Hotel owner John McRae's wife gave birth to twins in May 1897. Dr. Herald, stationed at the Bullion Pit mine, made the three-mile journey down to the Forks where he spent the night delivering the babies. There is no mention of who delivered Mrs. Yee May Kim's children. Henry Vieth, brother of George, brought his wife from New Jersey to assist with operating Vieth and Borland's store at Quesnel Forks during the summer, but Mrs. Vieth became ill, and did not return the next year.

While her husband coped with his many responsibilities, Jennie Stephenson's mental health began to show the effects of 20 years of isolation. Now in her early 50s, she suffered from alcoholism and grew partially addicted to a morphine-based medication, chlorodyne. At 150 Mile House, Elizabeth Allen, the police constable's wife, had been treated with another opiate, laudanum. When Elizabeth attempted to commit suicide in 1892 by taking an overdose, she was committed to the Provincial Insane Asylum for four months.[30] Stephenson and his sons cared for Jennie with every kindness, but with increasing concern, until she became violent and suicidal and required care at the insane asylum, too.

With settlers moving into the west Chilcotin, and mining developing at Harper's Camp, Stephenson had an immense area of responsibility. The problems of administering the law in a rural district demanded greater amounts of time. Yet, as always, he had to operate on a strict budget, and be responsible for every cent he collected and spent. Reimbursement to witnesses who had travelled some distance for a court case posed a problem in May 1896. Stephenson wrote to the Superintendent of Police:

> Is it right to pay Witnesses in a Crown case such as I had at Soda Creek on the 2nd inst. when I had those men Wm. & John Moffitt up for cattle stealing?

I had five Witnesses summoned. One had to come twenty miles, one sixteen miles, two thirteen miles, and one was at Soda Creek. I paid $5.00 expenses of bringing those witnesses from Alexandria to Soda Creek but they claimed two days' time. This I would not pay until I got authority as I cannot find any regular scale of witness fees in such a case. Would you kindly let me know what to do re the matter.[31]

While Stephenson was at 150 Mile House in early January 1898, Benjamin Franklin, a settler and justice of the peace at Tatla Lake, arrived with a 16-year-old native prisoner. The young man, Samien, had shot and killed Lewis Elkins, who kept a trading post at Gootzine Lake. Stephenson wrote Superintendent Hussey concerning a reward for Franklin and the three special constables involved, Charles Skinner, Edmund Elkins (brother of the murdered man) and Patrick McClinchy. When the reward money was approved and forwarded to Stephenson, he travelled to Hanceville to deliver it to the recipients.

The murder underscored frequent requests for a mounted Provincial Police constable in the west Chilcotin. Robert Pyper was assigned to

150 Mile House, owned by Vieth and Borland, ca. 1898, *with a pack train loading up. The white bell mare always took the lead.*
(HP 46754, BCA)

patrol the area in February 1898, and Stephenson supervised the tendering for construction of a jail with two cells and a ten-foot by 14-foot front room at Hanceville. He then ensured that it was furnished with handcuffs, blankets and a stove.[32]

Although Stephenson was notified to be on the alert, the next fugitive from justice, Milton O. Howell, was apprehended without his help by Thiel Detectives in October 1899, near 150 Mile House. Howell was wanted for the murder of Thomas Rosling in Montana. His quick arrest and extradition seems to mark the end of the few years of crime in the Cariboo that was inevitable, given the publicity for the mines, and the large number of itinerant labourers "on the tramp." The crime wave peaked when Stephenson and Bowron were in their sixties, coping with increased hydraulic mining activity. It must have been the most difficult time of their careers.[33]

At the Ashcroft railway station, the amount of freight for the Cariboo increased each year, doubling in size between 1894 and 1895. The famous packer, Jean Caux, also known as Cataline, made a number of trips to Quesnel Forks in 1895 and 1896. Angus McRae, brother and partner of Quesnel Forks hotel/store owner, John McRae, Fook Sang Lung and other Chinese merchants brought in their own supplies. William Parker developed a stage and packing business, with the Bullion Pit mine as a major customer.

A road connecting Quesnel Forks with Horsefly was now necessary because John Hobson supervised both the Horsefly Hydraulic Mine and the Bullion Pit. There were two mines at Harper's Camp: R.T. Ward managed the Horsefly Gold Mine, formerly called the Harper lease, and Senator Campbell from California managed the Miocene Mine. Once the wagon road was built to Quesnel Forks and Horsefly, Vieth and Borland's 150 Mile House on the Cariboo Wagon Road became a major distribution centre for freight trains. In February 1899, a reporter for the *Ashcroft Journal* counted 30 freight trains and a number of passenger stages outside the hotel. Vieth and Borland were "at their wit's end" trying to cater to everyone.[34]

Hotels owned by Alex Meiss and H.L. Walters at Harper's Camp became rowdy gathering places for miners. After an inspection, Bain, reported to Hussey:

The fact is they are not conducted as they should be. 1st they are inclined to be dirty. 2nd there is plenty of food but it is not properly handled. 3rd they do not conduct their barrooms properly.

It appears to me that they are paying attention to a few drunken stiffs who do as they please and letting the better class of men and the travelling public look out for themselves.[35]

One of the topics of conversation at the stopping places would have been the new technology and how it was improving mining operations. The latest steam pumps were powerful enough to raise water from the river, and in 1899, the Gold Point claim, located across the South Fork River from Quesnel Forks, tried them out. Because the Horsefly area was flat, the Horsefly Gold Mine and Miocene Mine installed hydraulic elevators to aid in gold recovery. They could lift water and gravel to a height of 40 feet.

River dredging also became popular. In 1896 there were six dredges on the Fraser River and one on the Quesnel River. One dredge was hauled 600 miles upstream on the Fraser River to the junction with the Smoky River.[36] With the success of river dredging in California and especially New Zealand (where the industry grew to 201 dredges in 1902) promoters were optimistic about dredging the Quesnel River. A further encouragement was the size of the dredging leases — five miles of river bed against one mile in New Zealand. The Newell dredger was built and launched at Quesnel Forks in 1899, and floated 20 miles downstream where it operated with limited success. Near Quesnelmouth, on the Fraser River, two other dredges were unsuccessful. Despite all the monetary investment and activity, dredging does not appear to have been as lucrative as it was in New Zealand and California in the same time period.[37]

Within a few years, environmental damage grew to dangerous proportions because of hydraulic mining. All the tailings from the Bullion Pit mine operation were dumped into the South Fork River at Dancing Bill's Gulch. As happened in California, the gravel washed downstream, filling the river bed at Quesnel Forks. Running at a higher level, and swollen by a summer of heavy rain, the river undercut the slum banks opposite the village. The first major slide, on September 10, 1898, filled half the river bed. There was more to

Dancing Bill's Gulch and the Bullion Pit mine. Note the immense amount of gravel sluiced into the South Fork River, ca. 1898.
(ZZ-95376, BCA)

come. Two days later Stephenson reported to Arthur Stephenson, road superintendent at Lytton: "Last night at 9 o'clock the hill started for the river bed and this morning there is a pile of dirt over 100 feet long and 25 feet high, clear across the river. Had not the water been turned off [at the Golden River Quesnelle dam] nothing would have saved the south end of the bridge, the Govt. house and quite a slice off the front of the town." On closer inspection, Stephenson found the slide was 500 feet in length and up to 100 feet deep.[38]

Joseph Hunter kept the gates of GRQ dam closed, giving Stephenson time to install 136 pilings along the bank in front of his house and up river, to protect the bridge. A few days later, all nine gates of the dam were opened and the rush of water tore out 30 of the new pilings. Stephenson sent word to Hunter to close the gates immediately, then set to work to make repairs. Hunter opened the gates carefully the second time and the bridge and village were saved. Road Superintendent Stephenson despaired of ever building a decent road down the bluffs to the south end of the South Fork bridge. He suggested that the town be moved to a safer place, but Quesnel Forks remained.[39]

Yet another landslide on July 20, 1899, damaged the South Fork bridge. William Stephenson had gained permission for a leave of absence in order to take his ailing wife to Vancouver. But these plans were put aside until he dealt with the emergency. Fortunately for Quesnel Forks, the slide was not as extensive as the previous year.

Protecting Quesnel Forks and the South Fork bridge were uppermost on Stephenson's list of responsibilities, but the care of aging pioneers also required more attention. Because these men often remained in the Cariboo as long as possible, in many cases they needed to be transferred carefully but quickly to the Provincial Home for Men at Kamloops. Stephenson spent precious working time to ensure that a Negro miner at Horsefly, Edward Doherty, and C.H. "Judge" Heath of Quesnel Forks, were sent down to the Home in

Cariboo gold rush pioneers at 150 Mile House ca. 1897: (l. to r. back row) James Cummings, Fred Rose, and John "Gassy" Shaw; (l. to r. front row) Frank Guy, Robert Borland, and W. Thompson.
(G-09002, BCA)

April. Doherty suffered from frostbitten feet, and Heath, a resident in the Cariboo for 35 years, had been paralyzed since February and cared for by Quesnel Forks residents. Once again, Stephenson was forced to defend the extra travelling expense to John Bowron:

> I have the honour to acknowledge receipt of vouchers returned to me re expense incurred in sending C.H. Heath from here to Kamloops, also one Doherty from 150 Mile House to Kamloops. In reply I beg to state that I done the best I possibly could. C.H. Heath was totally helpless and it took two men to handle him for all natural purposes, day and night. Consequently I was compelled to get a man to assist Constable Bain. And then when I got that man Doherty at the 150 Mile House he was next to helpless except that he could use his hands which Heath could not. As to why both Heath & Doherty were not sent down in the same wagon, 1st it was not possible to make room for both men in the wagon (both men had to be on stretchers): 2nd the smell from Doherty's feet was so offensive that people could not remain beside him. To overcome the difficulty I put him on the back action of a freight team that promised to travel in company with the team that was taking Heath down. This was the only way I could get him down.
>
> I certainly tried to get things done as cheaply as possible and attended to the matter personally up to the time I started them from the 150 Mile House in charge of Constable Bain.[40]

In the last days of the century, William Stephenson's career suffered a jolt. Rumours had been circulating for several years that he might lose his position as government agent, and the bad news came in January 1900. The government discharged Stephenson, Bain, and Joseph St. Laurent at Quesnelmouth. When Stephenson and St. Laurent asked C.A. Semlin, the Provincial Secretary, for an explanation, they were told that it was not necessary to go into particulars: "the conclusion for dispensing with your services was arrived at after discussion with the representatives of your district and considered to be in the public interest."[41]

George Vieth's dissatisfaction with Stephenson's sale of Quesnel Forks lots in 1895 appears to have been resolved, because Vieth and

Borland once again gathered up signatures on a petition, this time to save an old friend. "Mr. Stephenson is an old and faithful public servant of acknowledged integrity, diligent, and impartial in the performance of his duty, and I decline to believe that you will countenance his dismissal and sacrifice him for political expediency." But that is exactly what happened. A young Ashcroft lawyer, James Murphy, son of Denis Murphy of 141 Mile, replaced Stephenson for the next 18 months. Out of loyalty for his father, Allen Stephenson resigned his position as clerk.[42]

Stephenson made no formal protest about his predicament. It would have been a waste of time, given the volatile political situation, with people voted in by personality rather than by political party affiliation. He had weathered many storms; this one would blow over, too.

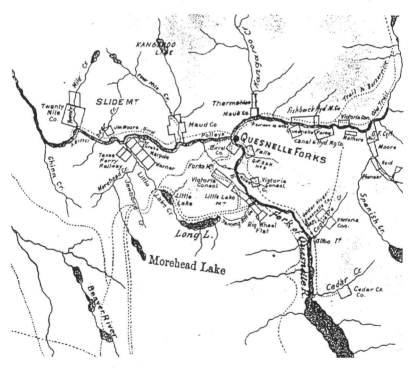

Portion of Lands and Works map showing mining claims, 1898.
(CM/C46, BCA)

CHAPTER NINE

A NEW CENTURY

"This old prostitute ... has given more trouble and
cost the Government more than any other of the
hard cases that we have had in this Section since she
came here in July 1896."[1]

William Stephenson

THE NEW CENTURY brought major changes. Within a decade
the hydraulic mining boom ended and Quesnel Forks became a quiet
backwater. Lode gold mining elsewhere in British Columbia quickly
took over as the major source of bullion.[2] However, until the Bullion
Pit closed in 1907, the mine continued to dominate social life at
Quesnel Forks. Two murders, and a sting operation involving
"Calamity Jane," enlivened the normal course of events.

James Murphy quickly took on Stephenson's responsibility for the
safety of the South Fork bridge and Quesnel Forks. During the spring
freshet in 1900, another slide forced the river to the north side. Four
buildings and a part of the bank 30 feet in width and 300 feet in
length were washed away. In the fall, a second slide came down near

the bridge, fortunately after the Golden River Quesnelle dam gates had been closed for the season, and there was not enough water left in the river to cause any damage. John McRae led a petition to install cribbing at both ends of the bridge, and along 600 feet of bank in front of Quesnel Forks. Murphy had spent $1,000 on crib work in April 1900. The petition requested that the cribbing be extended in January while the dam gates remained closed. When the cost ran over $10,000 the government questioned the project. A civil engineer, Thomas Drummond, residing at the Forks, was placed in charge.[3]

The government reinstated Joseph St. Laurent within a year of his dismissal, but Stephenson was kept waiting until October 1901. Stephenson's former police constable, James Bain, was not rehired. He worked for Hobson as a stage guard and later cruised for timber in the Quesnel Lake area and mined at the Maggie Mine, near Hat Creek. Stephenson's letters from this period record the demise of local residents. Both pioneer miner Martin Anderson at Pine Creek, and an unidentified Chinese at Quesnel Forks committed suicide, the latter because he had not done well in mining. William Lynch, a Negro cook at the Bullion Pit mine, died when he fell from his wagon in 1902.[4] As

At a court hearing, Soda Creek, ca. 1903: (l. to r.) Chipman Smith, Carlton Dunlevy, Allen Stephenson, D.M. Perkins, Gillespie Stephenson, William Stephenson, ?, James Murphy, and John Bowron.
(HP50829a, BCA)

the sequence of events at the Bullion Pit unfolded, Stephenson could do little but watch from the sidelines. He continued mining, working a claim near Kangaroo Creek with his two sons, then selling it to John Hobson in May 1906 for $5,000. Allen Stephenson took his father and brother to court, claiming that he was not paid for his share of the lease. Alternatively, he claimed wages of $1,400.[5]

William Parker's Cariboo Stage business reached its zenith in the early 1900s when he acquired two new passenger stages in addition to his freight teams. He now owned Lots 170 and 461 at Big Lake, comprising 640 acres, that provided ample pasturage for his horses. Every Monday, Parker's stages left Ashcroft for Horsefly and Quesnel Forks, or to connect with the steamer *Charlotte* at Soda Creek. His freight wagons serviced most of the Cariboo Road, as well as Quesnel Forks and Horsefly. Freight loads published in the *Ashcroft Journal* confirm that Parker was hauling a good percentage of the material transported on the road. Jealous of Parker's growing business, a group of freighters and associates formed the Cariboo Protective Union at Ashcroft, in January 1900. Their mandate was to control freight rates

William Parker's stopping house at Big Lake, Parker standing second from left.
(HP 9548, BCA)

and to ensure that each freighter in turn received a share of freight consignments. The slate of officers included M.P. Stewart, president and Isaac Lehman, vice president, with Ashcroft lawyers Stuart Henderson as secretary, and Denis Murphy as treasurer.

When Parker and a few other white and Chinese freighters refused to join the union, they were subject to harassment. During a loading session at Ashcroft, one saboteur spied the location of a whiskey keg on Parker's wagon. When the freight train stopped overnight at Cache Creek, he crawled underneath the wagon and drilled a hole through to drain the liquor. There was more in store for Parker. His horses were shot and wagons dismantled. The Provincial Police posted Reward notices to no avail. They were forced to take serious action when an incendiary targeted two of Parker's wagons in April 1902. The wagons, loaded with freight for James Reid's store at Quesnelmouth, had been left overnight on Ashcroft Hill (outside of town) in preparation for an early start in the morning. Both wagons and their contents were totally destroyed by the fire.

At the request of the Attorney General's department, Superintendent of Police Frederick Hussey enlisted the Thiel Detective Agency in Seattle, and they dispatched an undercover agent to Ashcroft in June 1902. During a six-month investigation, the agent strongly suspected freighter William Elmore of being the mastermind behind the ongoing sabotage. He plied Elmore with liquor, shared the same sleeping quarters, and travelled with him throughout the Ashcroft area, but could not gain a confession. After spending more than $1,500 on the case, Hussey felt there was not enough evidence for a conviction and had the agent recalled in January 1903. The agent wrote to Hussey a few months later, suggesting that Constable Joseph Burr at Ashcroft might have warned Elmore of the investigation. Parker became a local hero and continued his freight business until his death in 1927. For a time his sister, Mamie, helped to operate the ranch house at Big Lake which was used as a stopping house for travellers.

There was further environmental damage on the Quesnel River, this time caused by the Golden River Quesnelle dam. The provincial Act authorizing the dam had made no allowance for a fishway, yet a later report by the Fisheries Commissioner, John Pease Babcock, estimated that Quesnel Lake and its tributaries provided one-quarter of the sockeye spawning grounds in the Fraser River system. Joseph Hunter had installed, voluntarily, a fishway in the dam, but it was not built correctly. Unable to breach the dam, the enormous salmon run of 1901 floated downstream to decay on the river bank in front of Quesnel Forks. The British Columbia Cannery Association protested the dam blockage. Fears were expressed that should the dam give way during high water, "every bridge from Quesnel Lake down to the Gulf of Georgia, together with every dyke, cannery and habitation close to the present high water mark of the river, would be swept away."[6]

Future spawning disasters were avoided when the federal government installed a proper fishway in 1903 at a cost of $4,140. In 1905 the pack of canned salmon was 500,000 less than 1901, proving to many people in the fishing industry that the dam had been responsible for the low, fourth-year run. A watchman counted the fish using the raceway during spawning season. As an example of a large sockeye run, Robert Winkley reported over 4,000,000 salmon passed through in the month of August 1909.

By 1901 the Golden River Quesnelle Dam Company had closed down, as well as other large hydraulic operations such as Gold Point and Victoria Consolidated. At Keithley Creek, George Vieth and Robert Borland carried on their general store and their interests in various mines. In July 1902, the *Ashcroft Journal* announced, "The Onward Company's tunnel on Keithley Creek has broken into the old hill channel and the ground prospects well. An average of $6.44 to the pan was taken from the bedrock and $2.50 to the pan from the gravel. Vieth and Borland, the owners, will at once begin putting the property into shape for active mining, and should be washing dirt in three months."[7] At the same time, V&B also worked the Hayward Hydraulic and Golden Gate claims on Little Snowshoe Creek.

There was a minor gold rush to the country east of Horsefly in 1901 and 1902. The *Ashcroft Journal* did its best to promote the rush, printing a large map of the area. Sam Adler reconnoitred and declared the excitement a humbug. Mining continued at Senator Campbell's Miocene Mine and R.T. Ward's mine, using hydraulic elevators. Campbell spent $200,000 sinking a three-compartment shaft 555 feet deep, hoping to tap into a rich, buried river channel, but the shaft was abandoned because of water seepage. Gold production for the Horsefly River amounted to $289,849 between 1901 and 1905, then dropped to $3,750 between 1906 and 1910. Mining news was relayed more rapidly when a telegraph line from 150 Mile House to Quesnel Forks, badly needed for decades, was completed at the end of October, 1902. The line also connected to Harper's Camp and Polleys Lake.

With the participation of other mining districts in British Columbia (the Kootenays were now producting $2,000,000 annually in silver ore) John Hobson formed the British Columbia Mining Association in 1903. Hobson was very much opposed to provincial government regulations that required placer miners to expend $1,000 per year on developing individual claims. He felt this amount was too onerous for the average prospector, and strongly favoured the Crown granting of placer claims. A petition from Barkerville miners, presented by Cariboo MLA Joseph Hunter, rejected the idea. Hobson became vice president of the new association, and was named the "father of hydraulic mining in British Columbia." His admirers presented him with a diamond ring in recognition of his success in forming the association.[8]

Hobson's title was ironic, for despite 33 miles of flumes for the Bullion Pit mine, and the fresh water resources of Polleys, Bootjack and Morehead lakes, there was never enough water for hydraulicking. The longest mining period was 171 days in 1900 during which $350,085 in gold was recovered. In 1902 there were only 65 days of piping, and in 1903, 53 days. In 11 years the Consolidated Cariboo Hydraulic Mining Company spent $1,900,000 on equipment, and recovered $1,233,936 in gold. The Horsefly Hydraulic Mining Company spent $450,000 on equipment and recovered $180,000 in gold. Hobson claimed that all monies were put back into the company for development, but he lived well. During the winter he occupied an elegant home, Gisburn, at the corner of Moss and Belcher streets in Victoria, or journeyed to California.[9]

As the Bullion Pit grew larger, extending farther away from the river, hydraulicking was hampered by the long sluices necessary to wash gravel into the South Fork River. The mine's sluices extended 2,300 feet in length, making it difficult to maintain the correct slope. To shorten the distance, and to provide enough of a drop for the gravel to wash through the sluices easily, Hobson commenced boring a tunnel through the wall of hard, intrusive rock (a stock) that separated the Bullion Pit from the river. If done correctly, the tunnel would penetrate the stock and end slightly beneath the bedrock over which lay the Bullion Pit gravel deposits. A vertical tunnel, or raise, would then be made at the end of the horizontal tunnel, like a periscope at the end of a submarine. Powerful monitors projecting heavy streams of water would wash the gravel down the raise and over long riffles made of wood and iron, laid in the horizontal tunnel. On reaching the mouth of the tunnel the tailings would fall into the South Fork River. (If engineering calculations proved incorrect, and the horizontal tunnel broke through into the gravel some distance above bedrock, there would be a major problem. The important bedrock gravel, which contained considerable gold, could not be washed upwards.) The concept was identical to the hydraulic methods Hobson had seen or used in California, where volcanic overburden could be 600 feet thick. Unfortunately, despite the use of modern drills, the pace was slow. The stock proved difficult to penetrate and Hobson never saw the tunnel finished. (When finally completed in 1928, the 1,500-foot tunnel ended, successfully, 32 feet below bedrock. A vertical raise 119 feet in height was made into the gravel.) In 1905 Hobson installed an hydraulic elevator plant and a Loveridge derrick to aid the sluicing.

Following a number of dry years the Consolidated Cariboo Company wanted to withdraw its investment in the Bullion Pit mine. In 1905 Hobson went to New York to interest the Guggenheim Exploration Company (known as Guggenex), the exploration division of the Guggenheim Company of New York, in taking over the claims. While living in California, he had been friends with the company's flamboyant consulting engineer, John Hays Hammond. Hammond sent Charles Hoffman, a placer deposit expert, to the Bullion Pit mine to examine Hobson's operation. Final arrangements for the sale of the property to Hammond, on behalf of Guggenex, were made on February 28, 1906. In June 1906, Hobson also sold Hammond claims at Spanish Creek and at 4 Mile Creek on the Quesnel River.

With a promise of $500,000 from the Guggenheims, Hobson, continuing on as managing engineer, proceeded to spend $97,300 in 1906 on a new water system from Spanish Lake to the Bullion Pit. At the lake's outlet, he constructed a dam of barked spruce logs in cribs, extending 298 feet in length and 31 feet in height. Hobson advertised in the *Ashcroft Journal* for 100 mine labourers and axe men, wages two dollars and board, and for 500 labourers "accustomed to railway construction or excavation work, wages $1.50 per day and board,"[10] but he did not get enough men to carry out his plans for the summer. Two enormous traction steam shovels, ordered from the Vulcan Iron Works (later the Bucyrus Erie Company) of Toledo, Ohio, arrived by railroad at Kamloops in late summer. Although bridges along the Cariboo Road were reinforced for the heavy loads, the machinery was not delivered on site until the spring of 1907. To make matters worse, Vulcan had provided the wrong buckets; the teeth were for vertical excavation of ore bodies, and were useless for digging horizontal ditches.[11]

The influence of the Guggenheims on the mining industry of the Americas was immense. Their vast interests included silver, copper, gold and tin mines along the cordilleras of North and South America, from Alaska to Chile. By shutting down small mining operations, the Guggenheims' Smelter Trust had already caused "a blight of ghost towns" in the Colorado Mountains. In early July 1907, Guggenex's hydraulic mining expert, O.B. Perry, drove from Ashcroft to the Bullion Pit in a 35-hp Peerless, the first motor vehicle to travel the Cariboo Road. He had taken a side jaunt from Vancouver, en route to the Yukon to inspect one of Guggenex's latest developments, the Yukon Consolidated Goldfields (later named Yukon Gold Company). Hobson's mine and claims in the Spanish Lake area were no match for the immense Yukon interests, and orders for closure of the Bullion Pit arrived in mid-July.[12]

The closure was a dreadful blow to the local economy, but Hobson was not finished yet. Claiming that he still had a financial interest in the Bullion Pit mine, he attempted a clean-up operation with a Japanese crew, in the summer of 1907, but the Guggenheims obtained an injunction that permanently severed Hobson's connection with the mine. He was now in his 60s and could have retired, but the gravel of the Cariboo held a continuing promise of riches. He bought claims from William Stephenson and others in the Spanish Lake area. At the same time, he converted one of the Golden River Quesnelle

Dam buildings into a hunting lodge, Casa Blanca, at the present site of Likely. Hobson died in Victoria, of heart failure, on January 10, 1912, just as the Spanish Lake mine went into production.[13] An attempt to estimate Hobson's personal worth in British Columbia by examining his will proved futile. Hobson's executors reported that his financial holdings were nil, possibly because he had transferred all his money to California.

Always incredibly energetic and a born fighter, R.T. Ward had taken on Hobson and the Canadian Pacific Railway consortium in the 1890s, to defend his water rights to Moffat Creek for the Horsefly Gold Mining Company. In 1913, he became embroiled in more litigation when he acquired the mining claims to the Bullion Pit from the Guggenheims' Cariboo Gold Mining Company. John Hopp of Seattle challenged Ward's right to the claims. Hopp had supervised a number of mining ventures at Barkerville, and subsequently acquired the Hobson/Guggenheim property at Spanish Creek. He claimed that Ward had not taken out the requisite mining licence. The resulting series of court cases spanned a period of five years, during which time Ward was not allowed to work the mine. In 1916 the provincial government granted Hopp three placer mining leases to cover the Cariboo Hydraulic Mining Company leases (originally awarded to Hobson in 1894 and 1896). Ward kept fighting. In a final appeal to the Privy Council in July 1919, Hopp's 1916 leases were declared null and void. The judgment went to Ward. By a provincial act, Hobson's original leases were renewed to Ward's Cariboo Gold Mining Company for 30 years, from May 1919, with water rights to Six Mile Creek and Morehead Lake not to exceed 5,000 miner's inches. Ward's fight for the Bullion Pit mine had cost him $15,000 in legal fees, and, unfortunately, he did not live to enjoy his victory. He was trying to attract American investors to develop the mine when he died at age 76, in January 1923, in Vancouver.[14]

The only other mining excitement was generated by the development of the Quesnel Hydraulic Gold Mining Company, on the Quesnel River at Twenty-mile Creek, a decade later in 1911. Paid-up capital amounted to $1,750,000. Mining engineer H.W. DuBois was supposed to have carefully sampled the gravel before extensive work began. Water was brought from the Swift River, through an immense flume made of wooden staves, to the mine site on the Quesnel River. There was ample water, excellent gravel deposits with no overburden — but no gold. The developers had estimated from sampling that the returns would be 5¢ to 8¢ a cubic yard, but mining in 1912 recovered no more than 2¢ a cubic yard. After enormous expenses the mine was closed and the equipment moved to the Kitchener Mine on Keithley Creek. Failure of the Quesnel Hydraulic Gold Mining Company led to DuBois' suicide.[15]

Shortly before his retirement, William Stephenson was involved in the two sensational deaths at the Bullion Pit mine. Sam Lock (a.k.a. Chong Kee You), a cook who had been in Hobson's employ for 38 years, murdered a Chinese kitchen helper, Chew Hong, on July 15, 1906. Lock fled the murder scene and went into hiding. Stanley Prior found Lock on his farm at Little Lake and brought him to Stephenson at Quesnel Forks. The inquest, supervised by Dr. Cecil Boyd and Stephenson, showed that Chew Hong had been killed by a direct stab to the heart. The first trial, held at Clinton in October 1906, resulted in a hung jury. The second trial, in May 1907, ended in a sentence of death by hanging which was appealed. The third trial in October upheld the death sentence, with the date of the execution set for December 4, 1907.

During the first trial, Hobson, his foreman, W.N. Bissett, and his bookkeeper, E.H. Pollexfen, tried to convince the jury that Lock deserved compassion. He was about 60 years old, and had been a trusted employee for more than 30 years. They claimed that Lock was a victim of deceit and the animosity of the Quesnel Forks Chinese Tong. He was supposed to have given money to Chew Hong over a period of years, to send to China to care for his wife and child. Recently, Lock had found out that his family had died a number of years earlier yet Hong was still collecting money on their behalf. Petitions signed by the mayors of Victoria and Kamloops, respected clergymen, Chinese and white merchants in Victoria and Vancouver, and many residents of Kamloops and the Cariboo begged for clemency, but despite all their efforts Sam Lock was hanged in Kamloops in December 1907.[16]

In July 1907 one of the Japanese clean-up crew at the Bullion Pit, Y. Mikami, shot and killed another Japanese miner named Kondo, supposedly in self defense. Joseph Burr, Chief Constable at Ashcroft, set out by special express to Quesnel Forks to take charge. On arrival at the village he found that Stephenson had held the inquiry without waiting for him. Burr could scarcely conceal his annoyance in his report to Superintendent Hussey.[17] He escorted the Japanese murderer to Kamloops where he was found not guilty. Neither the death of Chew Hong nor that of Kondo appear to have been premeditated, yet one man was hanged and the other set free.

The summer of 1907 was not yet over when Stephenson became an unsuspecting participant in a sting operation. Hotel owner John McRae had complained to Superintendent Hussey a number of times

Luella MacKenzie, "Calamity Jane."
(IP-0001, BCA)

that several Chinese merchants and Luella MacKenzie were selling liquor without a licence.

When the undercover agent, D.G. McNaughton, arrived at Quesnel Forks in July 1907, he expected to find a booming mining town. Instead, the recent Bullion Pit mine closure had left only three or four itinerant men in the village. Quickly changing his modus operandi, the agent took the alias "Hall," and announced that he was a salesman for Scotland Woollen Mills, "on a month's vacation." For three days, Luella, Stephenson, his son Gillespie, and the local residents feted Hall, unaware of his true identity. With an enormous capacity for beer and poker, he fitted easily into the routines of the village. Luella placed an order with him for a pair of trousers for Allen Stephenson. Eventually, the Chinese liquor sellers were brought before the magistrate at Quesnel Forks and found guilty. Luella insisted that her trial take place at 150 Mile House, claiming she wouldn't get a fair hearing at the Forks. She was found guilty and fined $100 and costs.

Within a week, Luella was back in court, this time at Quesnel Forks, and fined once again for selling liquor without a licence. When her lawyer, Denis Murphy, filed an appeal, Stephenson wrote to defend police constable Field Yolland of 150 Mile House, who had arrested Luella:

> This old prostitute that at present goes under the name of Mrs. M. MacKenzie, has given more trouble and cost the Government more than any other of the hard cases that we have had in this Section since she came here in July 1896. She then received letters from the Post Office as Luella Runyon.
>
> On October 5th 1896 Constable James G. Bain had her pulled for selling liquor in her brothel, then in Court she gave the name of Mrs. A.L. Welsh, convicted and fined under that name again on 23rd April 1897, she was convicted and fined for same offence selling liquor in her house.
>
> In October 1899 pulled, convicted and fined for keeping a bawdy house, then she gave her name as Mrs. A. L. Welsh; after that affair she has named herself Mrs. MacKenzie.
>
> In March 1906 committed for interfering with Peace Officers on duty, Clinton Grand jury let her out of that affair.

Such is the person we have so much trouble with and likely to have more as when Mr. Yolland served the last summons upon her she told him if people would not quit bothering her she would have to kill someone yet.[18]

Luella won her appeal and the fine of $300 was repaid. She did not get the court costs refunded, however, and ten years later she was still fighting for reimbursement.

Luella continued to live at Quesnel Forks for a number of years, probably on the property she owned, Lot 1, Block D. Eventually, she moved to Likely where she operated a small store until her health deteriorated. She died at the Provincial Insane Asylum, in Essondale, in December 1940. Through the years, Luella had remained good friends with Allen Stephenson and she willed her property and personal possessions to him.

Luella's trial was the last major event in Stephenson's career as government agent. He retired in 1908, at age 75. Over a span of 30 faithful years, his salary had decreased from $125 per month in 1877 to $110 in 1908. When he first came to Quesnel Forks there were seven government agents in all of British Columbia; there were 27 when he retired. He was one of only 13 superannuants in 1910, receiving a pension of $55 a month. He retained his appointment as justice of the peace, which allowed him to prepare legal papers for local residents, such as those required for admission to the Provincial Home for Men at Kamloops.

As a parting blow, the provincial government announced that it was moving the mining recorder's office to 150 Mile House where the next government agent would reside. A petition to the Provincial Secretary, signed by the Quesnel Forks Chinese, and said to represent 70 people, possibly helped in maintaining a sub-recorder at the Forks. Gillespie Stephenson filled this position until his untimely death in 1909.

Many of Stephenson's old friends had already passed away. He acted as pallbearer at Peter Dunlevy's funeral at 150 Mile in 1905. George Vieth died in Victoria in 1906. A year later, Stephenson accompanied John King Barker to Vancouver, hoping that there was still time for his family to take him home to Palmer, Massachusetts, but John died in Vancouver, on October 26, 1907.

Slowly but surely, other gold rush pioneers at Quesnel Forks or within Stephenson's area of responsibility were forced to choose the Provincial Home at Kamloops when they could no longer care for themselves: Kansas John Metz and Hizer Newell at Quesnel Forks, Ned Humphries at Soda Creek, and Moses Wiley from the Chilcotin. Metz and Newell arrived at Quesnel Forks at the beginning of the gold rush; Humphries was the ferryman at Soda Creek, and Moses Wiley was a rancher near Farwell Canyon. Long years of friendship made some cases very sad for Stephenson. Santiago Huertas wrote from Victoria for help. He was one of a group of Latin American packers who had supplied goods to the Cariboo during the gold rush. Later, he became a naturalized citizen and operated a small farm near 150 Mile House. Now, at 76, he suffered from deafness, and cataract of the left eye:

> I have been doctoring myself since I left 8 Miles Creek, Horsefly, and I don't seem to derive any benefit from them. I have almost spent what little cash I had paying doctors and buying medicines for my eyes and I don't seem to be improving. I trust you will do your best for me in my sorrowfull position and please give this your earliest attention.[19]

In 1899 Stephenson had arranged for a Mexican packer named Andreas to be admitted to the Provincial Home for Men. He wrote the Provincial Secretary immediately on receipt of Huertas' letter, requesting similar care for his old friend.

Robert Borland cared generously for oldtimers at his Keithley Creek ranch, and at 150 Mile House. Aurora Jack Edwards had boarded at Keithley Creek in October 1907, for a dollar a day. When Edwards died in the Provincial Insane Asylum in 1910, Borland submitted a statement for $475 for groceries and other sundries; he had not wanted to press Edwards for payment when he was ill.[20] In 1908 Borland requested financial assistance for Robert Barr and John Malcolm, and Stephenson wrote letters to the Provincial Secretary to gain help.[21]

Sadly, Stephenson's most difficult case was within his own family. By the end of 1903, Jennie's mental condition had deteriorated to the point where she became violent toward her husband, and set their house on fire. She suffered from delusions of persecution, and threatened to drown herself. With medical reports from Dr. S. Mostyn Hoops at Soda Creek, and Dr. O.M. Jones of Victoria, Stephenson reluctantly applied to have Jennie committed to the Provincial Insane Asylum at New Westminster. Mr. and Mrs. Paterson, owners of the Vernon Hotel in Victoria, where the Stephensons sometimes stayed, and John and Julia Hobson vouched for the good care that William and his sons had given Jennie as she steadily declined over the past four to five years. Her addiction to chlorodyne partially contributed to her condition. She was educated, neat and clean, and looked "well cared for," arriving at the hospital wearing gold jewellery, and a sable fur cape and muff valued at $400. (Stephenson eventually requested that Jennie's furs be returned to Quesnel Forks so he could preserve them from moths. He later sent down many of her every-day clothes, her wedding dress and riding habit, and some knitting wool.)

Chlorodyne has been described as "the Victorian patent medicine par excellence." It was promoted as a cure for sleeplessness, coughs, colds, stomach ache, bowel pains, diarrhoea and colic. A British Army surgeon, Dr. J. Collis Browne, invented the mixture as a remedy for

Vieth and Borland's Willow Ranch, Keithley Creek. George Vieth, far right, stands next to Aurora Jack Edwards.
(89173, BCA)

168

cholera. The formula contained, "two full grains of morphia, and lesser amounts of chloral and tincture of cannabis indica," and sold as "J. Collis Browne's Chlorodyne." There were several competitors, "Towle's Chlorodyne" and "Teasdale's Chlorodyne," and most chemists made up their own version. In 1899, about the time that Jennie became addicted to chlorodyne, home and export sales for J. Collis Browne's product amounted to £25,851.[22]

In the late 19th century, the majority of opium and morphine addicts in the United States were women, primarily of the upper and middle classes. They became addicted from doctor's prescriptions for "female complaints," nervousness, or the effects of alcohol. If a doctor lacked training or was too lazy to search for the medical reason, opiates provided an immediate, effective relief. Opium-based medicines became even more habit-forming if a substantial prescription was given to the patient to self-administer because of rural living conditions. Jennie's situation and the trauma endured by her husband and sons was duplicated many times over in North America and Europe.[23]

Within a month of her admission to hospital, Jennie was much better. Now weaned from chlorodyne, her mental condition improved and she was no longer violent. She began writing long letters to her youngest son, Gillespie, and then to her husband, begging to be taken home. Jennie's intelligence was revealed in the ingenious excuses she used to try to obtain her discharge. Since Stephenson and his sons were often absent from Quesnel Forks on government business, he wrote frequently to the Medical Superintendent, Dr. Manchester, asking for updates on his wife's health, and for assurance that her statements were untrue, that she would not be discharged until completely well again. With the exception of Luella MacKenzie, there was no white woman available at Quesnel Forks to care for Jennie, and he feared an immediate relapse "to her old ways" should she return home too soon. Manchester repeatedly assured Stephenson that he should not believe Jennie's letters. She would always find something to complain about, and would never again be completely well, mentally.

Perhaps because of her status as the wife of a government agent, the superintendent took a close interest in Jennie's case. At Stephenson's request, Manchester provided her with a private room at the asylum, and with subscriptions to the Montreal *Family Herald* and *Weekly Star* and the San Francisco *Weekly Examiner*. After permitting Jennie several excursions to Vancouver, he felt she was well enough to live as an out-patient, near the hospital, in the home of a former asylum nurse, Mrs. Brown. The transfer took place in April 1904. Jennie remained under the close supervision of Manchester and Mrs. Brown, Stephenson paying for her board through the hospital's accounting system. (At one point Manchester did wonder if Jennie was obtaining cholorodyne on the sly during her visits to Vancouver.)

Jennie continued writing letters to Stephenson, blaming him for keeping her in care. Stephenson began to think that the only solution was to continue to pay board indefinitely. In late January 1905, Jennie wrote to Charles Wilson, the attorney general, asking for his help. Claiming that "both husband and wife are very dear friends of mine" and that he was "absolutely incompetent, on account of the regard I have for both of them, to properly investigate the matter," Wilson passed the letter to the Provincial Secretary's office. Dr. G.E. Doherty, Manchester's replacement as medical superintendent at the asylum, replied:

> I might say that she is recorded on the books of this institution as a case of alcoholic insanity, with considerable evidence of dementia. When first admitted she had delusions of great persecution, the imaginary source being her husband and her own children. I would advise the cancellation of her probation and her re-admission to the asylum unless she becomes more contented in her present quarter.[24]

With Stephenson's approval, Jennie was formally discharged from the hospital on July 31, 1905. She moved from the Browns' to the home of Mr. and Mrs. Robert J. Skinner in Vancouver. Stephenson knew Skinner, who had managed the Hudson's Bay Store at Barkerville, and was now Provincial Timber Inspector. It is not clear when Jennie rejoined her family. She may have spent winters in Vancouver and the warmer months at Quesnel Forks. Jennie's son, Allen, is quoted as saying his mother was in a nursing home in New Westminster when Gillespie died from meningitis, in October 1909.

Jennie lived only three years after Gillespie's death. Ironically, after all the concern about fire, the Stephenson house burned down in March 1912. They were able to save their furniture, but forced to move into a small cabin. No doubt deeply affected by this loss, Jennie died two months later, on May 29, 1912. Stephenson buried her beside Gillespie, and marked their graves with Vermont marble headstones. Jennie may have remained in the shadows during her lifetime, but her headstone showed that there was a complex, feminine side to the history of Quesnel Forks that should not be forgotten.

In Stephenson's last years, the Barkerville Freemasons honoured him on July 6, 1912, with a life membership.[25] He was reconciled with his son Allen and carried on placer mining near Quesnel Forks. A few Chinese merchants, pioneer miner Andrew Burrill, also from the Maritimes, and telegraph operator Grant Grinder were the only residents to keep them company at the Forks.

Farther afield, there were still a few other gold rush pioneers left in East Cariboo, including Robert Borland and Jimmy Adams at

R.W. Harrison, manager of the Kitchener mine, Jimmy Adams, W. Moore, and Dr.
Hodgson, at Willow Ranch.
(43089, GSC)

171

Keithley Creek and James Cummings at 150 Mile House. In 1913 Stephenson was supervising a claim on the North Fork and Robert Borland and Jimmy Adams had been prospecting on Little Snowshoe Creek. William Stephenson died at age 83, on January 5, 1916, Burrill at age 84 in 1918, Cummings, at age 86 in 1918, and Borland at age 83, in 1923. Jimmy lived the longest, to 90 years, and died at the Provincial Home in Kamloops, in September 1934. [26]

EPILOGUE

W HEN SURVEYOR R.W. HAGGEN visited Quesnel Forks in 1916, a few months after Stephenson's death, he found that fire had destroyed the best buildings. The government agent's house, Vieth and Borland's store, Helgesen's hotel and McRae's hotel were all gone. Only three white men and a few Chinese miners lived there, manning a store, post office and telegraph station. "Herr Tom," a Chinese cook, was in charge of the Ritz Cafe, and another Chinese resident operated a pack train to Keithley Creek.

The village remained undisturbed until the second Cedar Creek gold rush in 1921. Unlike the other Cariboo "rushes" this one had the added convenience of the Pacific Great Eastern Railway which was completed to Williams Lake in January 1919. On the advice of local resident John Likely, two prospectors, A.E. Platt and John Lynes, staked claims on Cedar Creek. Their claims were within a short distance of Captain Isaiah Mitchell's old trail and in the same area where Aurora Jack Edwards had mined in 1867. Unfortunately, when final surveys were made, Platt learned that his best ground belonged to the newcomers. Platt recovered 205 ounces of gold, worth $4,000, but was forced to give the owner of the adjacent claim 45 ounces. Both Lynes and Platt sold out in 1922, and litigation and wildcat promotion took up most of the following decade. The *Mining and*

Engineering Record gives the total production between 1921 and 1923 as 10,800 ounces of gold.

There were two positive results from the Cedar Creek rush. The little village of Williams Lake received an economic boost when hundreds of miners arrived by train for the Cedar Creek gold diggings, and a through road was made to Keithley Creek. Although well constructed, the Golden River Quesnelle dam had become a safety risk because of the rotting timber. Even the fishway had sagged under water, once again preventing sockeye from spawning. Public Works made a 250-foot breach in the dam for the fish, and began construction of a bridge. Six 60-foot king trusses with trestle approaches were built on the foundations of the dam in 1922. The completion of a second bridge, across the North Fork (Cariboo) River at Spanish Creek, allowed vehicle traffic at long last to reach Cariboo Lake. In the 1930s, Barney Boe took over mining at the Cedar Creek site and at Pine Creek on Cariboo Lake, using a plane to commute to his home at Williams Lake.

Mining at the Bullion Pit continued in coughs and sputters until the 1930s. In 1928 Carinelle Placers Limited completed the sluice tunnel started by Hobson in 1905. The company extended the ten-by-ten-foot tunnel 165 feet farther, making the total length 1,500 feet. A vertical raise, eight by six feet, 119 feet high, connected it to the gravel in the pit. The tunnel was electically lit, and a service car ran along the top of the flume. At his Likely sawmill, Gavin Hamilton cut all the lumber and spruce blocks to line the bottoms of the flumes. An aerial tram conveyed this material from the north bank of the South Fork River to the mouth of the tunnel. Miles of wooden structures were replaced with Dutcher suspended metal flume. The new system was ready for water within three and a half months but operations were suspended in 1929.

When Great Britain went off the gold standard in September 1931, and the United States in April 1933, the increased value of gold, from $20 an ounce to $34, encouraged intense development of the Bullion Pit. In 1933, mining supervisor Ray Sharpe, working for Bullion Placers Limited, cleaned out the tunnel, and had three shifts of 80 men employed. In 1934, control of Bullion Placers was transferred to E.B. Ridsdel, in England. Ridsdel retained Sharpe as manager, and hired

174

Bert "Taffy" Williams with hydraulic monitor in the Bullion Pit, ca. 1935.
(Courtesy Margaret Henderson, Dave Falconer collection)

Charles Stewart, as consulting engineer, to devise an efficient water scheme. Once the mine was in full operation, Sharpe boasted that the daily water supply exceeded that of the city of Vancouver. The mine continued operation until Ridsdel's death in 1939, when litigation and the outbreak of World War II ended large-scale operations.

In spite of the activity at the Bullion Pit mine, by 1934 most of the gold in British Columbia came from lode mining. Only approximately seven per cent of the province's total gold production was from placer mining.[1] During the 1930s, almost all the surface of Yanks Peak was staked by various mining companies, but the numerous tunnels drilled into the mountain failed to tap a mother lode. Nearby, on the Snowshoe Plateau, Fred Wells, who had successfully developed the Island Mountain Mine near Barkerville, opened the Snowshoe and Cariboo Hudson mines which only operated briefly.

There were various small-scale placer mining operations on the Horsefly River and at the south end of Beaver Valley. After 40 years, the Hobson ditch and flume to Moffat Creek was still usable. A local resident, A.H. Walker and his associates, repaired the ditch line in 1938 and brought water to a hydraulic operation near China Cabin

Creek.[2] Despite a mini-boom in placer mining at Horsefly in the 1930s, times were tough. During the winters, men trapped to keep bread on the table. The Corner House, built for Mr. and Mrs. J.P. Patenaude in 1910, was bursting at the seams. Expanded to ten rooms, it became the social centre of Horsefly under the genial ownership of the large Campbell family. Twenty-year-old schoolteacher Mary Lane boarded there in the late 1930s, as did many teachers before and after her. She enjoyed the card games and all-night dances with music provided by the Patenaude orchestra; weekends were spent horseback riding or camping. The conviviality that carried residents of Horsefly and young teachers from Vancouver through the Depression continues on to this day.

With the Bullion Pit mine in full operation, tons of tailings were once again being dumped into the South Fork River only a few miles above Quesnel Forks, and the danger to the village and bridge returned. In 1935, 45 residents petitioned the provincial government to repair two piers and the southern approach to the South Fork bridge. Names on the petition included Heng Lung Co., merchants, Mrs. May Kim, and 12 Chinese miners. The work was completed in 1936, but the bridge did not last much longer. There were many close calls because of extremely high runoff. Eventually part of the bridge structure was torn away, and a large section of bank on either side of the north end of the bridge, including the site of the government agent's house, disappeared into the river. The bridge was never replaced; instead, the old road on the north side of the river, from Quesnel Forks to the Golden River Quesnelle dam, was improved for vehicle traffic.

In 1938-39, Quesnel Forks hosted one of the "make work" programs devised for unemployed men, the Dominion-Provincial Placer Mining Training School. The camp at Quesnel Forks was used for the third, or final session of the school. The young men who attended these schools were not the "down and out," but came from well-educated, middle-class homes in the Lower Mainland. Most returned to their homes once the program ended, rather than use their new-found skills.[3]

By 1935 many of the older residents of Quesnel Forks, including Luella MacKenzie and Allen Stephenson, had moved to the GRQ dam

176

The Quesnel Forks jail as it looked in 1935.
(Courtesy Margaret Henderson, Dave Falconer collection)

site, renamed Likely, ten miles up river from Quesnel Forks. Likely was named after a miner from New Brunswick, John Plato Likely. It thrived during the Cedar Creek rush in the 1920s and the Bullion Pit mining in the 1930s. The GRQ mining building that John Hobson converted into a resort, Casa Blanca, was further renovated by Tom Bailey and H.W. Speed, and renamed Quesnel Lake Lodge, but it burned down in 1953. When the little community came together to celebrate the coronation of King George in 1938, Luella MacKenzie, as the oldest pioneer, was given the honor of planting a ceremonial tree. Alas, it was not allowed to take root. The new, idealistic young school-teacher did not approve of Luella's sudden rise to fame, so during the night some friends dug up the tree and threw it in the river.

Mrs. May Kim and her son Wong Kuey Kim continued on at Quesnel Forks. Mrs. Kim died in Williams Lake in 1948. Wong Kuey Kim died in the 1950s, one of the last caretakers of Chinese history in the village. For many years some of the log houses still held Chinese artifacts. A resident of Beaver Valley who lived at Quesnel Forks for a short time, Pearl DeBolt, purchased the altar furnishings of the Chee Kung Tong House for $100 and donated them to the Barkerville historic site.[4] They are now on display at an interpretive building there.

177

In recent years, local residents have taken a great interest in preserving East Cariboo history. The Likely Cemetery Society and friends have voluntarily spent a large amount of time restoring the Quesnel Forks cemetery and the cemetery at Keithley Creek. With a grant from B.C. Heritage Trust, the old cabins at the Forks have been stabilized and inventoried, and a replica of a two-storey log house erected. At Cedar Creek Park, near where Aurora Jack Edwards staked his discovery claim in 1866, local residents have restored one of the ill-fated traction steam shovels that Hobson abandoned in 1907 at Spanish Lake. The growing display of refurbished mining equipment includes hydraulic monitors (water cannon) and a pipe roller and pipe riveter rescued from abandoned mining sites. The historic trail kept open by William Barry, and made into a wagon road by Joseph Hunter, along the Quesnel (South Fork) River, from Quesnel Forks to the site of the Golden River Quesnelle dam, is being cleared of slides and reopened for public use.

Farther afield, Gary and Lana Fox of Quesnel, with the support of the Friends of Barkerville, have plotted and supervised the reopening of the original 40-kilometre gold rush trail from Keithley Creek to Barkerville. The project took six years, with financial support from the B.C. Forest Service, Forest Renewal, and West Fraser Mills, Quesnel.

Wong Kuey Kim with Lim Sing's dog, 1941, Quesnel Forks.
(Courtesy Margaret Henderson, Dave Falconer collection)

As a reminder that nature rules supreme in East Cariboo, a large landslide blocked the South Fork River in May 1997. It came down at the same site as the slides of the late 1890s. Once again, the Quesnel River began cutting an opening around the mud and gravel. Until this latest event, the pilings from the old South Fork bridge and part of the decking had always remained visible. One could stand on the river bank, near where William and Jennie Stephenson once lived, and marvel at the engineering that had maintained a road down the bluffs, and a bridge across the South Fork River for almost a century. The river has buried these last remnants of the old crossing by covering them with gravel.

Glossary of Gold-Mining Terms

CORNISH WHEELS: Large wheels, introduced by Cornish miners, that operated on the principle of a mill wheel. Water to make the wheel turn was usually brought in by a flume.

FLOUR GOLD: Very fine gold that required mercury to trap it.

GOLD FLAKES: Visible gold, up to an eighth of an inch in size.

GLORY HOLE: A specific deposit of gold, within definite boundaries, rather than the more common "strike" or layer of gold laid down by an ancient stream.

LONG TOM: A long trough, from 12 to 20 feet, for washing gravel. It was built of wood with perforated metal on the bottom to allow the smallest pieces of sand and gold to drop through.

MINER'S INCH: A flow of water equal to 1.68 cubic feet per minute, or 100 cubic feet per hour.

PENSTOCKS: Large pipes for water. In the Cariboo the term was used for the small holding ponds and flumes delivering water to a hydraulic mining site.

QUARTZ REEFS: Large outcrops of quartz, sought by prospectors because they were often a matrix for gold.

ROCKER: A portable sluice with a rocker base, operated by one or two men.

SLUICE: A trough, usually hundreds of feet long, with riffles or other gold-catching devices in the bottom, used to wash gold-bearing gravel.

SLUM: A mixture of silt, clay and sand that, when saturated with water, slid into rivers, mining tunnels and shafts, stopping operations.

STAMP MILL: Machine driven, vertical shafts with iron stamps on the bottom, used to pulverize ore-bearing rocks.

WING DAM: A dam projecting out at an angle into a river, to divert the water into a sluice or away from a mining site.

FOOTNOTES

INTRODUCTION

1. For the myriad of Kootenay ghost towns see, Elsie G. Turnbull, *Ghost Towns and Drowned Towns of West Kootenay*; for information on Ulkatcho and Kluskus see Elizabeth Furniss, *Changing Ways, Southern Carrier History, 1793-1940*, pp. 4-5, and Sage Birchwater, *Ulkatcho: Stories of the Grease Trail*, pp. 4 and 13.

2. Keynote Address by Patricia N. Limerick, *History News*, p. 7.

3. Douglas to Moody, Correspondence Book, MS, BCA, pp. 48-49, quoted in William H. Trimble, *The Mining Advance Into the Inland Empire*, p. 182.

4. The late R.C. Harris introduced me to an early Hudson's Bay Company map by Samuel Black showing the *"siffleur monts."* There are approximately 300 Mountain caribou in the Cariboo Mountains, and 1,500 Woodland caribou in the Itcha-Ilgachuz region of the Chilcotin. Advertisement by Cariboo Communities Coalition, *The Williams Lake Tribune*, November 4, 1997, p. 2.

5. L.C. Struik, *The Ancient Western North American Margin*, p. 8; *Structural Geology of the Cariboo Gold Mining District, East-Central British Columbia*, pp. 64-66.

6. John J. Clague, "Quarternary stratigraphy and history, Williams Lake, British Columbia," pp. 147-158.

7. John J. Clague, *Placer gold in the Cariboo district, British Columbia, Current Research*, Part E, Geological Survey of Canada, Paper 89-IE (1989), pp. 243-250; R.W. Boyle, *The Geochemistry of Gold and Its Deposits*, pp. 358-359.

8. For a superb treatment of a young man's correspondence during the California Gold Rush, see J.S. Holliday, *The World Rushed In*.

9. David R. Williams, *"The Man for a New Country"*, p. 150.

10. David R. Williams, *"The Man for a New Country"*, p. 98; Great Britain, Colonial Office, *Papers*, Despatch #4, June 15, 1858; and GR1486, Despatch #81, August 24, 1860, Microfilm Reel B1427. See *British Colonist*, September 15, 1860, p. 3, for

report on a native woman successfully laying a charge against Brown, a whiskey seller in Victoria.

11. Alexander Caulfield Anderson, in his *Handbook to the Gold Regions of Fraser's and Thompson's Rivers*, advised the miners to supply the Chief of the Natives at Similkameen Forks with a little tobacco that he could "smoke with his followers." Appendix, Part I, Great Britain, *Papers*.

12. Great Britain, *Papers*, Part 1, Despatch #4, June 15, 1858. During the mining season in 1858, a Texan, Captain Charles Rouse, led a contingent of miners up the Fraser River from Yale. They killed natives and destroyed five Indian villages. Daniel P. Marshall, "Rickard Revisited: Native 'Participation' in the Gold Discoveries of British Columbia," p. 96.

13. Alexander Begg, *History of British Columbia*, p. 283.

14. Colonial Secretary, correspondence outward, Douglas to Ball, October 10, 1859, Microfilm Reel B2651.

15. Anderson had been under observation by Magistrate Whannel at Yale, who wrote to warn Assistant Gold Commissioner Thomas Elwyn at Lillooet. After the shooting incident on Ferguson Bar, Anderson made his way to Point Roberts where he killed a man, supposedly in self defense. He was found not guilty, and disappeared from public records. *British Colonist*, December 11, 1860, p. 2.

16. "Welsh Miners in British Columbia," *B.C. Historical Quarterly* CXXI (1), p. 65.

17. Colonial correspondence, Elwyn, Letter F524/3, BCA.

18. Great Britain, *Papers*, Part IV, Despatch #13.

19. Colonial correspondence, H.M.Ball, Letter F95/22, July, 1860, BCA, cited in Averill Groenveld-Meuer, "Manning the Fraser River."

20. British Columbia, Colonial Despatches, Microfilm Reel B1427. See also Trimble, *Mining Advance*, pp. 154-155.

21. Trimble, *Mining Advance*, p. 154.

22. Colonial correspondence, Douglas Letterbook, BCA.

23. GR1486, Douglas to Newcastle, March 22, 1860, Microfilm Reel 1426; Margaret A. Ormsby, "Some Irish Figures in Colonial Days," pp. 61-82. One assistant gold commissioner not mentioned, John Boles Gaggin, briefly served at Quesnelmouth in 1864.

CHAPTER ONE: 1859

1. *British Colonist*, August 1, 1859, p. 3.

2. Pauline Jacobson, *City of the Golden Fifties*, pp. 6-7. Barry and Patten's saloon was located in the Brannan Building on Montgomery Street, San Francisco.

3. Californian filibusters, or military adventurers, were easy to recruit for General Walker's ill-fated expeditions to Nicaragua from the group of ex-miners that drifted into San Francisco. Walker was an adventurer, not a military man, but gained his title as "generalissimo" when attempting to take over Nicaragua. See Theodore H. Hittell, *History of California*, pp. 727-814. Three filibusters have been identified amongst the Cariboo miners: Moses Anderson, who shot a young native boy at the mouth of the Quesnel River in 1859, Robert Hamilton Smith, owner of the stopping house at Little Lake, and his friend Donald Monroe. Monroe died of

starvation near Barkerville when he became lost; Colonial correspondence, Begbie, F142e/7a, June 24, 1862.

4. Bishop Hills, Diary, Add MSS 1526. Hills met a young married woman at Hills Bar who was very lonely. The only other woman near Yale was not respectable. Hills used Johanna's name when he described their meeting at Williams Creek in August 1862.

5. *British Colonist*, August 1, 1859, p. 3.

6. *Ibid.*, p. 1.

7. Stuart S. Holland, *Placer Gold Production of British Columbia*, p. 9.

8. James May joined the rush to Omineca in 1873. He remained in the Omineca region for the rest of his life, spending his last years at Hazelton. Ralph Hall, *Pioneer Goldseekers of the Omineca*, pp. 40-53, and Walkem, *Stories*, pp. 206-207.

9. Nemiah T. Smith, Dancing Bill's partner, identifies him as Thomas Latham, a native of Rhode Island. Smith claimed they mined together during the fall and winter of 1859. Smith next prospected on Nelson and Williams creeks where he was given the name "Black Jack." Smith later met up with Latham in the Cassiar district. Latham died in the Cassiar in 1880. *British Colonist*, November 16, 1880, and November 17, 1880. See also Hall, *Pioneer Goldseekers,* p. 86; and Herman Francis Reinhart, *The Golden Frontier*, pp. 28, 29, 30, 33, 34-35, 118, 127.

10. Colonial correspondence, Nind, F1255/1, November 9, 1860; advertisement for sale of R.H. Smith's stopping house, *British Colonist*, November 27, 1863, p. 2.

11. Colonial correspondence, Elwyn, F524/9, September 20, 1859, BCA.

12. Colonial correspondence, Elwyn, F525/17, August 3, 1862, BCA.

13. Jean Murray Cole, *Exile in the Wilderness*, p. 231.

14. Colonial correspondence, Begbie, 1426/17, November 7, 1859, BCA. James Barry sold his saloon in January 1873 to W.R. McDonald (*Cariboo Sentinel*, January 11, 1873, p. 3). He was awarded the contract to paint the Alexandria Suspension Bridge in September 1871. (Colonial correspondence, Barry, F1306/1, BCA.)

CHAPTER TWO: 1860

1. Colonial correspondence, Begbie, F142d/11, April 1861, BCA.

2. *British Colonist*, July 14, 1860, p. 1.

3. Ballou sold out to Dietz and Nelson in November 1862, and Barnard took over the mail route for the Cariboo. *British Columbian*, November 22, 1862, p. 2,

4. Mining Statistics for the Year 1877, *B.C. Sessional Papers*, p. 389; Canada *Census*, 1881.

5. Great Britain, *Papers*, #84, August 28, 1860.

6. *Oregon Statesman*, February 14, 1860, p. 1; typescript of Joel Palmer's Pocket Diary for 1860, Oregon Historical Society, Portland, Oregon.

7. *Ibid.*

8. *Ibid.*; Fort Alexandria Letterbook, Folio 5/b/1, 1860-1865, p. 2, John Saunders to the Board of Management, Victoria, October 13, 1860. HBC Archives.

9. Typescript, Palmer's Diary, 1860, OHS.

10. *British Colonist,* July 7, 1860, p. 2.

11. *British Colonist*, September 11, 1860, p. 3.

12. *Ibid.*
13. Colonial correspondence, Begbie, F142d/11, April 1861, BCA; David R. Williams, *"The Man for a New Country,"* pp. 48-49.
14. Colonial correspondence, Nind, F1255/1, November 9, 1860, BCA.
15. Colonial correspondence, Nind, F1254/9, November 11, 1860, BCA.
16. *Ibid.*; see also GR216, Vol. 9, Letterbook, BCA.
17. Colonial correspondence, Nind, F1255/1, November 9, 1860, BCA.
18. *British Colonist*, January 23, 1861, p. 1.
19. *British Colonist*, December 25, 1860, p. 1.
20. *Province*, December 21, 1895.

CHAPTER THREE: 1861
1. Colonial correspondence, Nind, F1255/3, March 18, 1861, BCA.
2. *Ibid.*, March 27, 1861, BCA.
3. *Ibid.*
4. *Ibid.*
5. *Ibid.*; *British Colonist*, May 13, 1861, p. 3.
6. *Ibid.*, June 13, 1861, p. 3. Charles Blondin was a famous French acrobat and tightrope walker at that time.
7. *British Columbian*, June 13, 1861, p. 3.
8. Great Britain, *Papers*, Part IV, p. 53; Palmer diary, OHS.
9. *British Colonist*, August 12, 1861, p. 3; August 12, 1861, p. 3.
10. Colonial correspondence, O'Reilly, F1278/20, March 27, 1860, BCA. Nind's contribution of $20 is noted on a loose piece of paper, June 20, 1860.
11. Colonial correspondence, Moody, F963L, Lease of dam site, July 18, 1861.
12. Colonial correspondence, Nind, F1256/11, November 20, 1863.
13. GR216, Vol. 30, p. 39.
14. Colonial correspondence, Nind, December 11, 1861, F1255/34; see also correspondence from Elwyn, Gompertz and Fitzstubbs, June 6,1862, F525/9, BCA.
15. Kay Cronin, *Cross in the Wilderness*, p. 92.
16. *British Colonist*, July 29, 1861, p. 3.
17. GR216, Vol. 30, pp. 45 and 49, BCA.
18. *British Colonist*, August 2, 1861, p. 3.
19. John Saunders to P.H. Nind, April 28, 1861, Fort Alexandria Letterbook, B5/b/1, HBC Archives.
20. Fort Alexandria Letterbook, B5/b/1, HBC Archives.
21. *British Columbian*, August 22, 1861, p. 2.
22. *Ibid.*, July 11, 1861, p. 2.
23. Great Britain, *Papers*, Despatch #21, July, 1861, BCA.
24. *British Columbian*, August 28, 1861, p. 3.
25. Colonial correspondence, Nind, F1255/29, BCA.
26. Holland, *Placer Gold Production*, p. 52.
27. *British Columbian*, July 4, 1861, p. 2; *B.C. Sessional Papers*, 1903, Annual Report, Minister of Mines, p. H90.
28. A.J. Splawn, *KA-MI-AKIN, Last Hero of the Yakimas,* p. 167.

29. Colonial correspondence, Nind, F1255/14, May 6, 1861; Colonial correspondence outward, June 10, 1861; and GR1440, 109/82, P. O'Reilly to Lands and Works, January 24, 1882, BCA.
30. GR1486, September 16, 1861, [10505, CO 60/11] p. 34, BCA.
31. *Ibid.*
32. David R. Williams, "The Administration of Criminal and Civil Justice in the Mining Camps ...," p. 225; Nancy Parker, "Swift Justice and the Decline of the Criminal Trial Jury ...," p. 178.
33. Colonial correspondence, O'Reilly, November 15, 1861, F1280, BCA.
34. Dorothy Blakey Smith, "The Journal of Arthur Thomas Bushby," p. 144.
35. Colonial correspondence, Elwyn, F525/19, August 22, 1862, BCA.
36. Great Britain, *Papers*, Part IV, Despatch #24, October 24, 1861, BCA.
37. Colonial correspondence, Moody, F929/10, BCA.

CHAPTER FOUR: 1862
1. *British Colonist*, July 22, 1862, p. 3. The writer, S.G., remains anonymous.
2. Walkem, *Stories*, pp. 138-141.
3. *British Colonist*, January 9, 1862, p. 3, and April 14, 1862, p. 3.
4. *British Columbian*, June 11, 1862. In a later article in the *Columbian*, July 2, 1862, Millbury was made out to be a braggart.
5. Colonial correspondence, Elwyn, June 15, 1862, F525/10, BCA.
6. *Ibid.*
7. Bogart letter F775, Misc. Collection 1862, #13, Archives of Ontario. Information on Edward White supplied by United Church Archives, Victoria University, University of Toronto. See also, G.P.V. and Helen Akrigg, *British Columbia Chronicles,* pp. 244-245.
8. *British Colonist*, July 22, 1862, p. 3.
9. Colonial correspondence, O'Reilly, June 28, 1862, BCA.
10. Colonial correspondence, Elwyn, August 2, 1862, F525/16, BCA.
11. *British Columbian,* August 13, 1862, p. 1.
12. *Ibid.*
13. Colonial correspondence, Elwyn, August 2, 1862, F525/16, BCA.
14. *British Columbian*, October 4, 1861, p. 3.
15. *British Colonist*, July 23, 1862, p. 3, and January 30, 1863, p. 3.

CHAPTER FIVE: 1863-1870 — STAYING ON
1. Add MSS 2604, BCA.
2. Add MSS 2533, BCA.
3. *British Colonist*, February 18, 1863, p. 3.
4. British Columbia Supreme Court, Notes of Proceedings.
5. *Ibid.*
6. Colonial correspondence, Nind, F1256, letters 2 to10, BCA.
7. Nind to O'Reilly, October 28, 1866; Add MSS 412, BCA.
8. GR216, Vol. 77, p. 221, BCA.
9. Vertical file, BCA.

10. *Ibid.*
11. *Ibid.*, Vital Statistics, BCA.
12. *B.C. Sessional Papers,* 1903, Annual Report, Minister of Mines, p. H91.
13. Barkerville Correspondence, Microfilm Reel IM175, B12/b/1, HBC Archives.
14. Diary of Robert M. Scott, Add MSS 2604, BCA.
15. *Cariboo Sentinel,* March 13, 1873, p. 2.
16. John Roberts, "The Travails and Travels of a Pioneer."
17. *Cariboo Sentinel,* April/May 1867.
18. *Cariboo Sentinel,* September 2, 1867, p. 3.
19. GR216, Vol. II, Brew, September 22, 1868, BCA.
20. *Ibid.*

CHAPTER SIX: 1870-1880 — THE CHINESE TAKE OVER
1. Sessional Papers, 1877, Report of Minister of Mines, p. 420.
2. David Chuenyan Lai, "Home County and Clan Origins of Overseas Chinese in Canada in the Early 1880's," *B.C. Studies,* XXVII, Autumn 1975, pp. 3-27.
3. Parker, "The Decline of the Criminal Trial Jury," p. 178.
4. Information provided in introduction to Vital Statistics, BCA.
5. *Cariboo Sentinel,* June 18, 1870. p. 3.
6. GR216, Vol. I, Letter 116, Barry to Ball, November 23, 1870, BCA.
7. GR216, Vol. I, Letter 125, Chinese miners to Ball, December 9, 1870, BCA.
8. GR216, Vol. I, Letter 290, Hare to Ball, October 25, 1871, BCA.
9. GR216, Vol. I, Letter 376, Hare to Ball, June 26, 1872, BCA.
10. GR216, Vol. II, Letter 44, Hare to Ball, October 11, 1872, BCA; E. Gurnay built the North Fork bridge with a grant of $300 from the provincial government. *B.C. Sessional Papers* 1873/74, Report of Public Works, pp. 17 and 36.
11. GR1440, Letter 2041/74, BCA.
12. *Daily Colonist,* May 15, 1873, p. 3.
13. GR216, Vol. III, Letter 9, Hare to Bowron, June 18, 1873, BCA.
14. GR216, Vol. III, Letter 131, December 6, 1873, Hare to Ball, BCA.
15. GR216, Vol. IV, Letter 183, July 1, 1874, Hare to Bowron, BCA.
16. GR216, Vol. III, Letter 197, July 30, 1874, Hare to Ball, BCA.
17. GR216, Vol. III, Letter 210, September 8, 1874, Hare to Bowron, BCA.
18. *Cariboo Sentinel,* September 13, 1873, p. 3, and January 30, 1875, p. 3; GR526, Box 9, Letter 126/74; and Box 11, 138/75, BCA.
19. GR1440, Letter 2253, July 14, 1875, Microfilm Reel B2657, BCA.
20. *Cariboo Sentinel,* July 3, 1875, p. 3.
21. *B.C. Sessional Papers,* 1876, Report of Minister of Mines, p. 612.
22. *B.C. Sessional Papers,* 1877, Report of Minister of Mines, p. 420.
23. GR216, Vol. II, letter October 3, 1876, BCA; *Daily Colonist,* December 29, 1876.

CHAPTER SEVEN: A NEW ERA
1. GR216, Vol. IV, Part 2/229, BCA.
2. Dr. Margaret A. Ormsby examined the contribution made by Anglo-Irish administrators, in "Some Irish Figures in Colonial Days," pp. 61-82.

3. Ussher was shot by Archie McLean. See Mel Rothenburger, *'We've Killed Johnny Ussher!'* (Vancouver: Mitchell Press, 1973), pp. 40-41.

4. Quesnel Old Age Pensioners', *A Tribute to the Past*, pp. 81-82.

5. GR216, Vol. IV, Part 1/182, BCA.

6. Walkem had left the finances so badly managed that the Bank of British Columbia refused further credit to the government.

7. Margaret A. Ormsby, "Andrew Charles Elliott," pp. 299-301.

8. GR525, Box 19/323, BCA.

9. Provincial Archives of New Brunswick, Microfilm Reel F25; *Cariboo Sentinel*, April 29, 1871, p. 3.

10. *Colonist*, November 21, 1873, p. 3.

11. W.A. Johnston at Quesnel supervised roads in the Cariboo area until replaced by Joseph St. Laurent. GR 1440, letter 473/77, BCA.

12. GR868, Box 3, 1878/78 and 1879/78, BCA.

13. *B.C. Directory*, 1882-1883; GR55, Boxes 1, 5, 29, BCA.

14. GR216, Vol. III, 73, BCA.

15. GR216, Vol. III, 411, BCA.

16. GR1440, Microfilm Reel B2664, letter 730/80, BCA.

17. GR216, Vol. IV, Part 1/84, BCA.

18. GR216, Vol. IV, Part 2/229, BCA.

19. GR526, Box 24, Letter 7/84, BCA; Chinese Translation Contract-Phase 1, August 25 to September 8, 1988, prepared by David Chuenyan Lai for Barkerville Historic Town.

20. Timothy J. Stanley, " 'Chinamen, Wherever We Go'," p. 488.

21. Translation of posters of new members of the Chee Kung Tong, presumed to be from Quesnel Forks, made by Mavis Leung, Victoria. Posters catalogued as 980.414.1-.12, Archives, Barkerville Historic Town. Dr. David Chuenyan Lai has catalogued part of the inventory of Chinese material at the Barkerville Archives.

22. Harry Con, *From China to Canada*, pp. 31-32.

23. *Ibid*.

24. Barkerville Archives, Documents 980.414.1-11; 980.416.l; "Translation and Analysis of the Chee Kung Tong Material," David Chuenyan Lai, July 1989 (unpublished manuscript).

25. Consultation with Mavis Leung, formerly of Hong Kong, January 1999.

26. Timothy J. Stanley, 'Chinamen Wherever We Go,' p. 488.

27. *B.C. Sessional Papers*, 1885, "Chinese Regulation Act, 1884."

28. *Canada Parliament, Sessional Papers*, Vol. 18, No. 11, 1885.

29. File 980 415.1-4, Barkerville Archives, translated by Bil-Nor Cafe; and GR55, Box 27, letter from Stuart Henderson, solicitor for the Fook Sang Lung Co., to Superintendent of Police, June 8, 1899, BCA.

30 Canada, *Census*, 1901.

31. Conversation with Mrs. June Wall, granddaughter of May Kim, December 1998. The children were: Wong Young, born 1891, Wong Ying, born 1892, Wong Sue, born 1893, Wong Kuey Kim, born 1895, Wong Poo, born 1898, Wong King, born 1901, Wong Kim, born 1902, Wong Sin, born 1906, and Wong Ting, born

1911. 1901 Canada *Census*, and Likely-Quesnel Forks Tour Kit prepared for British Columbia Historical Federation, April 1996.

32. GR526, Box 27/594, BCA.
33. GR216, Box 5/269, BCA.
34. *B.C. Sessional Papers*, 1897, Petition, p. li.
35. GR216, Vol. V/368, BCA.

CHAPTER EIGHT: THE ROARING '90S

1. GR1440, Microfilm Reel 2714, letter 3767/98, BCA.
2. *B.C. Sessional Papers*, 1891, Mining Report.
3. GR868, Box 3, Letter 784/79, BCA.
4. *British Columbia Law Reports*, Vol. II, pp. 365-413.
5. *B.C. Sessional Papers*, 1898, Mining Report, p. 487.
6. Information provided by G.T. Markley, California, obtained from *History of Placer County, California* (1882), p. 216.
7. *B.C. Sessional Papers*, 1894/95, Public Accounts, July 1, 1892-June 30, 1893, pp. 23 and 119; see also pp. 709-717.
8. *The Mining Record*, Vol. VII, No. 4, April, 1900, pp. 119 and 120.
9. Some of the doctors were: 1896, Dr. Underhill; 1897, Dr. Herald; 1901-1904, Dr. Walter A. Wilkins; 1905, Dr. McKechnie.
10. Information gathered from various Bullion mine journals, BCA.
11. *Ashcroft Journal*, November 26, 1898, p. 1.
12. *B.C. Statutes*, Chapter 19, 1881, 1883; GR529, letter 283/82, Hunter to Minister of Mines, September 19, 1882, BCA.
13. GR1440, Lands and Works, Correspondence In, Letter 569, 1878, BCA, concerning an attempt to purchase land in the Bonaparte Valley and Scotty Creek areas. Hunter wanted to hold property in conjunction with his father-in-law, John Robson, while Dupont wanted property with I.W. Powell.
14. *The Inland Sentinel*, April 2, 1892, p. 1.
15. GR216, Vol. VI, Part 2/512, BCA.
16. Richard Wright, *Quesnelle Forks,* pp. 52-53.
17. GR1440, Microfilm Reel 2700, letter 2234/95, BCA.
18. *Ibid.*, Letter 2528/95 and *B.C. Sessional Papers*, 1898, p. 1039.
19. GR1440, Microfilm Reel 2714, 3767/98, BCA.
20. GR55, Box 16, Stephenson to Hussey, August 13, 1897, BCA.
21. *Ibid.*
22. GR1676, Vol. II, letter 150, BCA.
23. GR55, Vol. 7, Stephenson to Hussey, May 17, 1895, BCA.
24. GR429, Letter 3851/99, BCA.
25. GR55, Box 8, BCA. Within a short time after his arrival in Quesnelmouth, Anderson married Joseph St. Laurent's daughter, Luella. Quesnel Old Age Pensioners', *A Tribute to the Past*, p. 130.
26. GR55, Box 8, Hussey to Stephenson, August 23, 1895, BCA.
27. GR55, Box 8, Stephenson to Hussey, November 29, 1895, BCA.
28. GR55, Box 14, Stephenson to Hussey, March 19, 1897, BCA.

29. Conversation with Margaret Murray Henderson, 1994; Will of Luella MacKenzie, GR245, File 35/41; Luella died in the Provincial Insane Asylum in December 1940, age 76. GR2880/File 18,177, BCA.

30. GR55, Box 2; GR2880, File 502, BCA.

31. GR55, Box 7, Stephenson to Hussey, May 7, 1896, BCA.

32. GR526, 277/98, BCA.

33. GR55, Box 31, BCA.

34. *Ashcroft Journal*, February 18, 1899, p. 1.

35. GR55, Box 30, Bain to Hussey, August 25, 1899, BCA.

36. *Ashcroft Journal*, October 30, 1897, p. 1.

37. J.H.M. Salmon, *A History of Gold Mining in New Zealand*, pp. 233-236. Gold dredging in California is well illustrated in Wagner, *Gold Mines*, pp. 39-53.

38. GR1440, Microfilm Reel 2715, letter 6324, BCA.

39. *Ibid.*

40. GR1330, letter 861/99. Heath died in December 1900. GR1330, Box 54, letter 2427, BCA.

41. GR540, letter 92/100, BCA.

42. GR1330, letters 256/1900 and 413/1900, BCA.

CHAPTER NINE: A NEW CENTURY

1. GR55, Box 64, BCA.

2. A.H.A. Robinson, *Gold In Canada*, see Tables XIII and XIV, pp. 38 and 39.

3. GR2016, Legislative Assembly, Clerk of the House, Microfilm Reel B1397. Papers and documents referring to the proposed expenditure of $10,600 for the protection of the Quesnel River Bank at the Forks, tabled in the Legislature, May 3, 1901.

4. GR55, Box 71, death of Martin Anderson; GR55, Box 72, death of Chinese miner, BCA.

5. *Ashcroft Journal*, June 15, 1907, p. 4.

6. GR429, Box 10, Papers 2992, BCA; *B.C. Sessional Papers*, 1903, p. G11; *B.C. Sessional Papers*, 1906, pp. H5-6.

7. *Ashcroft Journal*, July 26, 1902, p. l; *B.C. Sessional Papers*, 1902.

8. Barman, *West Beyond the West*, Table 20, "Gross Value of Products Mined in British Columbia, 1860-1985"; *British Colonist*, January 17, 1903, pp. 1 and 2, and March 3, 1903, p. 8.

9. *B.C. Directory*, 1905.

10. *Ashcroft Journal*, March 10 and June 16, 1906, p. 1.

11. Both shovels are on display, one at Cedar Point Park, near Likely, and the other at Quesnel. The bucket and digging teeth of the steam-powered shovel at Cedar Point Park are in excellent condition. The entire machine has been preserved by local craftsmen, under the supervision of Clint Coleman, as part of a hydraulic mining display. Other equipment includes two hydraulic mine monitors, one pipe roller, one pipe riveter, and one large water pump. (Information sheet, Likely Chamber of Commerce Tourist Information Centre, Likely, prepared by D.G. Falconer.)

12. Harvey O'Connor, *The Guggenheims*, pp. 190-200; *Ashcroft Journal*, June 29 and

July 20, 1907; Lewis Green, *The Gold Hustlers*, pp. 109-120, 165.

13. Vital Statistics, BCA.

14. "Cariboo Claims go to Mr. Ward," *British Colonist*, October 23, 1919, p. 2; British Columbia Statutes, 1920, Chapter ll, Cariboo Hydraulic Mining Company (Amendment); *Ashcroft Journal*, January 27, 1923, p. 1.

15. *B.C.Sessional Papers*, 1914, Mining Report, pp. 61-66.

16. Record Group 13, Volume 1452, file 387a, NAC.

17. GR55, Box 38, Burr to Hussey, July 16, 1907, BCA.

18. GR55, Box 64, BCA.

19. GR1330, Microfilm Reel B4544, Stephenson to Provincial Secretary, January 17, 1907, BCA. Huertas was admitted to the Provincial Home in June, 1907. GR624, Box 3, BCA.

20. GR2880, File 2276, BCA. After leaving Keithley Creek, Edwards spent some time at the St. Alice Hotel, Harrison Hot Springs, and was transferred from the Vancouver General Hospital to the Public Hospital for the Insane in October 1908. He died January 12, 1910, from senile dementia. His estate held a net amount of $2,879.35, for which there was no next of kin.

21. GR1330, Box 92, letter 1989, and Box 93, letter 2119, BCA.

22. Terry M. Parssinen, *Secret Passions, Secret Remedies: Narcotic Drugs in British Society 1820-1930* (Philadelphia: Institute for the Study of Human Issues, 1983), pp. 34-35 and 230.

23. David T. Courtwright, *Dark Paradise*, pp. 36, 48-51.

24. GR1330, 748/1905, BCA.

25. Add MSS 676, Box 6, BCA.

26. *B.C. Sessional Papers*, 1914; Vital Statistics death certificates.

EPILOGUE

1. A.H.A. Robinson, *Gold in Canada*, p. 38.

2. *B.C. Sessional Papers*, 1938, Report of the Minister of Mines, p. C30.

3. Lesley Cooper, "Dominion-Provincial Placer Mining Training School, Quesnel Forks, 1938-1939," *Likely Cemetery Society Newsletter*, 1993-94, unpaginated.

4. Irene Stangoe, *Cariboo-Chilcotin: Pioneer People and Places*, p. 48.

BIBLIOGRAPHY

PUBLISHED SOURCES

Akrigg, G.P.V. and Helen. *British Columbia Chronicles, 1847-1871*. Vancouver: Discovery Press, 1977.

Bancroft, Hubert Howe. *History of British Columbia, 1792-1887*. San Francisco: History Company, 1887.

Barman, Jean. *The West Beyond the West: A History of British Columbia*. Toronto: University of Toronto Press, 1991.

Beeson, Edith, ed. *Dunlevey, From the diaries of Alex P. McInnes*. Lillooet: Lillooet Publishers Ltd., 1971.

Begg, Alexander. *History of British Columbia*. Toronto: William Briggs, 1894.

Berton, Pierre. *The National Dream*. Toronto: McClelland and Stewart Limited, 1970.

Birchwater, Sage. *Ulkatcho: Stories of the Grease Trail*. Quesnel: Spartan Printing, 1993.

Boyle, R.W. *The Geochemistry of Gold and Its Deposits*. Bulletin 280. Ottawa: Geological Survey of Canada, 1979.

British Columbia, Department of Mines. *Notes on Placer-Mining in British Columbia*. Victoria: King's Printer, 1938.

British Columbia Law Reports. Victoria: Province Publishing Company, 1895.

British Columbia. Ministry of Energy, Mines and Petroleum Resources. *Geology of the Central Quesnel Belt, British Columbia*. Open File 1990-31. Victoria, 1990.

British Columbia. Ministry of Forests. *Biogeoclimatic Zones of British Columbia*. Map. Victoria, 1988.

British Columbia. *Colonial Despatches, British Columbia*; Vancouver Island.

British Columbia, *Sessional Papers*.

Brooks, Julian. "Joseph Hunter: Forgotten Builder of British Columbia," *B.C. Historical News*, Vol. 28, 2 (Spring 1995): pp. 27-31.

Canada. *Census*, 1881, 1891, 1901.

Canada. *Geological Survey Report Vol. 3, Part 4, 1887-88.* Maps of the Principal Auriferous Creeks of the Cariboo Mining District, British Columbia, Surveyed and Drawn by Amos Bowman, Mining Engineer. Ottawa: Geological Survey of Canada, 1895.

Cheadle, Walter B. *Cheadle's Journal of a Trip Across Canada, 1862-63.* Edmonton: M.G. Hurtig, Ltd., 1971.

Chen, Yong. "The Internal Origins of Chinese Emigration to California Reconsidered," *Western Historical Quarterly* XXVIII, 4 (Winter 1997): pp. 521-546.

Clague, J.J. *Quarternary Stratigraphy and History of Quesnel and Cariboo River Valleys, British Columbia: Implications for Placer Gold Exploration.* Paper 91-1A. Ottawa: Geological Survey of Canada, 1991.

_____. "Quarternary stratigraphy and history, Williams Lake, British Columbia," *Canadian Journal of Earth Sciences,* Vol. 24, (1987): pp. 147-158.

Cole, Jean Murray. *Exile in the Wilderness.* Don Mills: Burns & McEachern Limited, 1979.

Con, Harry, et al. *From China to Canada; A History of the Chinese Communities in Canada.* Toronto: McClelland and Stewart Limited, 1982.

Courtwright, David T. *Dark Paradise: Opiate Addiction in America before 1940.* Cambridge: Harvard University Press, 1982.

Cronin, Kay. *Cross in the Wilderness.* Vancouver: Mitchell Press Limited, 1960.

Davis, John H. *The Guggenheims, An American Epic.* New York: William Morrow and Company, Inc., 1978.

DeSmet, Pierre J. *Western Missions and Missionaries.* New York: James B. Kirker, 1863.

Duthie, D. Wallace. *A Bishop in the Rough.* London: Smith Elder & Co., 1909.

Elliott, Gordon R. *Barkerville, Quesnel & the Cariboo Gold Rush.* Vancouver: Douglas & McIntyre, Ltd., 1978.

Fields, Albert E. *Fields of Endeavour.* Kelowna: Self published, 1993.

Forbes, Molly. *Lac La Hache: Historical Notes on the Early Settlers.* Quesnel: Big Country Printers, undated.

Furniss, Elizabeth. *Changing Ways: Southern Carrier History, 1793-1940.* Quesnel: Spartan Printing & Advertising Ltd., 1993.

Great Britain, Colonial Office. *Papers Relating to the Affairs of British Columbia.* London: G.E. Eyre and W. Spottiswoode, 1859-62.

Green, Lewis. *The Gold Hustlers.* Anchorage: Alaska Northwest Publishing Company, 1977.

Hall, Ralph. *Pioneer Goldseekers of the Omineca.* Victoria: Morriss Publishing, 1994.

Hardwick, F.C., ed. *East Meets West: The Chinese in Canada,* Canadian Culture Series No. 5. Vancouver: Tantalus Research Limited, 1975.

Hayden, Brian. *A Complex Culture of the British Columbia Plateau.* Vancouver: University of British Columbia Press, 1992.

Higgins, D.W. *The Mystic Spring.* Toronto: William Briggs, 1904.

Hittell, Theodore H. *History of California,* Vol. III. San Francisco: N.J. Stone & Company, 1898.

Holland, Stuart S. *Placer Gold Production of British Columbia.* Bulletin No. 28, British

Columbia Department of Mines. Victoria: Queen's Printer 1987. (Reprint of 1950 edition.)

Holliday, J.S. *The World Rushed In*. New York: Simon and Schuster, 1981.

Hong, W.M. *...And So...That's How It Happened*. Quesnel: Spartan Printing, 1978.

Howay, F.W. *British Columbia, From the Earliest Times to the Present*. Vol. II. Vancouver: The S.J. Clarke Publishing Company, 1914.

Jacobson, Pauline. *City of the Golden Fifties*. Berkeley: University of California Press, 1941.

Kelley, Robert. *Battling the Inland Sea*. Berkeley: University of California Press, 1989.

_____. "Forgotten Giant: The Hydraulic Gold Mining Industry in California," *Pacific Historical Review*, 23, (1954): pp. 343-356.

Lai, David Chuenyan. "Classification and Analysis of Chinese Documents and Field Surveys, July 1990." Prepared for Friends of Barkerville, Barkerville, B.C.

_____. *The Forbidden City Within Victoria*. Victoria: Orca Book Publishers, 1991.

_____. "Shipment of Bones to China." *Likely Cemetery Society Newsletter*, 1991.

Levson, Victor M. and Giles, Timothy R. *Geology of Tertiary and Quaternary Gold-Bearing Placers in the Cariboo Region*. Bulletin 89, Geological Survey Branch. Victoria: Ministry of Energy, Mines and Petroleum Resources, 1993.

Limerick, Patricia Nelson. "Keynote Address," AASLH, *History News*, Vol. 51, 1 (Winter 1996): p. 7.

Loo, Tina. *Making Law and Order*. Toronto: University of Toronto Press, 1994.

Macdonald, Norbert. "The Canadian Pacific Railway and Vancouver's Development to 1900," *B.C. Studies*, 35 (Autumn 1977): pp. 3-35.

Marshall, Daniel P. "Rickard Revisited: Native 'Participation' in the Gold Discoveries of British Columbia," *Native Studies Review* II, No. 1 (1996): p. 96.

May, Robin. *The Gold Rushes*. Melbourne: The Macmillan Company of Australia, 1970.

Melvin, George H. *The Post Offices of British Columbia*. Vernon: Privately Published, 1972.

Napier, R. Ross. "Government Agencies of British Columbia," *The 6th Report of the Okanagan Historical Society*. Vancouver: Wrigley Printing Co. Ltd. 1936: pp. 214-218.

O'Donnell, Terence. *An Arrow in the Earth*. Portland: Oregon Historical Society Press, 1991.

O'Connor, Harvey. *The Guggenheims: The Making of an American Dynasty*. New York: Covici Friede Publishers, 1937.

Ormsby, Margaret A. *British Columbia: a History*. Toronto: The Macmillans in Canada, 1958.

_____. "Andrew Charles Elliott," *Dictionary of Canadian Biography* XI. Toronto: University of Toronto Press, 1982: pp. 299-301.

_____. "Some Irish Figures in Colonial Days." *B.C Historical Quarterly* 14 (1950): pp. 61-82.

Palmer, Joel. "Pocket Diary," Transcript. Oregon Historical Society, Portland.

Parker, Nancy. "Swift Justice and the Decline of the Criminal Trial Jury: The Dynamics of Law and Authority in Victoria, B.C., 1858-1905," In *Essays in the*

History of Canadian Law, II. Eds. Hamar Foster and John McLaren. Toronto: University of Toronto Press, 1981.

Patenaude, Branwen C. *Trails to Gold*. Victoria: Horsdal & Schubart Publishers Ltd., 1995.

Paul, Rodman W. *California Gold*. Cambridge: Harvard University Press, 1947.

Petralia, Joseph. *Gold! Gold! A Beginner's Handbook: How to Prospect for Gold*. Vancouver: Hancock House Publishers Ltd., 1980.

Preston, Richard Arthur, ed. *For Friends at Home; A Scottish Emigrant's Letters from Canada, California and the Cariboo 1844-1864*. Kingston: McGill-Queen's University Press, 1974.

Quesnel Old Age Pensioners' Organization. *A Tribute to the Past*. Quesnel: Privately published, 1985.

Reinhart, Herman Francis. *The Golden Frontier*. Austin: University of Texas Press, 1962.

Roberts, John. "The Travails and Travels of a Pioneer," *Williams Lake Advocate*, October 20, 1993: p. 10.

Robin, Martin. *The Rush For Spoils*. Toronto: McClelland and Stewart Limited, 1972.

Robinson, A.H.A. *Gold in Canada 1935*. Ottawa: Department of Mines, 1935.

Roy, Patricia. *A White Man's Province: British Columbia Politicians and Chinese and Japanese Immigrants, 1858-1914*. Vancouver: University of British Columbia Press, 1989.

Salmon, J.H.M. *A History of Gold Mining in New Zealand*. Wellington: Government Printer, 1963.

Simon, Matthew. "New British Investment in Canada, 1865-1914," *Canadian Journal of Economics*, III, 2 (May, 1970): p. 2.

Smith, Dorothy Blakey. "The Journal of Arthur Thomas Bushby, 1858-1859," *B.C. Historical Quarterly* XXI: pp. 83-160.

_____. "Thomas Elwyn," *Dictionary of Canadian Biography*, XI. Toronto: University of Toronto Press, 1982: pp. 301-302.

Splawn, A.J. *KA-MI-AKIN, Last Hero of the Yakimas*. Portland: Binford & Mort, 1944.

Stangoe, Irene. *Cariboo-Chilcotin Pioneer People and Places*. Surrey: Heritage House, 1994.

Stanley, Timothy J. "'Chinamen, Wherever We Go,' Chinese Nationalism and Guangdong Merchants in British Columbia, 1871-1911," *The Canadian Historical Review*, Vol. 77, 4 (December 1996): p. 488.

Struik, L.C. *The Ancient Western North American Margin: An Alpine Rift Model for the East-Central Canadian Cordillera*, Paper 87-15. Ottawa: Geological Survey of Canada, 1987.

_____. "Imbricated Terranes of the Cariboo gold belt with correlations and implications for tectonics in southeastern British Columbia," *Canadian Journal of Earth Sciences*, Vol. 23, 8, 1986.

_____. *Structural Geology of the Cariboo Gold Mining District, East-Central British Columbia*, Memoir 421. Ottawa: Geological Survey of Canada, 1988.

Trimble, William H. *The Mining Advance Into the Inland Empire*. Madison: University of Wisconsin Press, 1914.

Turnbull, Elsie G. *Ghost Towns and Drowned Towns of West Kootenay.* Surrey: Heritage House, 1988.

Wagner, Jack R. *Gold Mines of California.* Berkeley: Howel North Books, 1970.

Walkem, W. W. *Stories of Early British Columbia.* Vancouver: News-Advertiser, 1914.

Watson, Rosalind. "A Trip Through the Cariboo," *The Mining Record,* Vol. X (November 1903).

Williams, David Ricardo. "The Administration of Criminal and Civil Justice in the Mining Camps and Frontier Communities of British Columbia," In *Law and Justice in a New Land, Essays in Western Canadian Legal History.* Ed. Louis A. Knafla. Toronto: The Carswell Company Limited, 1986.

_____. *"The Man For a New Country" Sir Matthew Baillie Begbie.* Sidney: Gray's Publishing Ltd., 1977.

Williams, R.T. *Williams British Columbia Directory.* Victoria: R.T. Williams, 1892.

Wiltsee, Ernest A. *The Pioneer Miner and the Pack Mule Express.* San Francisco: California Historical Society, 1931.

Wright, Richard Thomas. *Overlanders.* Saskatoon: Western Producer Prairie Books, 1985.

_____. *Quesnelle Forks, A Gold Rush Town in Historical Perspective.* Barkerville: Friends of Barkerville, 1987.

GOVERNMENT AND OTHER RECORDS

Government Records, British Columbia Archives:
    BC Mental Health Services, GR 2880
    Attorney General, GR 429
    Colonial Correspondence, Inward, GR 1372
    Colonial Correspondence, Outward
    Gold Commissioner, Lillooet, GR 3048
    Government Agency, Cariboo, GR 216, 255
    Lands and Works, GR 868
    Lands Branch, GR 1440
    Premier's Papers, GR 441
    Provincial Court, 150 Mile House, GR 596
    Provincial Police Force, GR 55, 56
    Provincial Secretary, GR 526, 529, 624, 1330
    Vital Statistics, Deaths and Marriage Records

Manuscript Records, British Coumbia Archives:
    Add MSS 676, Louis LeBourdais Papers
    Add MSS 767, Joseph Hunter Papers
    Add MSS 1526, Bishop Hills Diaries
    Add MSS 2532, Consolidated Cariboo Hydraulic Mining   Company
    Add MSS 2561, South Fork Hydraulic Mining Company
    Add MSS 2604, Diary of Robert Scott
    Robert Harkness Papers

Government Records, National Archives of Canada:
   Post Office Inspectors' Reports, RG3, RG13
   Record Group 13, Vol. 1452

Hudson's Bay Archives, Winnipeg:
   Barkerville Correspondence, B12/b/1
   Fort Alexandria Letterbook, B5/b/1; Fur Accounts, B5/d

Archives of New Brunswick
Archives of Ontario
Barkerville Historic Site Archives
Oregon Historical Society Archives
United Church Archives, Victoria University, University of Toronto
Williams Lake Archives

NEWSPAPERS
Ashcroft Journal (B.C. Mining Journal)
British Columbian
Cariboo Sentinel
The Daily Evening Post
Kamloops (Inland) Sentinel
San Francisco Chronicle
Vancouver Province
Vancouver Sun
Victoria Daily Colonist
Victoria Daily Times
Williams Lake Advocate
Williams Lake Tribune

MISCELLANEOUS PUBLICATIONS
Likely Cemetery Newsletter
The Mining Record
The Mining and Engineering Record
Wells History and Self Tour

UNPUBLISHED THESES
Averill Groenveld-Meuer, "Manning the Fraser River," 1994, University of British
   Columbia.
J.H. Stewart Reid, "The Road to Cariboo," 1942, University of British Columbia.

INDEX